Mind, Machine, and Will

Determinism, Responsibility, and Agency in the Age of AI

nova science publishers

www.novapublishers.com

The Future of Artificial Intelligence Series

Democratized Generative AI: Principles, Challenges and Applications
S. Balasubramaniam, PhD
and Seifedine Kadry, PhD (Editors)
ISBN: 979-8-89530-684-0
eBook ISBN: 979-8-89530-786-1

Divine Feminine Energies in Vedic Anthologies: A Scientific Inquiry Using AI and Large Language Models
Chandrasekar Vuppalapati
ISBN: 979-8-89530-583-6
eBook ISBN: 979-8-89530-706-9

Navigating the Future: Embracing Advances in AI and Digital Transformation and Seamlessly Integrating ESG Across Sectors
Michail Chalaris, PhD,
Christina Patitsa, PhD
and Stavros Kalogiannidis, PhD
(Editors)
ISBN: 979-8-89530-461-7
eBook ISBN: 979-8-89530-571-3

Real-World Applications of Artificial Intelligence and Machine Learning in Power Systems: A Code Approach
T. Mariprasath, ME, PhD
and V. Kirubakaran
ISBN: 979-8-89530-228-6 (Hardcover)
eBook ISBN: 979-8-89530-332-0

More information about this series can be found at
https://novapublishers.com/product-category/series/the-future-of-artificial-intelligence/

Daniel Plate
James Hutson

Mind, Machine, and Will

Determinism, Responsibility, and Agency in the Age of AI

nova science publishers
www.novapublishers.com

DOI: https://doi.org/10.52305/GIGY3687

Library of Congress Cataloging-in-Publication Data

ISBN: 979-8-89530-934-6 (Hardcover)
ISBN: 979-8-89530-952-0 (eBook)

Published by Nova Science Publishers, Inc. † New York

This manuscript is dedicated to our families, whose unwavering support and encouragement have been the cornerstone of our journey. To our parents, we express deep gratitude for instilling in us a thirst for knowledge and the determination to pursue our passions. Your belief in our abilities and unwavering support have propelled us forward.

To our spouses and partners, we extend heartfelt appreciation for standing by our side throughout the long hours of research and writing. To our children, we are grateful for your inspiration and the joy you bring to our lives. Your presence reminds us of the importance of our work and motivates us to strive for excellence. To our extended families, friends, and loved ones, we thank you for your encouragement, words of wisdom, and unwavering belief in our abilities. In particular, James Hutson would like to thank his wife Piper and children Bishop and Aurora.

Your support has been a source of strength and inspiration. We acknowledge the sacrifices you have made and the understanding you have shown, allowing us the time and space to pursue our scholarly endeavors. This manuscript stands as a testament to your love and support. With deepest appreciation and heartfelt gratitude, we dedicate this work to our families.

Contents

List of Figures

List of Tables

Acknowledgments

The authors express profound appreciation to the myriad individuals and institutions whose contributions and unwavering support have been pivotal in the genesis and fruition of this tome. At the vanguard of acknowledgment stands Dr. John Porter, whose innovative leadership in aligning the adoption of emergent technologies like AI with educational initiatives has left an indelible mark on this work's evolution.

Acknowledgment is due to Dr. Kathi Vosevich, Dean of the College of Arts and Humanities, for her steadfast encouragement and support of the research culminating in this publication. Vosevich's guidance and confidence in the authors' academic endeavors have been fundamental in sculpting the contours of this volume.

The authors extend their gratitude to the research team responsible for composing this manuscript and acknowledge the critical insights and contributions of various colleagues and co-authors from ancillary projects. James Hutson extends thanks to Professors Ben Fulcher, Jeremiah Ratican, Joe Weber, Ben Scholle, and Dr. Trent Olsen.

The authors also convey their deep appreciation to the administrative leaders at all of the institutions that participated in the study for their relentless support and dedication to creating an environment conducive to academic excellence and scholarly exploration. The leadership, encompassing Presidents, Provosts, and Deans at these institutions, has been instrumental in providing the necessary guidance and resources for this research and writing project.

To those that provided insight into their experiences as leaders in industry and education, we are indebted and thank you for your invaluable time and efforts in helping others navigate this unpredictable time. Finally, the authors are thankful for the insights and constructive feedback from colleagues and fellow researchers throughout this project. Their contributions have significantly enriched the work and helped to refine the ideas encapsulated within this volume.

About the Authors

Dr. Daniel Plate, a scholar in the field of composition pedagogy and educational technology, focuses his research on the integration of generative artificial intelligence with pedagogical methodologies. Educated with a Bachelor of Arts in English and Philosophy from Taylor University, a Master of Fine Arts in Creative Writing from the University of Arkansas, and a Ph.D. in Literature from Washington University in St. Louis, Plate presently serves as a faculty member at Lindenwood University. There, he teaches courses in creative writing, literature, composition, and applied AI. Beyond his creative writing contributions, he has co-authored numerous case studies that explore the nuanced applications of AI in classroom settings. These scholarly works not only contribute to the existing body of literature but also offer practical insights for educators interested in leveraging generative AI to enrich the learning experience. Plate's scholarly endeavors straddle the intersection of technology and pedagogy; he divides his professional time between developing code to augment teaching methods and conducting empirical research to better understand the symbiotic relationship between AI and innovative pedagogy. His latest publications are *Generative AI in the English Composition Classroom: Practical and Adaptable Strategies* (2024) and *Beyond Code: Redefining Programming Education Beyond STEM* (2025).

Dr. James Hutson specializes in multidisciplinary research that encompasses artificial intelligence, neurohumanities, neurodiversity, immersive realities, and the gamification of education. Earning a Bachelor of Arts in Art from the University of Tulsa, a Master of Arts in Art History from Southern Methodist University, and a Ph.D. in Art History from the University of Maryland, College Park, he later acquired additional Master's degrees in Leadership and Game Design from Lindenwood University and additional PhD in Artificial Intelligence at Capitol Technology University (2023). Over the span of his academic career since 2006, Hutson has held various pedagogical and administrative positions across five universities, including

Chair of Art History, Assistant Dean of Graduate and Online Programs, and most recently, Lead XR Disruptor and Department Head of Art History, AI, and Visual Culture. Notably, his scholarly portfolio includes several books on the application of artificial intelligence in education and cultural heritage, such as *Creative Convergence: The AI Renaissance in Art and Design* (2024), as well as numerous articles and case studies.

Foreword

At a moment when institutions and publics are struggling to adjudicate agency in an algorithmic century, this work offers an argument as precise as it is courageous. The volume contends that three crises—the authorship crisis in copyright law, the free-will crisis in neuroscience, and the understanding crisis in artificial intelligence—arise from a common philosophical error: the attempt to ground responsibility in private mental states rather than in public practices. The authors assemble a program that treats meaning, authorship, and accountability as achievements of participation that can be observed, corrected, and taught. Their analysis of Wittgenstein's later philosophy dislodges the intuition that inner episodes settle questions of intention; their reconstruction relocates normativity in shared forms of life in which rules are followed, contested, and revised. The result is neither cynical reductionism nor naïve optimism; it is a rigorous account of how communities actually stabilize knowledge and responsibility over time. Readers encounter a narrative that moves fluently from rule-following considerations to courts wrestling with machine-assisted creation, and from readiness potentials in motor cortex to policy architectures for automated systems. In place of metaphysical guarantees, the book defends procedural transparency and public contestability as the right kind of "seeing inside." That stance is not an abdication of ethics; it is a bet on the durability of institutions that can learn in public. The wager is that such institutions will preserve what matters about freedom—competence, corrigibility, and stewardship—even when causal stories do most of the explanatory work.

This argument unfolds across a carefully staged itinerary that begins with philosophical foundations and culminates in design blueprints and legal reforms. The foundational chapters show why the private language temptation fails and why agency belongs with the public criteria that make correction and error possible. The middle chapters draw on neuroscience to demonstrate that conscious will is often a narrative overlay on prior neural events, and they argue that the right response is not fatalism but the construction of scaffolds that expand responsible participation. A parallel legal story tracks courts and agencies as they grope toward practice-based standards—transformative use, documented curation, accountable workflows—instead of occult appeals to inner spark. Case studies from authorship disputes to AI liability reveal how doctrine improves when it asks what creative or organizational practices are *actually* in play. The volume repeatedly distinguishes productive transparency—procedures that enable audit, appeal, and repair—from metaphysical transparency—impossible audits of inner causes. That distinction clarifies why hybrid human–machine work can be governed without policing an ever-receding line between "the human part" and "the machine part." By the time readers reach the design chapters, "meaningful human control" has been reframed as "meaningful human practice," a change that directs engineers and regulators toward participatory mechanisms rather than dashboard switches. Across fields, the criterion for legitimacy becomes the capacity to join shared games of giving and asking for reasons. That is a criterion that social systems can measure, improve, and teach.

The achievement of this book is to replace an exhausted metaphysics with an actionable ethics of public practice, one that researchers, judges, clinicians, designers, and policy leaders can implement tomorrow. Scholars will value the synthesis of Wittgenstein, contemporary neuroscience, and jurisprudence that underwrites the program's conceptual clarity. Practitioners will value the operational guidance: document curation and intervention; build contestability into workflows; align accountability with observed competence; reward transformation and stewardship over mystique. Institutions will find here not only a diagnosis of responsibility gaps but also architectures for closing them through traceability, participatory review, and forward-looking remedies. Above all, readers will find a humane replacement for retribution and romantic authorship: a model in which responsibility is owned in public, distributed according to capacity to prevent and repair harm, and continually renewed through collective learning. In an era when science complicates stories of self-origination and automation complicates authorship, this book shows how to preserve the goods that freedom was always meant to secure. Its contribution is to turn a set of crises into a coherent research and governance agenda, and to do so with intellectual rigor and civic seriousness. For those seeking a map from metaphysics to practice—and from anxiety to institutional confidence—this volume is the necessary companion.

Preface

The rapid convergence of neuroscience, legal doctrine, and artificial intelligence in the early twenty-first century has occasioned a profound transformation in the way agency, responsibility, and creativity are conceptualized. Where once these notions rested comfortably on metaphysical assumptions about private mental states, contemporary developments increasingly reveal the inadequacy of such frameworks. In neuroscience, the rise of determinist models has called into question the very existence of free will, suggesting that conscious choice may be a *post hoc* rationalization rather than an originating cause. In law, particularly in copyright and criminal justice, the challenges posed by machine authorship and algorithmic decision-making demand an account of authorship, liability, and culpability that does not simply default to the inscrutability of individual intention. Meanwhile, artificial intelligence systems routinely perform tasks such as composing music, drafting legal opinions, and generating scientific hypotheses that, not long ago, were seen as the sole province of sentient, intentional agents. The question that unites these developments is deceptively simple: what is the ontological status of agency when the grounds for attributing it are public, procedural, and technologically mediated? This book aims to interrogate the legacy of inner-state theories, examine their gradual displacement, and chart the emergence of a practice-based alternative. By foregrounding both the conceptual and practical stakes of this transition, the work aspires to illuminate a path forward for scholars, policymakers, and practitioners grappling with the reconfiguration of mind, machine, and law.

At the heart of this inquiry is the insight, drawn from the later philosophy of Ludwig Wittgenstein, that meaning and agency are not private phenomena but are embedded in the social practices and public criteria that make sense of our actions. Wittgenstein's critique of private language and his account of rule-following upend the Cartesian tradition that sought the source of agency in the mysterious recesses of subjective consciousness. This philosophical revolution, however, remains only partially assimilated by the disciplines most affected by it. The persistence of mentalistic frameworks in neuroscience, legal reasoning, and AI ethics often obscures the fact that our attributions of understanding, authorship, and accountability are operationalized through communal norms and collective judgment. What does it mean, then, to claim that a machine understands, that a corporation is responsible, or that a defendant deserves blame, if these are not reducible to facts about inner states? The answer, this book contends, lies not in retreating to metaphysical speculation but in analyzing the forms of life through which meaning is conferred and maintained. As scientific and technological systems increasingly function as interlocutors and participants in these practices, traditional boundaries between human and machine, person and artifact, must be renegotiated. This negotiation is neither purely theoretical nor merely institutional; it is, in the deepest sense, philosophical, demanding the articulation of new criteria for agency, value, and justice.

Such reexamination is urgent, not only because of the technical acceleration of AI and neurotechnology, but also because of the accelerating pace at which law and policy are being forced to adapt to realities they were never designed to address. Consider the ongoing debates in copyright law, where the requirement for human authorship is routinely challenged by creative outputs generated through machine learning and algorithmic recombination. Similarly, in criminal justice, neuroscientific evidence has begun to erode the foundational presumption that individual actors possess the kind of metaphysical freedom required for desert-based punishment. These crises do not occur in isolation; rather, they are symptoms of a deeper philosophical unease regarding the sufficiency of inner-state explanations. The theoretical scaffolding of law, science, and technology is, in this moment, exposed and destabilized, inviting a reckoning with the assumptions that have long governed our most basic attributions of meaning, authorship, and blame. If society is to meet these challenges with intellectual integrity and ethical clarity, it must ask: what must be preserved, and what can be relinquished, as we transition to a post-Cartesian order?

The framework advanced in this book is unapologetically interdisciplinary, synthesizing analytic philosophy, philosophy of science, contemporary legal scholarship, and empirical research from neuroscience and AI. This approach is predicated on the belief that the complexity of the questions at hand cannot be satisfactorily addressed within the siloed methods or vocabularies of any single field. By juxtaposing case law, philosophical argument, and empirical evidence, the analysis seeks to reveal the mutual entanglement of conceptual problems and practical predicaments. This entanglement, far from being a source of confusion, is precisely what enables a robust interrogation of the categories of intention, understanding, authorship, and responsibility upon which so much theoretical and institutional labor depends. The book aspires not to resolve these tensions once and for all, but to render them productive, sharpening the philosophical questions and offering frameworks that facilitate ongoing critical engagement. Ultimately, the reader is invited not merely to witness a theoretical debate, but to participate in the active reconstruction of the categories that structure contemporary thought and practice.

A distinctive feature of the book's approach is its insistence on confronting the speed and scale of societal transformation occasioned by advances in science and technology. No previous generation has had to assimilate conceptual revolutions in neuroscience, jurisprudence, and machine intelligence at such a breakneck pace. The velocity with which courts must decide the legal status of AI-generated works, or neuroscientists must opine on the limits of moral responsibility, outstrips the capacity of existing epistemic and institutional frameworks to respond with coherence and foresight. As a result, the questions posed here are not simply academic; they are pressing social, ethical, and political matters whose answers (or lack thereof) will shape the conditions of human and machine agency for decades to come. How should the law assign liability in cases of distributed technological action? What norms of fairness and equity should prevail in a world where machines participate in meaning-making? Can traditional notions of justice, autonomy, and personhood survive contact with a deterministic neuroscience and algorithmic governance? These are the crucibles in which the future of agency is being forged.

Central to the book's method is the ongoing dialogue between conceptual analysis and concrete case studies. While analytic rigor remains indispensable, the abstraction of philosophical inquiry is continually brought into contact with the stubborn facts of legal precedent, neuroscientific experiment, and technological innovation. Each chapter poses its own set of questions, often drawn from headline-making controversies or landmark court decisions, and explores them through the prism of philosophical critique. This iterative movement between the universal and the particular, the normative and the empirical, constitutes the book's distinctive analytic rhythm. The goal is not only to clarify, but also to historicize and contextualize, demonstrating how the stakes of agency, responsibility, and creativity are inseparable from the historical moment in which they are debated. In this respect, the work is not only a contribution to theory but a map of the terrain in which theory and practice intersect.

A further aim is to resist the seduction of simplistic binaries (human versus machine, intention versus behavior, freedom versus determinism) that so often dominate public and academic discourse. While these dichotomies have heuristic value, they frequently occlude the complexities and ambiguities that define actual practice. The analytic framework developed here is designed to expose these ambiguities and to make visible the ways in which agency is always already distributed, negotiated, and contingent. Rather than seeking an elusive essence of agency or a final criterion for responsibility, the book advocates for a pragmatic and pluralistic approach, sensitive to context, community standards, and the open-ended evolution of social practices. This orientation is not a retreat from rigor, but a commitment to intellectual honesty in the face of unprecedented change.

The argument proceeds by stages, each addressing a distinct but interrelated dimension of the overall problem. The opening chapters lay the philosophical groundwork, tracing the genealogy of inner-state theories and their discontents through Wittgenstein and his interpreters. Subsequent chapters move through the domains of neuroscience and law, examining how empirical findings and judicial decisions increasingly converge on practice-based criteria for agency and responsibility. Later sections turn to the challenges posed by artificial intelligence, both as a technical phenomenon and as a philosophical provocation to inherited categories of mind and meaning. Throughout, the reader is encouraged to attend not only to what is changing, but to the forms of continuity and resilience that persist within the shifting landscape.

The sense of urgency that animates the book is both intellectual and civic. The accelerating tempo of change ensures that the lag between scientific discovery, legal adaptation, and ethical reflection is growing, not shrinking. This temporal gap is itself a source of risk, as decisions made in haste or ignorance can have far-reaching consequences for individuals, institutions, and societies. By foregrounding the speed and unpredictability of these transformations, the book seeks to foster a more reflective, deliberate mode of engagement—one capable of holding open the space for critical deliberation even as the pace of change threatens to overwhelm inherited capacities for judgment.

The following aspires to provide an integrative and conceptually robust framework for understanding the future of agency in an age of deterministic science and intelligent machines. It is a book for philosophers, scientists, jurists, and all those who are compelled by the question of what it means to act, to choose, and to be responsible in a world where the grounds for such attributions are everywhere contested. The wager of the work is that, by turning our attention to practices rather than inner states, we can recover both the coherence and the humanity of agency, even in the midst of technological upheaval. The challenges are formidable, the answers provisional, but the inquiry is indispensable. The future of agency, and of the societies in which it is embedded, will be determined not only by what we discover, but by how we learn to think (and rethink) the categories through which discovery becomes possible.

Introduction: Three Crises, One Solution

Abstract

The introduction articulates the convergence of three foundational crises—the human authorship crisis in copyright law, the free will crisis in neuroscience, and the understanding crisis in artificial intelligence—arguing that each exposes the limitations of explaining agency and creativity through private mental states. Drawing on Wittgenstein's reconceptualization of meaning as inherently public and practice-based, this chapter reframes the challenges faced in law, science, and technology as manifestations of a single philosophical error. It demonstrates how contemporary developments in each field force a reassessment of traditional accounts of authorship, choice, and understanding, revealing a shared theoretical impasse. Rather than treating these crises as isolated, the analysis establishes a unified lens through which the problem of agency must be addressed in the twenty-first century. The chapter foregrounds the necessity of a practice-centered account, arguing that agency, creativity, and responsibility are best understood as emergent from participation in social practices rather than rooted in internal, inaccessible phenomena.

0.1. Beyond Private Language: Meaning as Public Practice

The problem of private language, most famously articulated by philosopher Ludwig Wittgenstein (Figure 0.1) in his later work, lies at the core of contemporary debates on agency, responsibility, and understanding across disciplines. Wittgenstein rejected the notion that meaning is anchored in ineffable, inner mental states, marking a decisive break from Cartesian traditions, and this break reverberates through both analytic philosophy and the empirical sciences (Malcolm & Wittgenstein, 2001; Wittgenstein, 2003). Modern philosophy of mind has increasingly turned to the idea that language and meaning are fundamentally constituted by participation in public practices, rather than by subjective, introspective states (Hacker, 2014; Putnam, 1979). This view resonates with the social constructivist turn in psychology, where the focus shifts from the individual psyche to shared cultural scripts, institutional norms, and community standards as the bedrock of cognitive development and agency (Valsiner, 2014; Tomasello, 2009).

Figure 0.1. Portrait of Ludwig Wittgenstein, 1930.

Within sociology, meaning is similarly conceived as emerging from interaction and negotiation, rather than from private intentions or solipsistic cognition, an approach that foregrounds the centrality of social practices in the construction of knowledge (Berger & Luckmann, 2016). Neuroscience, too, has begun to recognize the profound social embeddedness of human cognition, with empirical research revealing that language processing and conceptual understanding depend on neural circuits shaped by social interaction and context (Hari et al., 2015; Frith & Frith, 2010). In the field of artificial intelligence, the shift from rule-based to data-driven and context-sensitive models, such as large language models, further underscores the limits of internalist accounts and the necessity of public practice for meaning and agency (Ahmed, 2025; Saeidnia & Nilashi, 2025). Across these fields, the critique of private language theory has become a touchstone for broader critiques of mentalistic and individualistic models of mind, law, and technology.

The dissolution of the private language myth entails significant philosophical and empirical consequences for our understanding of meaning and agency. For Wittgenstein, meaning is not a matter of private ostension but of public criteria—rules and practices shared within a linguistic community that enable the possibility of error, correction, and mutual understanding (Wittgenstein, 2009; Kripke, 1982). Psychological research into language acquisition supports this view, showing that children learn words and concepts through socially scaffolded interactions, not through isolated introspection (Vygotsky & Cole, 1978; Tomasello, 2009). From a sociological perspective, the institutionalization of language and the routinization of communicative acts reveal how deeply embedded meaning is in collective practices, ritual, and convention (Giddens, 1984; Berger & Luckmann, 2016). Neuroscience now documents that neural systems involved in language and meaning are profoundly shaped by the presence of others, as demonstrated by mirror neuron research and studies on social cognition (Hari et al., 2015; Frith & Frith, 2010). The evolution of models that generate language through exposure to vast corpora of public discourse, rather than introspective states or predetermined rules, reflects this same pattern of distributed meaning-making (Devlin et al., 2019). Agency and meaning are not privately manufactured, but collectively negotiated, enacted, and sustained.

Such a turn toward public practice has dramatic implications for the philosophy of action and theories of responsibility. If agency is not rooted in the opacity of inner states, but in the public performance of competence within socially recognized practices, then questions of intention, authorship, and blame must be reframed. Philosophers such as Elizabeth Anscombe and Donald Davidson have shown that attributing agency involves interpreting actions as rational and intelligible within a social context, rather than as the outcome of hidden, metaphysical will (Davidson, 1980; Stoutland, 2011). This interpretive, practice-centered orientation aligns with research in psychology on "theory of mind," which demonstrates that we understand others as agents by situating their actions within familiar scripts and practices (Apperly, 2010). Sociologists have likewise argued that accountability and responsibility emerge from the recognition and negotiation of expectations within shared practices, not from metaphysical notions of free will (Giddens, 1984; Garfinkel, 2023). Neuroscientific studies of volition and moral cognition reveal that the sense of agency is constructed and contextual, contingent on feedback from the environment and from social interactions (Haggard, 2017).

Research on explainability and alignment increasingly situates the intelligibility of machine behavior in transparent practices and externally verifiable outcomes, rather than in appeals to machine "intentions" (Doshi-Velez & Kim, 2017). This practice-based orientation provides a framework for understanding agency as a publicly recognizable achievement, rather than an inscrutable essence.

The displacement of private language theory also reconfigures debates on understanding and explanation in both science and technology. Where explanation once depended on uncovering hidden mental mechanisms, the current orientation emphasizes the external, rule-governed regularities that make explanation possible and meaningful within a community. In philosophy of science, this is reflected in the shift from internalist accounts of scientific discovery to models that privilege the social structure of scientific communities, peer review, and the replicability of practices (Kuhn, 1997; Longino, 2002). Psychologically, the social basis of explanation is evident in how children and adults alike prefer explanations that appeal to observable regularities and consensus, rather than private insight (Wellman & Liu, 2007). Sociologists studying scientific knowledge production have shown that what counts as a valid explanation is negotiated within the community through norms of evidence and methods (Latour, Salk, & Woolgar, 2013). Neuroscientific work has highlighted the extent to which explanatory satisfaction is context-sensitive, shaped by familiarity, expertise, and the cues provided by other agents (Lombrozo, 2012). At the same time, interpretability research has increasingly focused on creating models that can provide clear, actionable, and communal standards for explanation, echoing the broader turn toward public criteria (Hassija et al., 2024; Matthew et al., 2025). Across these disciplines, explanation is revealed not as the revelation of hidden causes, but as the deployment of shared practices that structure understanding.

Crucially, the rejection of private language illuminates the collective dimensions of creativity, authorship, and innovation, particularly in law and AI. In the legal domain, the notion that originality and authorship are the exclusive products of solitary genius has given way to models that recognize the irreducible role of collaboration, precedent, and institutional mediation (Woodmansee, 1984; Jaszi, 2017). Sociological and anthropological studies show that innovation is embedded in networks of practice, where ideas are developed, contested, and validated by reference to communal standards (Becker, 1984). Neuroscientific findings further support the social basis of creativity, demonstrating that brain regions implicated in creative thought are activated in collaborative and communicative contexts (Sawyer & Henriksen,

2024). The collective character of generative models is apparent: large language models synthesize public texts and encode patterns derived from distributed human input (Bengesi et al., 2024; Devlin et al., 2019). The upshot is a shift away from inner-state criteria for creative legitimacy toward external benchmarks of participation, transformation, and communal recognition.

The social-practice orientation equally transforms our approach to the attribution of responsibility, particularly as it pertains to emergent technologies and systems. As seen in the work of Pagallo (2013) and Matthias (2004), law and policy have long grappled with the challenge of assigning responsibility in contexts where agency is distributed across persons, institutions, and increasingly, machines. Psychological and sociological research reveal that collective responsibility is not merely an aggregation of individual guilt, but a product of institutionalized practices that articulate, enforce, and revise norms of accountability (Bratman, 1992). In neuroscience, studies of group decision-making show that the sense of responsibility is modulated by the perceived intentionality and presence of others, reinforcing the idea that agency is shaped by social context (El Zein, Dolan, & Bahrami, 2022). In computational studies, the debate over "responsibility gaps" highlights the inadequacy of individualistic models of fault and underscores the necessity of communal frameworks for liability and risk management (Matthias, 2004; Bryson, 2016). This reorientation points to the importance of designing social and technical systems that reflect and support the realities of distributed agency.

Perhaps the most significant implication of moving beyond private language is the transformation of our self-understanding as agents within a technologically mediated and legally regulated world. Where agency was once conceived as a metaphysical property of the solitary subject, it is now increasingly recognized as a practical achievement, visible in our ability to navigate, negotiate, and transform the norms and practices that constitute our social existence (Haslanger, 2012; Bratman, 1992). In philosophy of science, this practical turn is mirrored in an emphasis on scientific practice, experimental traditions, and the communal validation of knowledge claims (Kuhn, 1997; Longino, 2020). In psychology and neuroscience, agency is modeled as an emergent feature of dynamic interactions among embodied agents, tools, and environments (Clark, 2015). AI research, particularly in the area of human-AI interaction, highlights the emergent and negotiated character of agency as it is co-constructed in the ongoing flow of activity and communication (Seibt, Vestergaard, & Fossa, 2020). The shift from inner states to social practices enables a more nuanced, pluralistic, and context-sensitive understanding of agency, one that is responsive to the challenges of contemporary science, technology, and law.

Therefore, the critique of private language and the embrace of meaning as public practice mark a foundational shift in how agency, responsibility, and creativity are conceptualized and operationalized across philosophy, psychology, neuroscience, law, and AI. Rather than being the mysterious product of inner, unobservable states, these capacities are now understood as the outcome of participation in the dynamic, rule-governed practices that constitute our collective life. This orientation does not deny the reality of subjective experience, but it insists that such experience is intelligible only within the broader context of social norms, institutional frameworks, and public criteria. As science, technology, and law continue to evolve, the imperative is to develop frameworks that are robust enough to accommodate the realities of distributed, emergent, and technologically mediated agency. The abandonment of private language theory serves as both a diagnosis of conceptual error and a roadmap for the reconstruction of agency and meaning in the age of AI.

0.2. The Free Will Crisis in Neuroscience

The neuroscientific investigation of free will has generated profound challenges to traditional philosophical accounts of agency, intentionality, and moral responsibility. Empirical research since the late twentieth century has focused on identifying the neural correlates of conscious intention, with landmark studies like that of Libet et al. (1983) suggesting that the subjective experience of "willing" an action is preceded by unconscious neural activity. This result has been widely interpreted as evidence against the existence of free will in the metaphysical sense, since conscious volition appears to be a *post hoc* confabulation rather than an initiating cause (Double, 1996; Haggard, 2008; Vijayaraghavan & Felsen, 2025). Subsequent studies using more refined neuroimaging and computational techniques have largely confirmed Libet's findings, demonstrating that predictive neural patterns precede both simple and complex decisions by up to several seconds (Soon et al., 2008; Fried, Mukamel, & Kreiman, 2011). Philosophers and scientists alike have debated whether these findings eliminate the space for traditional notions of self-determination or simply reveal a more distributed, nonconscious form of agency (Dennett, 2015). What is clear, however, is that the folk psychological view of free will as the conscious selection of actions by an inner self is rendered deeply problematic by neuroscientific evidence (Roskies, 2010). This crisis has prompted a major re-examination of concepts like authorship, responsibility, and punishment in both academic and practical contexts, and this prior to advances in generative AI (Mele, 2014). The ongoing neuroscientific project continues to reframe free will as a question of how, rather than whether, the brain enables flexible and context-sensitive behavior.

The dissolution of free will as a metaphysical property has significant implications for the philosophy of mind, ethics, and the legal system. From a neuroscientific standpoint, the experience of agency and volition emerges from distributed processes that integrate sensory information, motor planning, and affective valuation (Dutta, 2025; Haggard, 2008). This distributed model stands in stark contrast to the classical Cartesian picture, in which an indivisible "I" acts as the ultimate source of choice and control (Baumeister, 2008). Experiments reveal that the readiness potential—a measurable buildup of electrical activity in the motor cortex—can occur long before an individual reports the intention to move (Libet et al., 1983; Schurger, Pak, & Roskies, 2021). Critics have noted that these experiments often involve arbitrary, trivial choices, and some argue that more complex forms of reasoning or deliberation may not be captured by the same mechanisms (Mele, 2014). Nevertheless, follow-up work has extended these findings to decisions involving value judgments, delayed gratification, and moral conflict (Soon et al., 2008; Fried, Mukamel, & Kreiman, 2011; Wittmann, Montemayor, & Dorato, 2025). The upshot is a growing consensus that conscious will may be less a causal driver than a narrative construction layered on top of unconscious neural computations (Chen & Bornstein, 2024; Gazzaniga, 2012). This reframing demands new theoretical models that can integrate the neuroscientific data with lived experience and normative concerns.

These neuroscientific findings have also catalyzed an interdisciplinary dialogue about the relationship between determinism and moral responsibility. Classical libertarian views, which posit that agents are the uncaused originators of their actions, appear increasingly untenable in light of empirical evidence (Caruso, 2012). Compatibilist philosophers argue that moral responsibility can still be grounded in the capacity to act in accordance with one's reasons and values, even if all actions are determined by prior causes (Dennett, 2015). Neuroscience complicates this picture by revealing the extent to which reason-responsive behavior is itself shaped by factors outside conscious awareness, such as genetic predispositions, environmental cues, and socialization processes (Greene & Cohen, 2004). Studies of individuals with brain lesions, psychiatric disorders, or developmental abnormalities illustrate how changes in neural circuitry can disrupt the normal experience of agency, sometimes abolishing the sense of responsibility altogether (Malik, 2023). The result is a landscape in which the boundaries of agency and accountability are increasingly seen as porous, context-dependent, and contingent on biological as well as social factors (Roskies, 2010). The free will crisis extends well beyond philosophy, prompting legal scholars and clinicians to reconsider the foundations of blame and punishment (Greene & Cohen, 2004). Neuroscience, in this sense, forces a reconceptualization of the human subject as a node within causal networks rather than as an autonomous metaphysical agent.

Recent advances in brain imaging and neuropsychology have further demonstrated that the construction of agency is intimately tied to the dynamics of the social and physical environment (Faraji & Metz, 2023). A sense of agency is now understood to arise from the integration of multisensory feedback, predictive motor signals, and external confirmation (Dutta, 2025; Haggard, 2017). This process is often disrupted in neurological and psychiatric conditions, such as schizophrenia or alien limb syndrome, where the boundaries of self-generated versus externally generated action become blurred (Blakemore, Wolpert, & Frith, 2002). Moreover, experiments show that the attribution of agency is highly context-sensitive, influenced by expectations, prior experience, and cultural scripts (Wegner, 2017). This context-dependence is mirrored in the operation of the "interpreter" module in the left hemisphere, which Gazzaniga (2012) argues constructs a narrative of selfhood by retrospectively integrating sensory, affective, and motor information. The implication is that agency is neither a fixed property nor a transparent experience, but a flexible, reconstructive achievement dependent on ongoing brain-environment interactions. These findings provide strong support for practice-based, rather than internalist, accounts of intentionality and moral responsibility (Haggard, 2017). By situating agency in public, embodied, and social practices, neuroscience aligns itself with the broader critique of private language and metaphysical voluntarism.

Accountability, in this light, depends not on a transparent audit of every neural precursor to action—an impossible task—but on an agent's participation within these public systems of reason-giving and correction. Any call for transparency is a call for contestable procedures, not for an exhaustive disclosure of causal origins. The practical consequences of the free will crisis are already manifest in law, clinical practice, and public policy. Courts and legislatures are increasingly confronted with neuroscientific evidence regarding diminished capacity, impulse control disorders, and the neural basis of addiction (Brown, 2021; Morse, 2005). This has led to contentious debates over the extent to which neurological deficits should mitigate culpability or affect sentencing, particularly in cases involving brain tumors, traumatic injury, or neurodevelopmental disorders (Reddy, 2025). The traditional reliance of the law on metaphysical notions of free will and rational self-control is now challenged by a science that uncovers the limits and contingencies of these capacities (Greene & Cohen, 2004). In practice, this has resulted in a gradual shift toward more nuanced, context-sensitive models of responsibility that incorporate neuroscientific findings without succumbing to reductive determinism (Morse, 2005). Some scholars advocate for a "public health" approach to criminal justice, emphasizing prevention, rehabilitation, and risk management over retribution (Caruso, 2012). The clinical sphere has likewise adapted, with psychiatric and neurological diagnoses increasingly framed as disruptions to the ordinary mechanisms of agency and self-regulation. As neuroscience continues to map the causal determinants of behavior, the institutions of law and medicine are compelled to reconsider foundational assumptions about accountability, intention, and personhood (Mele, 2014).

While some commentators warn of the dangers of "neuro-exceptionalism" and the overextension of neuroscientific findings to all aspects of human behavior, there is broad agreement that the crisis of free will is not simply an academic matter. It resonates deeply with public anxieties about autonomy, identity, and the capacity for genuine self-authorship in an age of scientific and technological determinism (Baumeister, 2008). At the same time, empirical studies reveal considerable variability in how individuals and cultures understand agency, responsibility, and blame, suggesting that scientific and legal models must remain sensitive to social and moral diversity (Bentahila, Fontaine, & Pennequin, 2021; Nichols, 2011). As philosophers and scientists seek to integrate the neuroscientific evidence with practical concerns, the question becomes how best to articulate a model of agency that is both empirically plausible and normatively robust. This has led to renewed interest in frameworks that foreground practice, community standards, and public accountability, rather than metaphysical speculation about uncaused causes (Dennett, 2015; Lehman, 2022). As such, neuroscience challenges us to reimagine free will as a relational, emergent, and socially mediated phenomenon. This reimagining opens the possibility for more humane, contextually grounded responses to human behavior—responses that recognize both the limits and the possibilities of agency in a deterministic universe.

0.3. The Understanding Crisis in AI

The accelerating sophistication of contemporary machine learning models, especially large language models (LLMs) and generative neural networks, has rekindled foundational questions regarding the nature of understanding in artificial systems. Recent scholarship highlights a growing consensus that the public, performative successes of such systems do not equate to genuine understanding in the philosophical sense; rather, they expose both the capabilities and the profound limitations of current architectures (Schlagwein & Willcocks, 2023). Despite their ability to generate highly plausible text and solve complex problems, these systems lack introspective awareness, subjective intentionality, and the capacity to ground meaning beyond pattern recognition. Philosophers and cognitive scientists argue that, while these models can simulate certain linguistic behaviors, they do so without any experience of meaning, making their "understanding" fundamentally different from human cognition (Yıldız, 2025). This distinction is now central to both philosophical debate and policy considerations as generative AI pervades research, education, and public discourse. The challenge, then, is to rigorously differentiate between the operational proficiency of these models and the qualitative, first-person features of understanding that characterize sentient beings. As Tredinnick and Laybats (2023) argue, the uncanny human-likeness of recent models risks blurring this boundary, tempting users to anthropomorphize algorithms in ways that outstrip their true cognitive architecture. Such concerns underscore the need for greater epistemic humility and conceptual clarity in our engagement with machine-generated language and apparent intelligence.

Recent philosophical and psychological research interrogates the pervasive human tendency to attribute complex mental states such as understanding and intention to systems that lack subjective consciousness. Yıldız (2025) contends that contemporary society is prone to "anthropomorphic projection," ascribing capacities like knowing, thinking, or believing to models that merely simulate these processes through statistical inference and large-scale data training. These attributions, while sometimes useful for communication and interface design, threaten to obscure the qualitative gap between human and artificial cognition. Empirical studies further reveal that the tendency to attribute mind to machines is influenced by contextual factors, such as task complexity and the linguistic fluency of the system (Cross & Ramsey, 2021; Wischnewski, 2025). Yet, as Ghiasi (2024) notes, the leap from intelligence to mind entails a transformation from systems that manipulate symbols to entities capable of integrating perception, emotion, and reflective judgment. The distinction between "artificial intelligence" and the more robust "artificial mind" becomes a central philosophical and practical question, one that cannot be resolved solely by advances in computation or engineering. As the line between machine-generated and human-generated outputs becomes increasingly difficult to discern in practice, public discourse and policy must be guided by principled philosophical analysis rather than technological hype. Current research emphasizes the importance of sustained critical inquiry into what is truly meant by understanding, intelligence, and mind in the context of artificial systems (Yıldız, 2025; Ghiasi, 2024).

The opacity of deep learning models, the so-called "black box" problem, poses a further obstacle to attributing genuine understanding to artificial systems. Schlagwein and Willcocks (2023) observe that while neural network models can produce outputs that appear meaningful and context-sensitive, the inner workings of these models remain largely inscrutable even to their creators. This lack of transparency raises epistemological and ethical issues: if we cannot explain how a system arrives at its conclusions, can we coherently claim that it "understands" anything at all? Kurilovich et al. (2024) emphasize that the epistemic opacity of such models complicates not only philosophical accounts of machine cognition but also efforts to regulate, audit, and ensure accountability in the deployment of these technologies. Furthermore, the rapid rise in the detectable presence of machine-generated content in scientific and scholarly communication suggests that questions of authorship, authenticity, and the nature of understanding are no longer merely theoretical concerns but have immediate, practical significance (Howard et al., 2024). The understanding crisis is as much a challenge for the philosophy of science and epistemology as for engineering and applied research.

Comparative philosophical work has increasingly turned to historical frameworks such as Kantian and Marxist theories of mind to provide fresh perspective on the challenges of defining and evaluating artificial understanding. Grigorova and Komarov (2024) analyze the limits of computational architectures through the lens of Kant's account of judgment and imagination, arguing that the synthesis of perception and reason in the human mind cannot be reduced to calculation alone. Lan and Shu (2024) bring historical materialism and the philosophy of mind into dialogue, showing that both the technical progress of artificial intelligence and the conceptual evolution of understanding require grounding in social, ethical, and cultural practices. These approaches suggest that the question of understanding in machines is not merely a technical or individual cognitive matter, but an issue deeply entangled with the structures of social life and the ongoing negotiation of what counts as meaning, reason, and personhood. The contemporary debate situates the understanding crisis as part of a broader philosophical transformation, wherein the boundaries between technology, subjectivity, and culture are renegotiated with each technological advance (Lan & Shu, 2024; Grigorova & Komarov, 2024). In this light, the pursuit of "artificial mind" or machine understanding becomes inseparable from the collective project of defining the human.

Finally, the ethical, social, and policy implications of the understanding crisis demand urgent and ongoing attention from scholars and practitioners alike. Recent conference proceedings and policy analyses reveal a rapidly shifting landscape in which the proliferation of generative models outpaces society's ability to develop robust frameworks for regulation, accountability, and the assignment of responsibility (Schlagwein & Willcocks, 2023; Howard et al., 2024). As Tredinnick and Laybats (2023) point out, public anxiety about the existential risks and societal impacts of machine "understanding" is intensifying, even as scientific assessments emphasize the limited and fundamentally non-conscious nature of current systems. The ethical imperative is twofold: to resist both the exaggeration of machine capabilities and the complacency that can result from underestimating their effects on institutions, knowledge production, and individual agency. Current research calls for a multidisciplinary, practice-based approach to the understanding crisis, one that integrates conceptual analysis, empirical inquiry, and policy design. Such an approach must remain attentive to the evolving boundary between appearance and reality, simulation and understanding, artifact and agent in the age of advanced computation (Yıldız, 2025; Schlagwein & Willcocks, 2023).

0.4. The Wittgensteinian Unified Framework

The later philosophy of Wittgenstein stands as a decisive intervention in the perennial debates over mind, meaning, and agency. Rejecting the traditional quest for inner, private states as the source of meaning, Wittgenstein posited that language is fundamentally a public practice, grounded in rule-following and shared human activities (Wittgenstein, 1953/2009). His "private language argument" famously demonstrated that any purportedly private meaning is unintelligible, as criteria for correctness—what it is to mean or understand—are possible only in a public space, where error and correction can occur

(Baker & Hacker, 1984). This insight had radical consequences for how philosophers and scientists would come to understand mind, language, and social reality, shifting the focus from the "inner theatre" of consciousness to the lived, communal activities that constitute human life (Kripke, 1982). Contemporary philosophers of language and mind have elaborated on this framework, arguing that even our most intimate psychological states, such as pain or intention, are intelligible only through their manifestation in public practices and criteria (Putnam, 1979; Hacker, 2014). This "practice turn" dissolves the dichotomy between internal mental content and external behavior, replacing it with a more nuanced, holistic account of meaning as use. Wittgenstein's framework has become foundational for subsequent work not only in analytic philosophy, but also in the cognitive sciences and artificial intelligence, where the "problem of other minds" and the nature of understanding are constantly renegotiated in light of new technological developments (Baker & Hacker, 1984; Hacker, 2014). The enduring influence of the Wittgensteinian framework is visible in current debates about the status of agency, understanding, and meaning in both humans and machines.

This framework redefines what it means for a practice to be 'public.' This notion of public criteria is not a demand for the exhaustive disclosure of every influence on an action, but rather for a shared, contestable framework within which actions become intelligible and accountable. Central to the underlying framework here is the conception of rule-following, which underpins this account of linguistic meaning, intentionality, and the social construction of reality. Wittgenstein argued that following a rule is not a matter of consulting an inner template or private intention, but a skillful, embodied participation in forms of life, governed by public standards of correctness (Wittgenstein, 1953/2009). The so-called "rule-following considerations" reveal that no finite set of explicit instructions can determine all future applications of a rule; instead, it is the open-ended, socially negotiated practices of a community that give rules their force (Kripke, 1982). This understanding challenges both the "mentalistic" and "mechanistic" models of mind: neither an isolated consciousness nor a purely syntactic algorithm can account for the creative, context-sensitive ways in which humans deploy and revise the rules of language and action (Baker & Hacker, 1984). Recent research in developmental psychology and cognitive science corroborates Wittgenstein's insight, showing that children acquire language, concepts, and norms not through introspection but through social scaffolding, imitation, and correction (Nawaz, Nizamani, & Hameed, 2024; Tomasello, 2019). Similarly, neuroscientific studies of social cognition underscore that even basic forms of understanding and action recognition are dependent on shared attention, mutual responsiveness, and culturally transmitted practices (Hari et al., 2015; Frith and Frith, 2010). The rule-following problem becomes a lens through which to view both the distinctiveness of human understanding and the challenges faced by artificial systems attempting to emulate or participate in such practices. The Wittgensteinian framework ultimately foregrounds the irreducibility of sociality to either internal states or computational rules.

The dissolution of the boundaries between language, action, and life bears directly on questions of agency, responsibility, and authorship. The analysis of the philosopher reveals that agency is not a metaphysical property located "inside" the subject, but an attribution made possible by participation in recognizable patterns of action and social expectation (Hacker, 2014). This shift resonates strongly with contemporary practice-based accounts of responsibility in philosophy, law, and cognitive science, where attributions of intention, blame, or credit are negotiated within communal practices and institutional settings (Bratman, 1992; Garfinkel, 2023). The influence of Wittgenstein is particularly salient in debates over authorship and creativity in the age of distributed cognition and technological mediation; the question "Who is the agent?" is increasingly reframed as "Which practices, norms, and institutions constitute the act and its recognition?" (Jaszi, 2017; Woodmansee, 1984). This perspective destabilizes the notion of the "isolated genius" or "original author," foregrounding instead the collaborative, context-sensitive, and rule-governed dimensions of agency. Recent scholarship on collective intentionality, distributed cognition, and the sociology of knowledge further extends Wittgenstein's insight, demonstrating that agency and creativity are never merely individual achievements but are always embedded in social and historical practices (Becker, 1982; Longino, 2020). This unified framework provides not only a diagnosis of the conceptual errors of traditional philosophy, but also a positive program for understanding agency, meaning, and creativity as emergent features of human forms of life.

The ramifications of the framework extend into contemporary neuroscience and technology, particularly as these fields grapple with the challenges of understanding, simulation, and consciousness. In neuroscience, the turn toward "embodied cognition" and the recognition of the social brain reflect Wittgensteinian insistence that mind and meaning cannot be understood apart from the practices in which they are instantiated (Clark, 2015). Studies show that neural activity underlying language, empathy, and intention is shaped by social interaction and contextual embedding, not merely by isolated information processing (Hari et al., 2015; Oesch, 2024). Similarly, debates about the understanding crisis in artificial intelligence are increasingly informed by Wittgensteinian skepticism about the possibility of genuine machine understanding without shared forms of life (Yıldız, 2025; Schlagwein & Willcocks, 2023). Philosophers and technologists alike are confronted with the limits of "simulation" or "performance" in the absence of true participation in the practices that give content to concepts and intentions (Putnam, 1975; Kripke, 1982). As machine learning models become more sophisticated, this framework urges us to ask not just "What can the machine do?" but "What practices does it participate in, and what forms of recognition, correction, and normativity are available to it?" This question is central to ongoing debates about the limits and possibilities of artificial minds.

Finally, Wittgenstein's unified framework compels a methodological humility and pluralism, challenging the search for final, foundational answers in philosophy, science, or technology. For Wittgenstein, the work of philosophy is not to build new theoretical structures atop questionable foundations, but to clarify the forms of life and patterns of practice that already undergird our concepts of mind, meaning, and agency (Wittgenstein, 1953/2009). This "therapeutic" approach dissolves pseudo-problems and reframes philosophical debate as an ongoing activity of elucidation, critique, and reorientation (Baker & Hacker, 1984). In the context of contemporary crises—whether in neuroscience, law, or artificial intelligence—Wittgenstein's method demands a renewed attention to how our categories and frameworks are shaped, maintained, and revised in practice. Rather than treating agency, understanding, or responsibility as metaphysical mysteries, we are invited to view them as emergent, contingent, and open to transformation as our practices evolve (Longino, 2020; Tomasello, 2009). In this way, this unified framework provides not only a philosophical diagnosis but a critical resource for navigating the conceptual, scientific, and social challenges of our age.

0.5. Structure of the Book

The architecture of this volume is deliberately designed to traverse—and synthesize—the conceptual terrains of philosophy, neuroscience, law, and technology. The structure reflects the conviction that the crises of authorship, freedom, and understanding are not discrete puzzles, but entangled phenomena demanding integrative, practice-based analysis. This book proceeds from a detailed philosophical and historical foundation, through empirical and legal case studies, to a set of forward-looking frameworks for ethical, technological, and legal reconstruction. The movement is dialectical: each part revisits the questions posed in the introduction, offering increasingly robust resources for navigating a world in which the meaning of agency, responsibility, and creativity is no longer a metaphysical inheritance but an object of ongoing negotiation and collective design.

The book is organized into four thematic parts, each corresponding to a distinct layer of the contemporary crisis in agency. *Part I: The Philosophical Foundation* develops the theoretical groundwork, tracing the transition from mentalist to practice-based accounts of meaning, agency, and responsibility. It situates Wittgenstein's revolution against inner states as the decisive philosophical context, then explores how contemporary neuroscience (especially Sapolsky's determinism) and copyright doctrine reveal the inadequacy of traditional, intention-based models. *Part II: The Pattern of Agency* moves from theory to comparative analysis, examining how both human and machine agency are shaped by participation in public practices. Here, the focus is on the limits of libertarian freedom, the construction of meaning in language and communication, and the irreducibility of social context in both human and artificial systems.

Part III: Legal and Ethical Reconstruction addresses the transformative pressures exerted by technological advances on legal reasoning, moral theory, and institutional practice. It critically evaluates the ongoing evolution of copyright, criminal justice, and liability frameworks, highlighting the need to replace metaphysical models of agency with ones grounded in participation, transformation, and collective standards. *Part IV: The Post-Inner-State World* looks ahead, articulating the implications of these transformations for the ethical design of artificial systems, the evolution of legal and constitutional principles, and the search for meaning and community after the decline of the Cartesian subject. Each part builds on the last, culminating in a unified, pragmatic approach that redefines transparency not as the impossible audit of inner states or causal chains, but as the public act of taking responsibility within shared practices. This distinction between procedural transparency and the flawed pursuit of metaphysical disclosure will be a central thread of the analysis that follows.

The narrative journey of this book moves from the Introduction here to Chapter 1: Wittgenstein's Revolution Against Inner States, which reconstructs the dissolution of the philosopher of the private language myth and his argument for meaning as a matter of use within public practices. This chapter illuminates how the rule-following considerations and the rejection of mentalist explanations ground a fundamentally social conception of language, intention, and agency. In Chapter 2: Sapolsky's Challenge and the Determinist Insight, the lens shifts to neuroscience, with a particular focus on Robert Sapolsky's empirical and philosophical work. This analysis reveals how deterministic accounts of human behavior disrupt metaphysical models of self-origination and force both philosophy and law to reconsider the nature of freedom and responsibility.

Chapter 3: The Copyright Laboratory draws on recent case law and doctrinal evolution to interrogate the ongoing debates around AI-generated works and the human authorship requirement. The chapter demonstrates how courts and policymakers are gradually moving away from intention-based frameworks, often under practical pressure, toward standards rooted in participation, transformation, and public practice. With this philosophical and legal foundation in place, the book transitions in Chapter 4: AI Understanding Without Inner Experience to explore whether advanced computational systems can exhibit genuine understanding. It interrogates the irreducibility of public linguistic practice and community validation, highlighting the deep challenges facing attempts to simulate or reproduce human understanding technologically.

Subsequent chapters elaborate these core themes across broader domains. Chapter 5: Human Agency Without Libertarian Freedom explores the consequences of relinquishing metaphysical accounts of agency, advocating a practice-based view of responsibility and revealing the parallel structure of decision-making in both human and machine agents. Chapter 6: Speech Acts, Intentions, and the Social Construction of Meaning extends the inquiry into the philosophy of language, analyzing how both human and artificial communication are grounded in shared practices, with intentionality emerging not from inner states but from social performance.

The argument's trajectory continues in Chapter 7: Toward Post-Cartesian Copyright, which charts the evolution of legal doctrine away from mind-centered standards of creativity toward new, practice-oriented benchmarks that better reflect the realities of collaborative and technologically mediated authorship. This legal transformation is mirrored in Chapter 8: Criminal Justice After Free Will, where the erosion of traditional free will conceptions under neuroscientific scrutiny motivates a rethinking of retributive justice and the development of alternative frameworks focused on competence, rehabilitation, and social protection.

Chapter 9: AI Liability and Systemic Responsibility takes up the challenge of assigning responsibility within distributed technological systems, emphasizing the need for legal and ethical frameworks that can accommodate collective and emergent forms of agency. The practical and normative insights generated in these legal and philosophical analyses are then brought to bear in Chapter 10: Designing Ethical AI Systems, which provides a pragmatic blueprint for embedding ethical values and social practices into the design and governance of artificial systems, going beyond superficial models of "meaningful human control."

The closing chapters widen the scope, considering the institutional and societal implications of this intellectual transformation. Chapter 11: The Broader Legal Transformation explores how the decline of inner-state-centric worldviews may reshape constitutional norms, principles of equal protection, and due process, advocating for a pluralistic, context-sensitive approach to justice. In Chapter 12: Living After the Cartesian Ghost, the text reflects on what is gained by relocating agency, responsibility, and meaning within the fabric of communal life and practice, and sketches new forms of community and policy for a determined age. The Conclusion: The Unexpected Unity draws together these arguments, highlighting the philosophical and practical necessity of grounding agency, meaning, and responsibility in social practices, and inviting readers to contribute to the ongoing work of conceptual and societal renewal.

References

Ahmed, I. (2025). Navigating Ethics And Risk In Artificial Intelligence Applications Within Information Technology: A Systematic Review. *American Journal of Advanced Technology and Engineering Solutions*, *1*(01), 579-601.

Apperly, I. (2010). *Mindreaders: the cognitive basis of" theory of mind."* Psychology Press.

Baker, G. P., & Hacker, P. M. S. (1984). On misunderstanding Wittgenstein: Kripke's private language argument. *Synthese*, 407-450.

Baumeister, R. F. (2008). Free will in scientific psychology. *Perspectives on Psychological Science, 3*(1), 14–19.

Becker, H. (1984). *Art worlds.* University of California press.

Bengesi, S., El-Sayed, H., Sarker, M. K., Houkpati, Y., Irungu, J., & Oladunni, T. (2024). Advancements in generative AI: A comprehensive review of GANs, GPT, autoencoders, diffusion model, and transformers. *IEEe Access*, *12*, 69812-69837.

Bentahila, L., Fontaine, R., & Pennequin, V. (2021). Universality and cultural diversity in moral reasoning and judgment. *Frontiers in psychology*, *12*, 764360.

Berger, P., & Luckmann, T. (2016). The social construction of reality. In *Social theory re-wired* (pp. 110-122). Routledge.

Blakemore, S. J., Wolpert, D. M., & Frith, C. D. (2002). Abnormalities in the awareness of action. *Trends in cognitive sciences*, *6*(6), 237-242.

Bratman, M. E. (1992). Shared cooperative activity. *The philosophical review*, *101*(2), 327-341.

Brown, T. R. (2021). Treating addiction in the clinic, not the courtroom: Using neuroscience and genetics to abandon the failed war on drugs. *Ind. L. Rev.*, *54*, 29.

Bryson, J. J. (2016). Patiency Is Not a Virtue: AI and the Design of Ethical Systems. In *AAAI Spring Symposia*.

Caruso, G. D. (2012). *Free will and consciousness: A determinist account of the illusion of free will*. Lexington Books.

Chen, J., & Bornstein, A. M. (2024). The causal structure and computational value of narratives. *Trends in Cognitive Sciences*, *28*(8), 769-781.

Clark, A. (2015). *Surfing uncertainty: Prediction, action, and the embodied mind*. Oxford University Press.

Cross, E. S., & Ramsey, R. (2021). Mind meets machine: Towards a cognitive science of human–machine interactions. *Trends in cognitive sciences*, *25*(3), 200-212.

Davidson, D. (1980). *Essays on actions and events*. Oxford University Press.

Dennett, D. C. (2015). *Elbow room, new edition: The varieties of free will worth wanting*. mit Press.

Devlin, J., Chang, M. W., Lee, K., & Toutanova, K. (2019, June). Bert: Pre-training of deep bidirectional transformers for language understanding. In *Proceedings of the 2019 conference of the North American chapter of the association for computational linguistics: human language technologies, volume 1 (long and short papers)* (pp. 4171-4186).

Doshi-Velez, F., & Kim, B. (2017). Towards a rigorous science of interpretable machine learning. *arXiv preprint arXiv:1702.08608*.

Double, R. (1996). *Metaphilosophy and free will*. Oxford University Press.

Dutta, A. (2025). Neurocomputational Mechanisms of Sense of Agency: Literature Review for Integrating Predictive Coding and Adaptive Control in Human–Machine Interfaces. *Brain Sciences*, *15*(4), 396.

El Zein, M., Dolan, R. J., & Bahrami, B. (2022). Shared responsibility decreases the sense of agency in the human brain. *Journal of Cognitive Neuroscience*, *34*(11), 2065-2081.

Faraji, J., & Metz, G. A. (2023). Toward reframing brain-social dynamics: current assumptions and future challenges. *Frontiers in Psychiatry*, *14*, 1211442.

Fried, I., Mukamel, R., & Kreiman, G. (2011). Internally generated preactivation of single neurons in human medial frontal cortex predicts volition. *Neuron*, *69*(3), 548-562.

Frith, U., & Frith, C. (2010). The social brain: allowing humans to boldly go where no other species has been. *Philosophical Transactions of the Royal Society B: Biological Sciences*, *365*(1537), 165-176.

Garfinkel, H. (2023). Studies in ethnomethodology. In *Social Theory Re-Wired* (pp. 58-66). Routledge.

Gazzaniga, M. (2012). *Who's in Charge?: Free Will and the Science of the Brain*. Hachette UK.

Ghiasi, M. (2024). From artificial intelligence to artificial Mind: A paradigm shift. *IEEE Potentials*.

Giddens, A. (1984). *The constitution of society: Outline of the theory of structuration*. Univ of California Press.

Greene, J., & Cohen, J. (2004). For the law, neuroscience changes nothing and everything. *Philosophical Transactions of the Royal Society B: Biological Sciences*, *359*(1451), 1775.

Grigorova, Y. V., & Komarov, S. V. (2024). Analyzing the problem of artificial intelligence through the prism of immanuel kant's philosophy. *Философия. Психология. Социология 2024*, 464.

Hacker, P. M. (2014). Two conceptions of language. *Erkenntnis*, *79*(Suppl 7), 1271-1288.

Haggard, P. (2008). Human volition: towards a neuroscience of will. *Nature Reviews Neuroscience*, *9*(12), 934-946.

Haggard, P. (2017). Sense of agency in the human brain. *Nature Reviews Neuroscience*, *18*(4), 196-207.

Hari, R., Henriksson, L., Malinen, S., & Parkkonen, L. (2015). Centrality of social interaction in human brain function. *Neuron*, *88*(1), 181-193.

Haslanger, S. (2012). *Resisting reality: Social construction and social critique*. Oxford University Press.

Hassija, V., Chamola, V., Mahapatra, A., Singal, A., Goel, D., Huang, K., & Hussain, A. (2024). Interpreting black-box models: a review on explainable artificial intelligence. *Cognitive Computation*, *16*(1), 45-74.

Howard, F. M., Li, A., Riffon, M. F., Garrett-Mayer, E., & Pearson, A. T. (2024). Characterizing the increase in artificial intelligence content detection in oncology scientific abstracts from 2021 to 2023. *JCO Clinical Cancer Informatics*, *8*, e2400077.

Jaszi, P. (2017). Toward a theory of copyright: the metamorphoses of "authorship." In *Intellectual Property Law and History* (pp. 61-108). Routledge.

Kripke, S. A. (1982). Wittgenstein on Rules and Private Language: An Elementary Exposition. Harvard University Press.

Kuhn, T. S. (1997). *The structure of scientific revolutions* (Vol. 962). Chicago: University of Chicago press.

Kurilovich, I. S., Golubov, M. D., Perova, N. V., & Zanina, A. P. (2024). Artificial Intelligence as a Metaphor, Object, and Subject of Philosophical Analysis. *VOPROSY FILOSOFII*, (9).

Lan, X., & Shu, H. (2024). The breakthrough of philosophy of mind in the construction of artificial intelligence concepts in Marxist philosophy. *Trans/Form/Ação*, *47*(6), e02400332.

Latour, B., Salk, J., & Woolgar, S. (2013). Laboratory life: The construction of scientific facts.

Lehman, G. (2022). *Accountability and transparency in the modern anthropocene*. Springer.

Libet, B., Gleason, C. A., Wright, E. W., & Pearl, D. K. (1983). Time of conscious intention to act in relation to onset of cerebral activity (readiness-potential) the unconscious initiation of a freely voluntary act. *Brain*, *106*(3), 623-642.

Lombrozo, T. (2012). 14 Explanation and Abductive Inference. *The Oxford handbook of thinking and reasoning*, 260.

Longino, H. E. (2020). Science as social knowledge: Values and objectivity in scientific inquiry.

Malcolm, N., & Wittgenstein, L. (2001). *Ludwig Wittgenstein: a memoir*. Oxford University Press.

Malik, R. (2023). *Neurocognitive Mechanisms & Genetic Variants Underlying Apathy in Neurodegenerative Dementias* (Doctoral dissertation, The University of Western Ontario (Canada)).

Mathew, D. E., Ebem, D. U., Ikegwu, A. C., Ukeoma, P. E., & Dibiaezue, N. F. (2025). Recent emerging techniques in explainable artificial intelligence to enhance the interpretable and understanding of AI models for human. *Neural Processing Letters*, *57*(1), 16.

Matthias, A. (2004). The responsibility gap: Ascribing responsibility for the actions of learning automata. *Ethics and information technology*, *6*(3), 175-183.

Mele, A. R. (2014). *Free: Why science hasn't disproved free will*. Oxford University Press.

Morse, S. J. (2005). Brain overclaim syndrome and criminal responsibility: A diagnostic note. *Ohio St. J. Crim. L.*, *3*, 397.

Nawaz, M., Nizamani, M., & Hameed, R. (2024). Analyze how children acquire language and the cognitive processes involved, including the role of environmental and social factors. *Bulletin of Business and Economics (BBE)*, *13*(3), 239-247.

Nichols, S. (2011). Experimental philosophy and the problem of free will. *science*, *331*(6023), 1401-1403.

Oesch, N. (2024). Social brain perspectives on the social and evolutionary neuroscience of human language. *Brain Sciences*, *14*(2), 166.

Pagallo, U. (2013). The laws of robots. *Crimes, Contracts and Torts,* Cham.

Putnam, H. (1979). *Mind, language and reality* (Vol. 2). Cambridge University Press.

Reddy, K. J. (2025). Mitigation and Sentencing in Criminal Cases. In *Foundations of Criminal Forensic Neuropsychology: Bridging Mind, Law, and Criminal Justice* (pp. 341-377). Cham: Springer Nature Switzerland.

Roskies, A. L. (2010). How does neuroscience affect our conception of volition?. *Annual review of neuroscience*, *33*(1), 109-130.

Saeidnia, H. R., & Nilashi, M. (2025). From MYCIN to MedGemma: A Historical and Comparative Analysis of Healthcare AI Evolution. *InfoScience Trends*, *2*(6), 18-28.

Sawyer, R. K., & Henriksen, D. (2024). *Explaining creativity: The science of human innovation*. Oxford university press.

Schlagwein, D., & Willcocks, L. (2023). 'ChatGPT et al.': The ethics of using (generative) artificial intelligence in research and science. *Journal of Information Technology*, *38*(3), 232-238.

Seibt, J., Vestergaard, C., & Fossa, F. (2020). Towards a taxonomy of social robots. *International Journal of Social Robotics, 12*(1), 27–46.

Schurger, A., Pak, J., & Roskies, A. L. (2021). What is the readiness potential?. *Trends in cognitive sciences*, *25*(7), 558-570.

Soon, C. S., Brass, M., Heinze, H. J., & Haynes, J. D. (2008). Unconscious determinants of free decisions in the human brain. *Nature neuroscience*, *11*(5), 543-545.

Stoutland, F. (2011). Introduction: Anscombe's Intention in context. In *Essays on Anscombe's Intention* (pp. 1-22). Harvard University Press.

Tomasello, M. (2009). *The cultural origins of human cognition*. Harvard University Press.
Tredinnick, L., & Laybats, C. (2023). The dangers of generative artificial intelligence. *Business Information Review*, *40*(2), 46-48.
Valsiner, J. (2014). An invitation to cultural psychology.
Vijayaraghavan, S., & Felsen, G. (Eds.). (2025). *Neuroscience and Society*. CRC Press.
Vygotsky, L. S., & Cole, M. (1978). *Mind in society: Development of higher psychological processes*. Harvard university press.
Wegner, D. M. (2017). *The illusion of conscious will*. MIT press.
Wellman, H. M., & Liu, D. (2007). Causal reasoning as informed by the early development of explanations. *Causal learning: Psychology, philosophy, and computation*, *261279*.
Wischnewski, M. (2025, April). Attributing mental states to non-embodied autonomous systems: A systematic review. In *Proceedings of the Extended Abstracts of the CHI Conference on Human Factors in Computing Systems* (pp. 1-8).
Wittgenstein, L. (2003). *Ludwig Wittgenstein*. Bloomsbury Publishing PLC.
Wittgenstein, L. (2009). *Philosophical investigations*. John Wiley & Sons.
Wittmann, M., Montemayor, C., & Dorato, M. (2025). Stoicism, mindfulness, and the brain: the empirical foundations of second-order desires. *Frontiers in psychology*, *16*, 1569237.
Woodmansee, M. (1984). The genius and the copyright: Economic and legal conditions of the emergence of the'author'. *Eighteenth-century studies*, *17*(4), 425-448.
Yıldız, T. (2025). The minds we make: A philosophical inquiry into theory of mind and artificial intelligence. *Integrative Psychological and Behavioral Science*, *59*(1), 10.

Part I: The Philosophical Foundation

Chapter 1

The Wittgensteinian Revolution Against Inner States

Abstract

This chapter examines the philosophical revolution initiated by Ludwig Wittgenstein, challenging the primacy of private mental states in the constitution of meaning and agency. Through an exploration of the private language argument and the problem of rule-following, the discussion shows that meaning arises not from internal experiences but from participation in shared linguistic and normative practices. The analysis considers how the critique of Wittgenstein extends to the ascription of intention, responsibility, and understanding, demonstrating that these concepts rely fundamentally on community standards and external criteria. A skeptical interpretation, as developed by Saul Kripke, is brought into dialogue to highlight the centrality of communal agreement in fixing meaning and attributing agency. By tracing the historical and philosophical implications of the Wittgensteinian approach, the analysis displaces inner states from a privileged theoretical position, inaugurating a practice-based account of action and thought. This orientation toward practice serves as a foundation for the critical investigations of agency that unfold in subsequent chapters.

1.1. Beyond Private Language: Meaning as Public Practice

The philosophical argument known as the private language argument represents a foundational moment in twentieth-century philosophy of mind and language. Ludwig Wittgenstein proposed that language cannot function as a private phenomenon, accessible only to a solitary consciousness, but must instead exist within the context of shared social practices and communal criteria (Wittgenstein, 1953/2009; Baker & Hacker, 1984). Any attempt to construct a language intelligible only to a single speaker founders on the absence of external standards for correctness, error, or understanding. Without public criteria, there can be no meaningful distinction between seeming to follow a rule and actually following it, rendering the notion of purely private meaning incoherent (Kripke, 1982). Philosophical and empirical research in psychology corroborates this argument, demonstrating that language acquisition and conceptual understanding emerge through social interaction, imitation, and correction, not through introspective acts of private naming (Tomasello, 2009; Vygotsky & Cole, 1978). Sociological analyses further illuminate how meaning becomes institutionalized through patterns of behavior, ritual, and norm enforcement, reinforcing the centrality of communal practice (Giddens, 1984; Berger & Luckmann, 2016). This perspective challenges Cartesian traditions that privilege inner mental content as the origin of language and meaning, shifting the analytic focus to observable, public activity (Putnam, 1975). The result is a robust, practice-based account of meaning that undergirds subsequent developments in philosophy, cognitive science, and law.

Rule-following emerges as a central theme in Wittgenstein's later philosophy, offering a lens through which to understand both linguistic competence and the sociality of mind. Wittgenstein argued that no finite set of explicit rules or mental representations can determine all future applications of a rule; instead, mastery of a rule is demonstrated through participation in socially negotiated practices (Wittgenstein, 1953/2009; Kripke, 1982). The open-ended character of rule-application necessitates that individuals rely on community standards for guidance, correction, and validation. Cognitive scientists have extended this analysis, finding that even basic conceptual abilities and inferential reasoning are shaped by scaffolding, shared attention, and culturally embedded routines (Tomasello, 2009). Neuroscience further supports the view that neural circuits for language and action develop within social contexts, with activity in the so-called "social brain" modulated by patterns of joint attention, cooperation, and feedback (Hari et al., 2015; Frith & Frith, 2010). The social dimension of rule-following displaces the idea that mental content resides exclusively within the subject, relocating meaning within the flow of practical activity. This perspective has profound implications for legal theory, educational practice, and the design of artificial systems, all of which depend on reliable standards for ascribing competence and agency. Wittgenstein's critique demonstrates that meaning is never a matter of private intuition but always of public negotiation and recognition. Here, "public" refers to the accessibility of the practice itself, not to a requirement for total transparency of an individual's methods or motivations. The focus is on the shared game, not on revealing every card in one's hand.

The consequences of this framework extend to the ascription of intention, responsibility, and understanding. Wittgenstein contended that these concepts, too, derive their intelligibility from participation in socially recognized forms of life, rather than from any hidden, subjective states (Wittgenstein, 1953/2009; Hacker, 2014). Philosophers have developed this point by showing that intentional action is attributed not on the basis of introspective access, but through the interpretation of observable behavior in light of shared scripts, norms, and expectations (Bratman, 1992). Psychological research on theory of mind supports this analysis, revealing that individuals attribute intentions and beliefs to others by reference to familiar patterns of action and public context (Apperly, 2010). Law and ethics have followed suit, increasingly grounding assessments of responsibility and accountability in community standards, institutional practices, and the capacity to engage in social reasoning (Garfinkel, 2023; Longino, 2020). The shift away from mentalistic explanations of agency enables more pluralistic, context-sensitive approaches to justice, pedagogy, and social regulation. Rather than seeking metaphysical guarantees of intention, public practices become the criterion for both competence and culpability. In this sense, Wittgenstein's framework not only challenges traditional philosophy but also reorients foundational assumptions across the social sciences and humanities.

A central contribution of Wittgenstein's analysis lies in the critique of the sharp boundary between inner and outer, mental and behavioral. Rather than viewing behavior as a mere outward sign of hidden mental content, Wittgenstein presented human action as itself the bearer of meaning, intention, and understanding. Philosophers of language and mind have extended this anti-dualistic insight, showing that concepts such as pain, belief, or promise are meaningful only insofar as they are manifested in the regularities of public life (Putnam, 1979; Baker & Hacker, 1984). Neuroscientific research into mirror neurons and social cognition reinforces this point, demonstrating that the perception and attribution of agency rely on embodied, interactive processes, not introspective inference (Eickers, 2024; Hari et al., 2015). In practical terms, this means that education, law, and technological design must attend to the ways in which standards of meaning, agency, and competence are constructed and maintained within the community. The rejection of the inner-outer dichotomy provides not only a philosophical diagnosis but a methodological imperative: to study the forms of life and shared practices that constitute mind and meaning. This practice-oriented methodology stands in contrast to introspective or computational approaches that seek the origins of meaning in private or algorithmic domains. Wittgenstein's analysis encourages ongoing investigation of how social practices enable, constrain, and transform agency across contexts.

Recent scholarship has highlighted the enduring relevance of the practice-based framework of Wittgenstein in addressing challenges posed by technological and social change. As machine learning models and artificial agents increasingly participate in domains traditionally reserved for humans, questions about the nature of understanding, creativity, and responsibility become pressing (Schlagwein & Willcocks, 2023; Yıldız, 2025). Researchers argue that the standards for ascribing agency or understanding to machines must be grounded in their ability to engage in communal practices, be subject to correction, and generate outcomes intelligible to human participants (Yıldız, 2025; Zafar, 2025). The ongoing debates in law, policy, and philosophy of technology reflect the need for public, practice-based criteria in attributing authorship, intention, or blame, especially as technological systems grow more complex and autonomous (Jaszi, 2017; Woodmansee, 1984). The critique of private language provides not only a theoretical foundation for rethinking agency, but a practical guide for responding to contemporary problems in science, law, and society. By insisting that meaning is constituted through participation, negotiation, and communal validation, Wittgenstein's framework equips scholars and practitioners with the tools to navigate an era of rapid conceptual and technological transformation.

In sum, the rejection of private language and the embrace of meaning as public practice serve as a foundation for a pluralistic, adaptive, and resilient understanding of mind and society. This framework empowers scholars, policymakers, and technologists to move beyond the search for hidden mental essences and instead to construct standards of competence, understanding, and responsibility through visible, corrigible, and participatory practices. The approach scales from the micro-level of conversation and education to the macro-level of governance, law, and technology, providing a methodological anchor for navigating ambiguity, disagreement, and innovation. In an era marked by distributed agency, whether through collaborative research, complex institutions, or AI-driven systems, the need for practice-based benchmarks is more urgent than ever. By foregrounding the processes by which meaning is enacted, debated, and revised, Wittgenstein's account ensures that our criteria for agency, legitimacy, and value remain open to negotiation and growth. This orientation not only demystifies language and mind but also fosters the collective creativity and accountability needed to address the ethical, legal, and existential challenges of the twenty-first century. Ultimately, it is through shared practices rather than private introspection that society continually remakes the conditions for meaning, understanding, and collective flourishing.

1.2. The Rule-Following Considerations and the Death of Inner Determination

The analysis on the part of Wittgenstein of rule-following represents a radical departure from theories that ground meaning and intentionality in private mental content. According to this framework, following a rule is not a solitary exercise of consulting internal representations, but a social activity that unfolds within the context of training, habit, and communal standards (Langseth, 2008; Kamota & Ndemo, 2024). The correct application of a rule is determined not by introspective access to private intentions, but by regularities in action, social expectation, and the consequences of practical engagement (Heath, 2008). As Miller (2024) notes, Wittgenstein's emphasis on "blind rule-following" underscores that normativity is established through manifest competence in public practices, rather than through mental rehearsal or private interpretation. This perspective dissolves the idea that an inner act of meaning-bestowal or decision serves as a final arbiter of correctness, replacing it with the iterative, communal negotiation of standards (Kamota & Ndemo, 2024). The skepticism that arises from considering how one could ever be sure of following a rule "correctly" leads to the insight that the stability of meaning and intentionality is a function of public regularities, not internal determination (Shahryari, 2021). Such a shift destabilizes classical accounts of the will, agency, and authorship by removing the metaphysical "ghost in the machine" and placing responsibility within the pattern of communal practice. Recent work continues to explore the implications of this move for ethics, social theory, and legal reasoning (Ogleznev, 2020).

The so-called "paradox of rule-following" (Figure 1.1), famously crystallized by Saul Kripke, argues that no fact about an individual, not even an explicit set of intentions, can determine the correct way to apply a rule in novel circumstances (Shahryari, 2021). Any purported mental blueprint can be interpreted in multiple ways, making the very notion of "inner determination" unstable. As a result, Wittgenstein's analysis compels us to accept that the ability to follow a rule is grounded in the lived practices of a community, where deviation is corrected through training and negotiation, not through appeal to hidden inner facts (Langseth, 2008). Recent studies show that even mathematical practices, often held up as paradigms of logical necessity, are deeply infused with social and grammatical conventions rather than being reducible to objective, context-free rules (Ravn & Skovsmose, 2019). The turn away from inner determination marks the "death" of the search for metaphysical criteria of correctness, highlighting the pragmatic dimension of rule-governed activity (de Silva Pinto, 2024). Rule-following is revealed as a form of life, a complex ensemble of habits, expectations, and responsive adjustments embedded in the ongoing flow of social interaction (Gürsoy, 2024). This view aligns with the increasing recognition in anthropology and sociology that normative competence is inseparable from the capacity to engage in shared, improvisational practices. The consequence is a vision of normativity and meaning as essentially public, context-sensitive, and evolving.

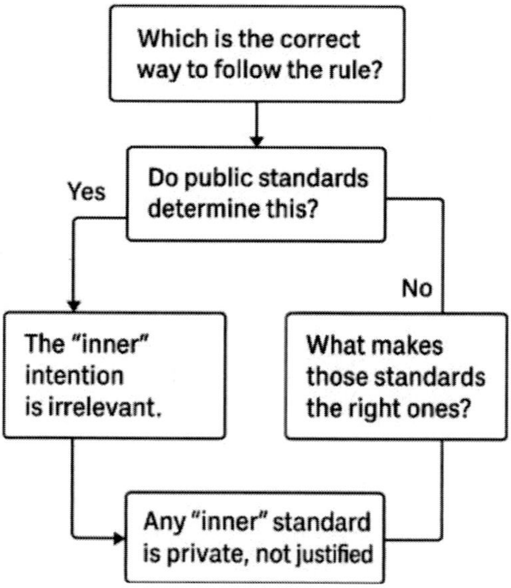

Figure 1.1. Rule-Following Problem.

The social character of rule-following has profound implications for understanding agency and responsibility in modern society. Nowak (2019) and others argue that moral judgment and discursive competence are possible only because individuals manifest a normative competence that is recognized and reinforced through collective practice. As well, Langseth (2008) contends that Wittgenstein's perspective demonstrates the limits of individual interpretation: criteria for correct rule-following are supplied by public responses, not by private conviction. In legal philosophy, this insight has prompted scholars to reconsider how legal standards and precedents function as shared resources, subject to contestation, reinterpretation, and gradual evolution (Ogleznev, 2020). The pattern of correction, challenge, and modification forms the backbone of institutional practice, providing both flexibility and stability in systems of meaning and governance (Elliott, 2024). In the design of technological and social systems, understanding rule-following as an emergent property of collective life shifts attention from the encoding of rules to the cultivation of practices capable of adapting to change (Pérez-Escobar & Sarikaya, 2024). The resulting account rejects metaphysical models that seek grounding in inner determination and instead locates agency in the ongoing achievement of competence within a community's evolving forms of life. Rule-following, in this light, becomes the central phenomenon through which human beings create, sustain, and revise the normative landscape.

Critics have sometimes challenged the practice-based approach to rule-following, raising concerns about relativism, arbitrariness, or the loss of objectivity. Recent scholarship, however, suggests that communal standards and forms of life offer both stability and the capacity for rational critique (de Silva Pinto, 2024). Rather than grounding correctness in private insight, the public nature of rule-following allows for collective reflection, mutual correction, and innovation within the bounds of shared language games (Kamota & Ndemo, 2024). Miller (2024) argues that understanding, meaning, and intentional content are not reducible to simple dispositional or behavioral facts, but are realized in the intention to exercise abilities within the horizon of a community's standards. This anti-reductionist perspective preserves the critical distinction between merely acting in accordance with a rule and genuinely following a rule, a distinction only meaningful in a context where others can judge, correct, or challenge one's actions (Child, 2024). The death of inner determination does not entail the disappearance of rationality or objectivity, but their relocation into the dynamic processes of communal life. Rules and meanings remain robust so long as they are maintained, revised, and justified through actual practices and dialogic engagement. This account opens new avenues for understanding learning, change, and disagreement as constitutive features of normative life, rather than as problems to be eliminated. The implications reach beyond philosophy into law, education, and technological design, each domain drawing strength from the public, corrigible character of normativity.

The ramifications of Wittgenstein's rule-following considerations extend into political theory, epistemology, and the philosophy of technology.

Scholars such as Elliott (2024) and Gürsoy (2024) have drawn on the idea that rules and forms of life are the loci of both constraint and emancipation, making possible the collective pursuit of justice, knowledge, and self-realization. The flexibility and resilience of social norms depend not on their foundation in inner determination but on the capacity of communities to recognize contradiction, innovate new practices, and adapt to shifting circumstances (Elliott, 2024). Studies in epistemology and mathematics reveal that rule-following is inseparable from the contingent, historical, and cultural factors that shape conceptual content (Ravn & Skovsmose, 2019; Gürsoy, 2024). Legal and ethical debates increasingly recognize that legitimacy and rationality reside not in metaphysical sources, but in the procedural and participatory character of social regulation (Ogleznev, 2020; Nowak, 2019). Rule-following is the central process by which meaning, authority, and accountability are both maintained and transformed. The replacement of inner determination with a social-practice model clarifies how agency and normativity can be both stable and open to evolution, grounded in actual human life rather than philosophical abstraction. As technological and institutional systems become more complex, the Wittgensteinian focus on communal competence and correction offers a guide for responsible adaptation and renewal.

The contemporary impact of Wittgenstein's account of rule-following is evident in the ongoing development of collaborative technologies, distributed legal regimes, and adaptive educational models. In digital environments such as open-source software communities, online dispute resolution platforms, and AI-assisted learning systems, the creation, interpretation, and enforcement of rules emerge from ongoing negotiation, peer feedback, and participatory correction rather than from top-down directives or fixed mental templates (Pérez-Escobar & Sarikaya, 2024; Langseth, 2008). These systems thrive when they embody mechanisms for communal scrutiny, iterative revision, and transparent governance, demonstrating that robust normativity can be achieved through the practical work of shared engagement. By foregrounding the social construction of meaning and the necessity of public standards for competence, Wittgenstein's insights enable more resilient and responsive forms of coordination, innovation, and collective agency across diverse domains. The "death" of inner determination is not a loss but a generative transformation, equipping contemporary societies to confront the challenges of pluralism, complexity, and continual change through the open-ended, dialogic refinement of their forms of life.

1.3. The Kripkean Skeptical Solution: Community Standards over Mental States

The influential reading of Wittgenstein on rule-following by American philosopher and logician Saul Kripke stands as a major intervention in the philosophy of language and mind. Kripke articulates a deep skepticism about the possibility that any private fact—mental state, intention, or interpretation—could determine how a rule is to be followed in new circumstances (Kripke, 1982; Shahryari, 2021). The so-called "Kripkenstein" paradox asks: what, if anything, could guarantee that a person means addition rather than "quaddition" (a deviant function) when using the symbol "+"? Every attempt to ground rule-following in a mental blueprint or internal plan collapses, as such mental facts are themselves subject to reinterpretation. Recent commentators have noted that this challenge undermines not only traditional mentalist accounts, but also dispositional or behaviorist attempts to fix meaning (Miller, 2024; Kamota & Ndemo, 2024). The skeptical solution Kripke develops contends that no fact about an individual, mental or physical, can secure the correct application of a rule in isolation. Instead, meaning and correctness are constituted by the regularities, expectations, and practices of a linguistic community. The act of following a rule is made possible only by public, social standards, not by inner determination.

The skeptical solution of Kripke moves the discussion from the metaphysics of mental content to the pragmatics of communal interaction. Correctness on this account does not reside in the private realm but in the actual patterns of response and agreement found among competent language users (Langseth, 2008; Child, 2024). When the use of a word on the part of an individual is challenged, the standard for deciding correctness is not introspective certainty, but the acceptance or rejection of that use by others who share the practice. Wittgenstein, as interpreted by Kripke, places the "bedrock" of normativity in the regularized social practices that structure our forms of life (Gürsoy, 2024). Public negotiation, correction, and reinforcement become the criteria by which meaning is established, maintained, and transmitted. The implication is not a slide into relativism, but a recognition that normativity is sustained through the dynamic interplay of communal life. Current research in social epistemology and legal philosophy confirms that stable standards of meaning and justification emerge not from private conviction, but from shared, historically embedded patterns of reasoning (Elliott, 2024; Ogleznev, 2020). This account suggests that the possibility of objective meaning and rationality depends on the social practices in which individuals participate.

The consequences of the skeptical solution of Kripke ripple out into many domains, including epistemology, law, and the philosophy of technology. In epistemology, the communal account of rule-following underpins theories that treat knowledge as a product of collective inquiry and institutionalized methods rather than as private possession (Langseth, 2019; Gürsoy, 2024). Legal theorists draw on these insights to argue that the legitimacy of laws and judgments is grounded in procedures that are publicly accessible and open to contestation, not in any official's or interpreter's mental state (Ogleznev, 2020). In the context of machine learning and algorithmic decision-making, the public character of standards for interpretation and correction becomes crucial for assessing accountability and transparency (Pérez-Escobar & Sarikaya, 2024). The reading by Kripke of Wittgenstein has helped to clarify the social underpinnings of normativity in an era where both human and artificial agents participate in complex, evolving practices. The maintenance of meaning, whether in law or technology, is achieved through ongoing public dialogue and institutional adaptation. Even as practices change, the public and corrigible nature of standards enables both stability and innovation. This social-practice orientation allows for the possibility of rational disagreement, correction, and ethical growth over time.

Despite its strengths, the Kripkean skeptical solution has attracted important criticism and has stimulated robust debate within philosophy. Some commentators have charged that communal regularities alone cannot explain why any particular response counts as correct rather than merely customary (Child, 2024; Miller, 2024). Others have defended the account by emphasizing the distinction between acting in accordance with a rule and genuinely following it, arguing that the latter is intelligible only within a context of mutual recognition and critique (Kamota & Ndemo, 2024). The practical ability to be trained, corrected, and justified to others is taken as the ultimate ground for normativity, with mental states playing only a secondary, interpretive role. This approach avoids both reductive behaviorism and solipsistic subjectivism, presenting a vision of meaning as an achievement of social life. The flexibility and openness of community standards permit both stability and transformation, as new challenges, technologies, and forms of life emerge (Elliott, 2024; Gürsoy, 2024). The skeptical solution encourages philosophers and social scientists alike to study the mechanisms by which communities negotiate, revise, and sometimes reinvent their practices.

The community-centered interpretation of Wittgenstein on the part of Kripke continues to shape contemporary research on meaning, agency, and normativity. Scholars now widely accept that private mental states, though important for motivation and individual perspective, cannot by themselves sustain the intricate web of rules, meanings, and responsibilities that constitute social reality (Shahryari, 2021). The ability to follow rules, give reasons, and be held accountable is intelligible only within a structure of mutual recognition and shared practice. In law, politics, and education, this insight has fostered a pluralistic, dialogic approach to normativity, one that values public debate, institutional responsiveness, and openness to reform (Ogleznev, 2020; Elliott, 2024). As digital and technological systems increasingly mediate human action, the Kripkean vision of normativity as public, procedural, and evolving remains a powerful guide for the construction of just, meaningful, and adaptive communities. The ongoing philosophical conversation continues to build on the Kripkean challenge, exploring new frontiers of collective understanding and agency in the twenty-first century.

The relevance of the Kripkean skeptical solution is only growing as society navigates the ethical and practical challenges posed by artificial intelligence, globalization, and rapid technological change. In these contexts, the adequacy of communal standards is continually tested and renegotiated, demanding mechanisms for transparency, participatory rule-making, and adaptive oversight (Pérez-Escobar & Sarikaya, 2024; Gürsoy, 2024). New forms of hybrid agency in which decisions are co-produced by humans and machines highlight the necessity of shared protocols for evaluation, correction, and legitimacy that go beyond any individual's mental states. The creation of interoperable norms in global trade, digital platforms, and cross-cultural governance further exemplifies how normativity is sustained by collective, iterative practice. As researchers, policymakers, and technologists seek to design fair and accountable systems, the Kripkean lesson remains vital. Only by embedding public, corrigible standards at the heart of our institutions can we ensure that meaning, agency, and justice remain accessible, revisable, and responsive to the needs of pluralistic communities. This ongoing commitment to practice-centered normativity will be indispensable for addressing the complexities and opportunities of collective life in the twenty-first century.

1.4. From Language Games to Practice-Based Agency

The Wittgensteinian concept of "language games" provides a bridge between his critique of private language and his positive account of agency as rooted in public practice. Language games are structured social activities in which meaning arises from the use of words within rule-governed contexts, encompassing not only speaking but also the doing that accompanies it (Wittgenstein, 1953/2009; de Silva Pinto, 2024). In this view, the mastery of language is not a matter of internalizing fixed definitions but of learning to participate competently in a variety of communal forms of life (Ravn & Skovsmose, 2019). Agency, then, becomes intelligible as the ability to navigate, innovate, and adapt within the ever-evolving games that structure social interaction (see Figure 1.2) (Tselishchev, 2021). Recent scholarship in the philosophy of mathematics and science underscores that even highly formal systems are embedded in language games, requiring practitioners to adjust, justify, and negotiate meaning in real time (Ravn & Skovsmose, 2019). This dynamic and context-sensitive account has proven fruitful not only in philosophy, but also in empirical studies of legal reasoning, scientific practice, and technological design (Ogleznev, 2020). As technological and institutional environments become more complex, the flexibility and adaptability of language games become essential resources for effective agency and innovation. Wittgenstein's approach redefines agency as a practical, socially achieved competence rather than an expression of private, inner states.

The language game framework also explains how agency is distributed, shared, and negotiated within communities. Contemporary theorists emphasize that rule-following and agency cannot be reduced to the acts of isolated individuals but must be understood in terms of the patterns of correction, challenge, and mutual recognition that sustain communal life (Nowak, 2019; Elliott, 2024). The negotiation of meaning and the adaptation of rules are ongoing processes, open to revision and contestation as participants encounter new circumstances and perspectives. Social scientists and philosophers of technology note that innovation frequently occurs at the margins of established language games, as practitioners experiment, deviate, and sometimes redefine the boundaries of accepted practice (Gürsoy, 2024; Pérez-Escobar & Sarikaya, 2024).

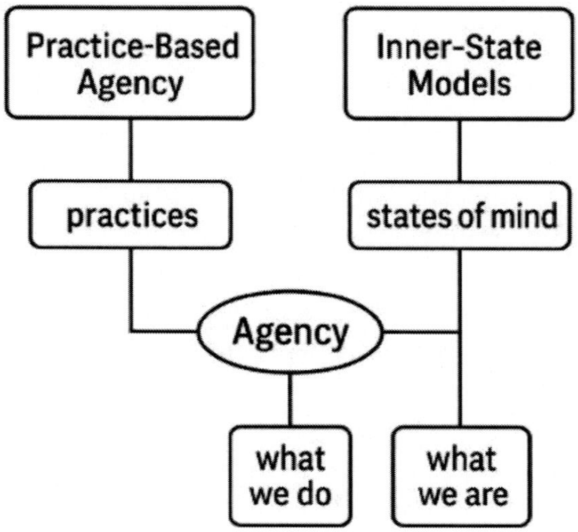

Figure 1.2. Agency Model.

Table 1.1. Metaphysical vs. practice-based agency

Criteria	Metaphysical Agency	Practice-Based Agency
Foundation of Agency	Internal, uncaused will or soul	Observable actions within shared norms
Assessment of Responsibility	Based on inner intent or free will	Based on adherence to public rules and social practices
Moral Evaluation	Determined by metaphysical desert (deserving praise/blame)	Determined by consequences and practical effects
Evidence for Judgment	Inferred internal states (beliefs, intentions)	External behaviors and contextual outcomes
Model of the Mind	Private, first-person, introspective	Public, behavioral, interactional
Legal Implication	Retributive justice rooted in culpability	Restorative/rehabilitative models grounded in accountability
Philosophical Source	Classical dualism, Kantian freedom, Cartesian mind	Wittgensteinian pragmatism, social epistemology
Vulnerability to Critique	Challenged by neuroscience and determinism	Critiqued for potential moral relativism or lack of inner depth
Nature of Transparency	Full disclosure of inner states or causal history to establish authenticity	Accountability through public, procedural standards and the social act of claiming responsibility

This process not only drives cultural and institutional evolution but also ensures that agency remains a living, responsive phenomenon. Legal philosophy, for example, recognizes that the legitimacy of judicial decisions depends on their justification within, and responsiveness to, shared legal language games (Ogleznev, 2020). Educational theorists similarly argue that learning is best understood as enculturation into the practices, norms, and values that constitute forms of agency within particular traditions (Tomasello, 2009). Wittgenstein's language games therefore underpin a pluralistic, participatory, and historically sensitive account of agency.

The transition from language games to practice-based agency has reshaped contemporary understandings of normativity, responsibility, and ethical life (Table 1.1). Agency on this view involves the ability to act in ways that are intelligible to others, accountable to shared standards, and open to public scrutiny and revision (Pérez-Escobar & Sarikaya, 2024; Gürsoy, 2024). This account underlines the connection between agency and moral judgment, suggesting that the capacity for ethical action is grounded in the ability to participate in, and sometimes challenge, the practices that define what counts as a reason, a justification, or a transgression (Nowak, 2019). Philosophical and empirical studies indicate that agents are recognized not by their internal deliberations but by their visible engagement in the collective maintenance and transformation of social norms (Langseth, 2008; Child, 2024). In practical arenas such as law, science, education, or technology, this means that the work of agency consists in the continuous negotiation, reinforcement, and reimagining of the rules and standards that structure collective life. The responses of the community to novel or ambiguous cases reveal the living character of agency, always at risk but also always capable of renewal. Practice-based agency enables both the persistence and the critique of existing social structures, making room for innovation and reform. Wittgenstein's framework, by rooting agency in practice, allows for a critical but non-utopian model of social change.

Empirical research in cognitive science and anthropology provides strong support for this practice-based account of agency. Developmental studies demonstrate that infants and children acquire both language and intentional agency through active participation in social routines, games, and shared tasks (Carpendale, Kettner, & Guevara de Haro, 2024; Horen et al., 2024). The ability to act with reasons, to give and receive correction, and to adapt to new circumstances emerges through immersion in the practices of a linguistic community, not from isolated cognitive achievement (Tselishchev, 2021). Neuroscientific investigations further confirm that the neural substrates of agency, decision-making, and moral judgment are activated within contexts of joint attention, mutual expectation, and social engagement (Hari et al., 2015). These findings reinforce the Wittgensteinian claim that agency is not a mysterious metaphysical faculty but a skill cultivated and exercised within a network of communal activities. As artificial systems are increasingly designed to interact with and learn from humans, the challenge lies in enabling machines to participate meaningfully in social practices, not merely to simulate isolated behaviors (Pérez-Escobar & Sarikaya, 2024). The social grounding of agency stands as both an empirical hypothesis and a philosophical imperative for future research. This alignment of philosophical and scientific inquiry signals the growing importance of practice-based approaches across disciplines.

The move from language games to practice-based agency also clarifies the sources of meaning, rationality, and autonomy in a pluralistic world. Rather than seeking absolute foundations or metaphysical guarantees, practitioners and theorists alike are called to attend to the concrete procedures, historical traditions, and collective negotiations that sustain and justify agency (Gürsoy, 2024). This orientation encourages humility and openness, as the standards for what counts as reason, understanding, or innovation remain perpetually subject to critical examination and communal deliberation (Nowak, 2019; Child, 2024). In law, science, and education, the Wittgensteinian approach enables robust but flexible systems of justification, suited to the complexities of modern life. Practice-based agency empowers individuals and groups to co-create, contest, and transform the rules that govern their interactions, enabling both continuity and creative rupture. As a result, social and institutional progress is understood as a function of collective agency, not as the outcome of detached theorizing or private intention. The legacy of Wittgenstein's language games endures in the ongoing effort to build forms of life where agency, responsibility, and meaning are sustained by shared and revisable practices.

The implications of this practice-based vision of agency are increasingly relevant as society navigates the integration of artificial intelligence, global communication networks, and multicultural forms of life. As new language games emerge around digital platforms, open-source collaboration, and cross-disciplinary innovation, the capacity for meaningful agency rests on communities' abilities to establish, maintain, and revise the rules that structure participation and sense-making (Pérez-Escobar & Sarikaya, 2024; Gürsoy, 2024). Rather than seeing agency as a fixed attribute or individual possession, the Wittgensteinian approach calls for designing systems that are explicitly open to feedback, renegotiation, and the contributions of diverse actors. This adaptability is vital for justice and innovation in pluralistic societies, as it ensures that norms can be challenged and recalibrated in response to changing contexts, new evidence, and evolving aspirations. Thus, grounding agency in practice empowers both humans and machines to engage in the dynamic work of building, contesting, and sustaining the shared realities that constitute our ever-shifting social world.

The discussion throughout this chapter illuminates the decisive shift away from inner mental states as the privileged locus of meaning, agency, and normativity. Through analysis of Wittgenstein's critique of private language, the exploration of rule-following considerations, and the examination of Kripkean skeptical solution, the chapter establishes that the grounding for linguistic meaning and intentional action resides not in individual consciousness but in the shared, corrigible practices of the community. The language games framework demonstrates that participation in public forms of life marked by rule-governed use, mutual recognition, and communal standards supplants the quest for metaphysical guarantees or private determinations. Rule-following is revealed as an essentially social phenomenon, one where the legitimacy of actions, utterances, and attributions of agency is achieved and maintained through ongoing negotiation, correction, and collective validation. The interpretation of Kripke intensifies this insight by showing that no fact about an individual, mental or behavioral, can fix meaning or correctness apart from the communal practices in which the individual is embedded. The resulting vision is one of normativity as both historically situated and open to transformation, with meaning emerging from dynamic interaction rather than static, internal facts.

The key takeaway from this chapter is the reorientation of philosophical inquiry from introspection and individual intention to the public, practical, and procedural dimensions of agency and meaning. This approach displaces the "inner determination" model and, instead, foregrounds the indispensable role of community, language games, and practice-based standards for the constitution of agency, responsibility, and understanding. In doing so, the chapter not only clarifies the conceptual basis for the arguments that follow but also sets the stage for the interdisciplinary application of these themes to neuroscience, law, and technology. The insights developed here invite a critical reconsideration of how society evaluates competence, culpability, and creativity and urges a move toward frameworks that privilege participation, mutual intelligibility, and collective life. As the subsequent chapters will demonstrate, the abandonment of metaphysical individualism in favor of practice-based agency promises more robust, adaptive, and ethically responsive models for confronting the challenges of the contemporary world.

References

Apperly, I. (2010). *Mindreaders: the cognitive basis of" theory of mind."* Psychology Press.

Baker, G. P., & Hacker, P. M. S. (1984). On misunderstanding Wittgenstein: Kripke's private language argument. *Synthese*, 407-450.

Berger, P., & Luckmann, T. (2016). The social construction of reality. In *Social theory re-wired* (pp. 110-122). Routledge.

Bratman, M. E. (1992). Shared cooperative activity. *The philosophical review*, *101*(2), 327-341.

Carpendale, J. I., Kettner, V. A., & Guevara de Haro, I. (2024). A genealogy of gestures: On the nature and emergence of forms of gestural communication within shared routines. *Human Development*, *68*(1), 30-43.

Child, W. (2024). "Following according to a rule is FUNDAMENTAL to our language-game." Rules and meaning in Wittgenstein. *Journal for the Philosophy of Language, Mind and the Arts*, *5*(3).

da Silva Pinto, V. M. (2024). *O epistémico e o simbólico: Wittgenstein, Cassirer e Langer* (Master's thesis, Universidade NOVA de Lisboa (Portugal)).

Eickers, G. (2024). *Scripts and social cognition: How we interact with others*. Taylor & Francis.

Elliott, R. J. (2024). Addressing 'the civic status of a contradiction': Wittgenstein and democratic self-realisation. *European Journal of Political Theory*, 14748851241266920.

Frith, U., & Frith, C. (2010). The social brain: allowing humans to boldly go where no other species has been. *Philosophical Transactions of the Royal Society B: Biological Sciences*, *365*(1537), 165-176.

Garfinkel, H. (2023). Studies in ethnomethodology. In *Social Theory Re-Wired* (pp. 58-66). Routledge.

Giddens, A. (1984). *The constitution of society: Outline of the theory of structuration*. Univ of California Press.

Gürsoy, Ö. (2024). Historical A Priori as Form of Life: The Rationality of Social Practices in Foucault's Archaeology in terms of Wittgensteinian Criteria. *Journal of the Philosophy of History*, *19*(1), 1-25.

Hacker, P. M. (2014). Two conceptions of language. *Erkenntnis*, *79*(Suppl 7), 1271-1288.

Hari, R., Henriksson, L., Malinen, S., & Parkkonen, L. (2015). Centrality of social interaction in human brain function. *Neuron*, *88*(1), 181-193.

Heath, J. (2008). *Following the rules: Practical reasoning and deontic constraint*. Oxford University Press.

Horen, N. M., Sayles, J., McDermott, K., Sippel-Klug, K., Drake-Croft, J., & Long, T. (2024). Infant and early childhood mental health (IECMH) and early childhood intervention: Intentional integration. *International journal of environmental research and public health*, *21*(7), 870.

Jandrić, N. (2022). Expressivism as normative social functionalism: Wittgenstein and Sellars. *Theoria, Beograd*, *65*(4), 17-31.

Jaszi, P. (2017). Toward a theory of copyright: the metamorphoses of "authorship." In *Intellectual Property Law and History* (pp. 61-108). Routledge.

Kamota, T. B., & Ndemo, G. (2024). International Journal of Social Science and Human Research.

Kripke, S. A. (1982). Wittgenstein on Rules and Private Language: An Elementary Exposition. Harvard University Press.

Langseth, J. (2008). Wittgenstein's account of rule-following and its implications. *Stance: An International Undergraduate Philosophy Journal*, *1*, 38-43.

Longino, H. E. (2020). Science as social knowledge: Values and objectivity in scientific inquiry.

Miller, A. (2024). *Wittgenstein and the Possibility of Meaning:" to Follow a Rule Blindly."* Oxford University Press.

Nowak, E. (2019). Wittgenstein: From Ethics to Blind Rule-Following and Back Again. *ETHICS IN PROGRESS*, *9*(2), 131–161. https://doi.org/10.14746/eip.2018.2.10

Ogleznev, V. V. (2020). Wittgenstein's Problem of Rule-Following and Legal Philosophy Studies. *Epistemology & Philosophy of Science*, *57*(3), 34-39.

Pérez-Escobar, J. A., & Sarikaya, D. (2024). Philosophical investigations into ai alignment: A wittgensteinian framework. *Philosophy & Technology*, *37*(3), 80.

Putnam, H. (1979). *Mind, language and reality* (Vol. 2). Cambridge University Press.

Ravn, O., & Skovsmose, O. (2019). *Connecting humans to equations*. Springer International Publishing.

Schlagwein, D., & Willcocks, L. (2023). 'ChatGPT et al.': The ethics of using (generative) artificial intelligence in research and science. *Journal of Information Technology*, *38*(3), 232-238.

Shahryari, S. (2021). A Critical Review of the Book Wittgenstein on Rules and Private Language. *Pizhuhish nāmah-i intiqādī-i mutūn va barnāmah hā-yi ʿulūm-i insāni (Critical Studies in Texts & Programs of Human Sciences)*, *21*(7), 165-190.

Tomasello, M. (2009). *The cultural origins of human cognition*. Harvard University Press.

Tselishchev, V. V. (2021). Rules, understanding and language games in mathematics. Правила, понимание и языковые игры в математике https://doi.org/10.17726/philIT.2021.1.2.

Vygotsky, L. S., & Cole, M. (1978). *Mind in society: Development of higher psychological processes*. Harvard university press.

Wittgenstein, L. (2009). *Philosophical investigations*. John Wiley & Sons.

Woodmansee, M. (1984). The genius and the copyright: Economic and legal conditions of the emergence of the'author'. *Eighteenth-century studies*, *17*(4), 425-448.

Yıldız, T. (2025). The minds we make: A philosophical inquiry into theory of mind and artificial intelligence. *Integrative Psychological and Behavioral Science*, *59*(1), 10.

Zafar, M. (2025). Normativity and AI moral agency. *AI and Ethics*, *5*(3), 2605-2622.

Chapter 2

The Sapolskyan Challenge and the Determinist Insight

Abstract

The second chapter addresses the neuroscientific assault on traditional conceptions of free will, focusing particularly on empirical arguments for hard determinism advanced by Robert Sapolsky. Through a careful review of neuroscientific evidence, the discussion demonstrates that choices and behaviors emerge from antecedent genetic, biological, and environmental causes, leaving no space for the metaphysical self-origination presupposed by libertarian accounts of free will. The analysis connects the position advanced by Sapolsky to themes in Wittgensteinian philosophy, suggesting that both traditions converge in their critique of mentalistic explanations of agency. Strategies of compatibilism, which attempt to reconcile determinism with meaningful notions of responsibility, are scrutinized and found wanting for their continued reliance on privileged accounts of inner states. The chapter articulates why practice-based models of agency and responsibility, grounded in observable participation and competence, better accord with both scientific evidence and philosophical coherence. This approach positions agency as an achievement within social and embodied practices, rather than as a product of uncaused mental volition. In so doing, the discussion prepares the ground for a conception of responsibility and agency that is fully consonant with a determined, causally structured world.

2.1. Determined: The Neuroscientific Case Against Free Will

Neuroscientific research over recent decades has fundamentally disrupted traditional philosophical conceptions of free will (Table 2.1). Experimental findings, most notably those initiated by Benjamin Libet (1916-2007) (Figure 2.1) and expanded by others, show that brain activity indicating an impending decision can be detected seconds before a person reports any conscious intention to act (Libet et al., 1983; Soon et al., 2008). These studies suggest that neural processes rather than conscious volition play the decisive role in generating choices and behaviors. More recent work employing advanced neuroimaging confirms that unconscious determinants of action are present even in complex, value-laden decisions (Bogataia, 2025; Fried, Mukamel, & Kreiman, 2011; Spaid, 2025). Such results leave little room for the metaphysical self-origination presupposed by libertarian theories of agency (Baumeister, 2008). Philosophers and neuroscientists argue that the sense of willing an action is more accurately interpreted as a *post hoc* rationalization, a narrative constructed after the relevant neural events have already determined the outcome (Haggard, 2008; Gazzaniga, 2012). The result is a growing consensus that free will, as traditionally understood, does not exist within the constraints imposed by biological causation. This determinist challenge poses major implications for concepts of responsibility, authorship, and justice.

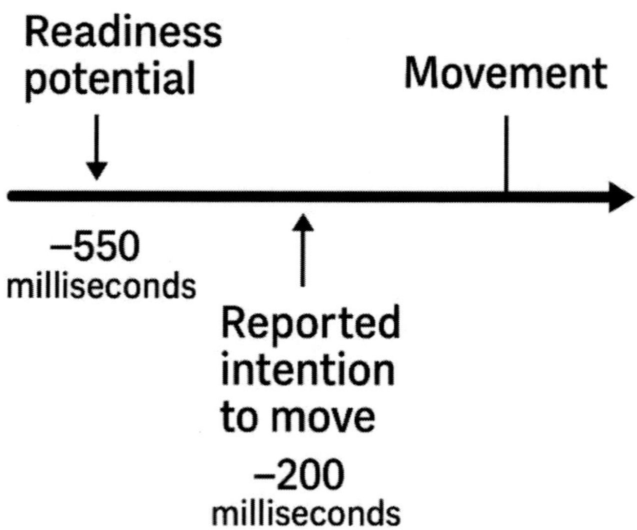

Figure 2.1. Libet Experiment Timeline.

The deterministic account finds further support in studies of pathological and atypical brains, where lesions or neurochemical imbalances reliably alter decision-making and impulse control (Malik, 2023; Roskies, 2010). Behavioral changes resulting from tumors, injury, or neurodevelopmental disorders illustrate how agency and moral responsibility fluctuate with underlying neural conditions. Empirical evidence points to a continuous, causally structured relationship between brain states and volitional behavior, rather than a sharp divide between "free" and "unfree" action (Blakemore et al., 2002; Kornhuber & Deecke, 2012; Watson, 2018). This body of research casts doubt on the idea that there exists an inner faculty capable of breaking free from causal chains. Instead, agency appears as an emergent property of neural systems shaped by genes, environment, and socialization (Baumeister, 2008; Greene & Cohen, 2004). In this model, responsibility must be rethought as a function of participation in shared practices, rather than as an expression of metaphysical autonomy. Neuroscientific discoveries have begun to shift public and legal discourse toward more context-sensitive, practice-oriented frameworks for judging culpability and competence (Argetsinger, 2023; Morse, 2005; Greene & Cohen, 2004). The scientific case for determinism undermines not only metaphysical accounts of free will, but also the institutional logics of blame and punishment that depend on them.

Table 2.1. Neuroscientific experiments on free will

Experiment	Method	Key Finding	Implication for Agency/ Free Will
Libet et al. (1983)	EEG to detect readiness potential before voluntary finger movement	Neural activity precedes conscious intention by ~350ms	Suggests unconscious brain processes initiate actions before conscious intent
Soon et al. (2008)	fMRI to predict decisions (left/right button) up to 10s in advance	Brain regions predicted decisions before participants were aware	Challenges the belief in conscious decision-making autonomy
Haggard & Eimer (1999)	ERP to assess timing of conscious intention	Found variability in perceived timing of "urge to act"	Casts doubt on reliability of subjective introspection
Haynes et al. (2007)	Multivariate pattern analysis on fMRI data	Classifier predicted binary decisions with significant accuracy	Suggests determinism in seemingly spontaneous choices
Fried et al. (2011)	Implanted electrodes in epilepsy patients	Neural buildup found seconds before awareness of intention	Reinforces Libet's findings with higher temporal resolution
Schultze-Kraft et al. (2016)	Real-time EEG to interrupt decisions mid-readiness potential	Subjects could still veto actions at the last moment	Supports possibility of a "free won't" mechanism

Neuroscientific findings also challenge compatibilist approaches that seek to preserve responsibility within a deterministic framework. Compatibilists claim that individuals can be held responsible if they act according to their desires and reasons, regardless of causal antecedents (Dennett, 2015; Hübner, 2025). However, neuroscience reveals that desires, values, and deliberative processes themselves arise from neural mechanisms subject to prior influences (Serra, 2021). The sense of "ownership" over one's actions, often cited by compatibilists as the basis for responsibility, turns out to be deeply contingent on both biological and social conditions (Haggard, 2008; Peroutka, 2022). Critics argue that compatibilist notions of control and autonomy are vulnerable to the same empirical objections leveled against libertarianism, since control is itself a product of causes outside the agent's conscious grasp (Baumeister, 2008; Mele, 2014). The implication is that compatibilist responsibility may be more a matter of legal and ethical convention than of scientific reality. Philosophical and neuroscientific work increasingly converges on the need for a practice-based conception of agency, grounded in observable competence and participation rather than inner mental freedom (Haggard, 2017; Greene & Cohen, 2004). This shift in perspective has begun to reshape theoretical and practical debates across multiple disciplines.

Empirical research continues to extend the deterministic paradigm, exploring the ways in which cultural, environmental, and genetic factors interact with brain development to produce patterns of action (Hua, 2025). Studies in developmental psychology demonstrate that early-life experiences, social learning, and exposure to environmental risks become encoded in neural circuits, constraining future possibilities for thought and behavior (Ellis et al., 2022; Malave, van Dijk, & Anacker, 2022). The social brain hypothesis, for example, posits that human cognition is fundamentally shaped by the demands of social participation and mutual coordination, further reinforcing the view that agency is a product of dynamic, context-sensitive processes (Gantley, McKeown, & Jiménez, 2022). Neuroscientific analysis of decision-making in groups also reveals that responsibility and intentionality are distributed, negotiated, and reinforced within collaborative activities (Blakemore et al., 2002; de Almeida et al., 2021). This practice-based, relational account of agency offers an alternative to models that privilege the inner life of isolated individuals. The scientific case against metaphysical free will paves the way for more robust, ethically responsive frameworks that situate agency within the practices, norms, and relationships of lived experience (Greene & Cohen, 2004; Haggard, 2017). The growing interdisciplinary literature points to the necessity of reconstructing responsibility and authorship as social and institutional phenomena.

The implications of the neuroscientific case against free will reverberate through law, medicine, education, and ethics. As empirical evidence for determinism accumulates, courts and policymakers have begun to reconsider the foundations of blame, mitigation, and retribution (Morse, 2006; Greene &

Cohen, 2004). Public health and criminal justice reforms increasingly incorporate neuroscientific insights, advocating for prevention, rehabilitation, and context-sensitive responses to behavioral problems (Caruso, 2012). In education and clinical practice, understanding agency as an emergent, context-dependent property opens possibilities for targeted intervention and support (Baumeister, 2008). Philosophers and scientists argue for a pragmatic reorientation, where the focus shifts from metaphysical speculation to the construction and maintenance of social practices that enable individuals to act competently, respond to feedback, and engage in communal life (Haggard, 2017). This new orientation does not eliminate moral and legal responsibility but redefines them as achievements of collective life rather than as inborn properties of isolated agents. The scientific case against free will challenges society to build systems of accountability and care that reflect the realities of causation, plasticity, and mutual dependence. In so doing, neuroscience fosters the emergence of a more humane, adaptive, and ethically grounded model of agency for the twenty-first century.

The neuroscientific dismantling of metaphysical free will also compels a reassessment of how institutions cultivate agency and foster personal development. In workplaces, schools, and communities, the deterministic perspective encourages the design of environments that support skill acquisition, self-regulation, and collaborative problem-solving, rather than attributing success or failure solely to personal willpower or moral character (Hua, 2025; Ellis et al., 2022). Such an orientation redirects resources from punitive interventions toward the cultivation of enabling conditions such as mentoring, access to health care, and enriched social networks. Structures such as these enhance individuals' capacities for participation and learning. By recognizing that agency emerges from structured opportunities for engagement, feedback, and correction, organizations can more effectively promote inclusion, resilience, and equitable outcomes. In this sense, the neuroscientific case against free will underwrites a new ethics of institutional responsibility, where the focus shifts from blaming individuals to creating practices and environments that enable flourishing.

At the philosophical level, the deterministic paradigm renews the call for a practice-based conception of agency that is attuned to pluralism, adaptability, and accountability. Rather than lamenting the demise of inner freedom, contemporary theorists advocate for models of responsibility and authorship that are transparent, revisable, and grounded in public participation (Baumeister, 2008; Greene & Cohen, 2004; Haggard, 2017). This view aligns with the Wittgensteinian and pragmatist traditions explored throughout this volume, in which meaning, normativity, and agency are constituted through shared forms of life and the open-ended negotiation of standards. Through situating agency within dynamic social practices, this account not only demystifies human behavior but also empowers communities to deliberate, critique, and improve the norms by which they live. Ergo, the neuroscientific challenge to free will is not a cause for pessimism, but an invitation to rebuild ethical, legal, and institutional frameworks that are empirically informed, socially responsive, and capable of supporting robust forms of individual and collective agency.

2.2. From Neurons to Choices: The Causal Chain Complete

A robust body of neuroscientific research now demonstrates that every conscious decision emerges from a seamless causal chain, beginning with molecular and cellular events in the brain and extending outward into complex behaviors. Functional neuroimaging and electrophysiological studies reveal that neural activation associated with decision-making can be detected well before individuals report any awareness of having made a choice (Libet et al., 1983; Soon et al., 2008). The readiness potential, a slow buildup of electrical activity in the motor cortex, serves as a marker for unconscious neural processes that precede overt voluntary action. These findings have been extended to more complex forms of decision-making, where value judgments and emotional appraisals are likewise predicted by brain activity observable seconds in advance of conscious intention (Lerner, Dorison, & Klusowski, 2024; Nambiar, 2024). This evidence suggests that choices, whether mundane or morally significant, are not initiated by an uncaused "act of will" but are the endpoint of interacting causal influences ranging from genetics and development to momentary context. The role of conscious awareness is reframed as a witness to neural events, rather than as a prime mover (Gazzaniga, 2011). Philosophers of mind and cognitive scientists now argue that the self-as-author model, once central to theories of agency, should be replaced with a model of the self as a locus of integration and narrative construction (Baumeister, 2008). The cumulative effect is a comprehensive account of agency as an emergent property of physical, psychological, and social causation.

The causal chain that links neurons to choices incorporates not only local brain activity but also the influence of environmental and developmental factors. Studies in developmental neuroscience and psychology show that early experiences, social learning, and environmental exposures shape the architecture of the brain, constraining the repertoire of possible actions and strategies (Liu et al., 2025; Wright, Adcock, & LaBar, 2024). Genetic differences, neurochemical modulation, and epigenetic factors further influence individual propensities toward risk, reward, and self-regulation (Mbiydzenyuy et al., 2024). At the same time, social norms and cultural practices learned through participation in communal life become encoded in neural circuits and guide patterns of attention, interpretation, and response (Godovanets et al., 2024). This web of causes means that agency is best understood not as an isolated faculty, but as a distributed process integrating brain, body, environment, and community. The so-called "social brain hypothesis" underscores that neural systems for decision-making evolved in response to pressures for cooperation, negotiation, and collective action (Gantley, McKeown, & Jiménez, 2022). Neuroscience thereby situates the origins of choices in the continuous feedback loop between organism and world. The resulting view is one in which each decision is the outcome of multiple, overlapping causal streams rather than an act of sovereign self-determination.

This thoroughgoing determinism does not eliminate the reality or importance of agency, but redefines it in terms of observable participation, competence, and responsiveness to feedback. On this view, agency is the ability to monitor, adjust, and refine actions in light of changing conditions, a capacity that depends on the flexible integration of information from diverse sources (Baumeister, 2008; Haggard, 2017). This capacity for self-control and planning is grounded in the brain's executive systems, which function by inhibiting impulses, updating goals, and weighing competing values (Hofmann, 2024). Social learning, institutional reinforcement, and feedback from others provide the scaffolding for the development and maintenance of agency over time. The deterministic model shifts responsibility from metaphysical will to practice-based achievement, where the attribution of agency is a judgment about an individual's participation in shared standards, responsiveness to correction, and capacity for improvement (Greene & Cohen, 2004). Crucially for this book's argument, observability pertains to the agent's performance within a social context, not to the impossible demand for a transparent causal ledger of every neuron, gene, and environmental factor. Accountability is located in the practice, not in the exhaustive mapping of its deterministic origins. This conception finds application in law, education, and clinical practice, where the focus is on fostering competence rather than searching for metaphysical sources of freedom. The practical consequence is a system of responsibility oriented toward empowerment, support, and remediation. Agency remains meaningful as the emergent outcome of complex causal processes, intelligible in terms of what individuals can actually do within their environments.

Recent research has begun to explore how this causal, practice-based model of agency might guide the design of institutions, policies, and interventions. In legal contexts, neuroscientific findings have prompted reforms that favor rehabilitation and prevention over retribution, grounded in an understanding of behavior as a product of modifiable causes (Coppola, 2021). In medicine and public health, the recognition that decision-making capacity depends on neural and environmental factors has led to targeted therapies and preventive strategies designed to enhance agency through education, treatment, and community engagement (Sox et al., 2024). Education researchers increasingly advocate for curricula that support the development of executive function, self-regulation, and collaborative problem-solving skills (Cumming et al., 2022). Philosophers and policy experts call for a reorientation toward "empowerment justice," where responsibility is reconceived as the capacity to participate in and benefit from social practices, rather than as an innate power of choice (Kapur, 2023). These innovations demonstrate that the causal chain from neurons to choices, far from undermining agency, provides new tools for its cultivation and ethical evaluation. The emerging synthesis across neuroscience, philosophy, and policy offers a foundation for more humane, effective, and equitable systems of support and accountability.

The implications of this integrated causal model extend well beyond the laboratory, shaping the structure and aims of contemporary institutions. In criminal justice, for example, the focus on neurobiological and psychosocial determinants of action has inspired the adoption of risk assessment tools, trauma-informed care, and diversion programs that seek to address the roots of harmful behavior rather than simply assigning blame (Coppola, 2021; Greene & Cohen, 2004). This shift mirrors parallel changes in medicine and mental health, where interventions now target modifiable risk factors and emphasize prevention, early detection, and the cultivation of resilience. As neuroscience continues to reveal the interplay between biology, environment, and social context, legal and clinical practices are increasingly oriented toward enabling individuals to regain or strengthen their capacity for agency within supportive communities.

Additionally, this practice-based, causal approach to agency has prompted a rethinking of moral and educational responsibility. Rather than holding individuals accountable for failing to transcend their causal histories, the emerging view seeks to empower them through access to resources, social capital, and opportunities for skill development (Cumming et al., 2022; Kapur, 2023). Educational systems that prioritize collaborative problem-solving, metacognitive reflection, and context-sensitive scaffolding reflect an appreciation for the plasticity of the brain and the role of social support in the cultivation of autonomy. In ethics, philosophers have argued that the attribution of responsibility should be responsive to individual circumstances and capacities, grounded in what a person can realistically achieve given their neural and environmental constraints. This perspective supports a more compassionate, adaptive, and pluralistic approach to justice and education, aligning the allocation of responsibility with the realities of neurobiological diversity and environmental complexity.

The recognition that agency is both determined and dynamic challenges outdated binaries between autonomy and causation. Instead of asking whether human beings are "truly free," the new paradigm asks how agency can be fostered, expanded, and recognized within the networks of causation that constitute lived experience (Baumeister, 2008; Haggard, 2017). This practical orientation has transformative consequences for the design of policies and institutions: it encourages ongoing investment in social infrastructure, targeted interventions for at-risk populations, and the continuous refinement of systems that promote learning, inclusion, and adaptability. As a result, responsibility and agency are understood not as metaphysical facts, but as achievements of practice, a practice that is emergent, corrigible, and subject to improvement through collective effort. By tracing the full causal chain from neurons to choices, society gains the tools needed to cultivate robust forms of agency and to build systems of support that are as complex and dynamic as the human beings they are meant to serve.

2.3. Hard Determinism as Implicit Wittgensteinianism

A growing strand of contemporary philosophy and neuroscience has begun to converge on a vision of agency that is both hard determinist and practice-based. This position aligns more closely with the later philosophy of Wittgenstein than is often recognized. Robert Sapolsky is among the most vocal proponents of hard determinism. His work marshals a wealth of neuroscientific evidence to argue that human choices, behaviors, and even moral impulses are products of prior genetic, environmental, and developmental factors (Sapolsky, 2017). For Sapolsky the idea of a metaphysically "free" agent capable of transcending causal chains is an illusion. This view resonates deeply with Wittgensteinian dissolution of inner states and his insistence that attributions of meaning, intention, and agency arise from participation in public practices rather than from any uncaused interior source (Wittgenstein, 1953/2009; Baker & Hacker, 1984). Both approaches reject the metaphysical and dualistic accounts of agency, situating the phenomenon within patterns of observable behavior, linguistic participation, and communal standards. Sapolsky extends this logic into legal and ethical discourse, advocating for systems of justice and care that focus on prevention, support, and rehabilitation, rather than on blame and retribution grounded in illusory freedom (Sapolsky, 2017). The alignment of neuroscientific determinism with Wittgensteinian practice theory offers a powerful critique of inner determination and supports a pragmatic reorientation of social and ethical life. The compatibility of these frameworks suggests that the challenge to metaphysical freedom is not a loss, but an opportunity for constructive transformation.

The work of Sapolsky has catalyzed renewed debate in philosophy, law, and social policy regarding the foundations of responsibility. Drawing on studies of brain lesions, genetic predispositions, and environmental influences, Sapolsky argues that every human action can ultimately be traced back to factors beyond conscious control. The striking implication is that no action is fully self-originating, a claim undermining the retributive logic still prevalent in much of law and public morality (Greene & Cohen, 2004; Morse, 2005). Wittgensteinian practice theory provides philosophical support for this position by grounding the attribution of agency not in the search for inner causes, but in the assessment of competence, participation, and responsiveness to feedback within communal forms of life (Baker & Hacker, 1984). On this view, to be an agent is to be recognized as such by others, to demonstrate the practical skills and social understanding needed to navigate rule-governed contexts. The traditional distinction between those who are "free" and those who are not gives way to more nuanced judgments about capacity, education, and support. Judgments of this sort, it is hoped, can be more empirically informed and context-sensitive. Sapolsky's call for compassion, prevention, and restorative approaches to justice is mirrored by Wittgenstein's rejection of metaphysical privilege in favor of practical achievement and social participation (Sapolsky, 2017; Wittgenstein, 1953/2009). The convergence of these perspectives underscores the necessity of reconstructing responsibility as a function of what agents do within their communities, not as a mysterious power to step outside causality.

This alignment between hard determinism and Wittgensteinianism is evident in current legal and ethical reform. As neuroscientific evidence for causal determinism mounts, courts and policy-makers are pressed to reconsider the legitimacy of practices rooted in blame, punishment, and desert (Freeman, 2011; McGeer, 2012). Practice-based standards, grounded in observable participation and demonstrated competence, offer more adaptive and humane alternatives. The account of rule-following and language games developed by Wittgenstein provides a model for evaluating agency in terms of engagement with communal norms, mutual correction, and ongoing learning. Proposals advanced by Robert Sapolsky for public health–oriented approaches to criminal justice employ similar logic, emphasizing the social scaffolding required for successful participation and the importance of context in judgments of accountability. In this light, to be responsible is not to possess an uncaused faculty of will, but to be able to participate, respond, and improve within a network of practices. The reforms inspired by these insights are increasingly reflected in restorative justice, education policy, and public health interventions (Caruso, 2012). The guiding principle becomes empowerment and inclusion, not metaphysical independence.

The philosophical implications of this convergence are profound. Both hard determinism and Wittgensteinian practice theory undermine the "inner theater" model of agency, instead locating meaning, action, and responsibility within the dynamic flow of communal activity (Baker & Hacker, 1984; Medina, 2013). The "death of inner determination" does not render agency or responsibility meaningless; instead, it reveals them as achievements of skillful navigation, social understanding, and mutual recognition (Garnett, 2017). Sapolsky's vision of a world where compassion replaces retribution, and where prevention supplants punishment, finds philosophical validation in Wittgensteinian framework of language games and forms of life. Practice-based agency, understood as a capacity to participate in and contribute to evolving communal standards, stands as a robust alternative to both libertarian and compatibilist models. This approach fosters flexibility, accountability, and continuous improvement, enabling societies to adapt their practices as new challenges and insights emerge. By reframing agency in these terms, philosophy and neuroscience jointly equip society to build more ethical, adaptive, and resilient institutions.

Finally, the convergence of neuroscience and Wittgensteinianism opens new directions for research and policy. Philosophers and scientists are called to collaborate in mapping the causal networks that shape human action, and in designing social systems that nurture competence, responsiveness, and mutual understanding (Haggard, 2017). The practice-based, determinist paradigm invites interdisciplinary exploration of how legal, educational, and technological practices can be reformed to reflect the realities of human causation and social embeddedness. Sapolsky's challenge, when combined with Wittgenstein's philosophical insights, encourages the development of policies that prioritize capacity-building, rehabilitation, and inclusion over blame and exclusion (Sapolsky, 2017; Caruso, 2012). As society moves further into an era defined by complex causal systems, the need for frameworks that support collective flourishing becomes ever more urgent. The death of inner determination, far from entailing nihilism, marks the beginning of a new ethics of participation, learning, and mutual care.

As this convergence gains traction, contemporary policy makers, clinicians, and educators are increasingly called to operationalize practice-based agency in real-world institutions. In criminal justice, restorative models are replacing punitive ones, focusing on repairing harm and equipping individuals for constructive participation rather than stigmatizing or excluding those deemed "irresponsible" by metaphysical standards (Caruso, 2012; Sapolsky, 2017). In mental health and disability policy, the emphasis shifts to identifying and nurturing the practical competencies that enable autonomy and social integration, rather than treating agency as a precondition for legal or moral recognition. In educational practice, scaffolding, differentiated instruction, and collaborative problem-solving replace rigid, blame-oriented assessments, cultivating an ethos of inclusion and continual improvement. These shifts demonstrate that the move from metaphysical freedom to practice-based competence is not merely philosophical. It is a practical, institutional, and ethical imperative. By foregrounding communal participation, mutual recognition, and skillful engagement, hard determinism and Wittgensteinianism together foster more just, responsive, and adaptable forms of life, guiding the evolution of collective norms and supporting flourishing within the constraints of a determined world.

2.4. Why Compatibilists Miss the Point About Inner States

The compatibilist position has long sought to preserve meaningful responsibility and moral agency within a deterministic framework by redefining free will as acting according to one's desires, reasons, or rational deliberation. This approach often focuses on an agent's internal states (preferences, intentions, or self-reflective attitudes) as the basis for ascribing accountability and autonomy (Dennett, 2015). However, this internalist orientation remains vulnerable to the same criticisms that undermine libertarian theories of free will, as empirical research demonstrates that desires, values, and cognitive processes are themselves products of causal chains extending beyond the agent's control (Baumeister, 2008; Haggard, 2008). The emphasis on mental content or subjective feeling as the criterion for responsibility risks reintroducing a metaphysical "ghost in the machine," subtly reinstating the dualism that determinist and Wittgensteinian analyses reject. Instead of providing a genuine solution to the challenge posed by neuroscience and hard determinism, the compatibilist model leaves unexplained why certain internal events should carry special normative weight if they are equally determined by antecedent causes.

Recent philosophical work has sharpened this critique by showing that attributing responsibility to internal deliberation does not escape the problem of regress. If an agent's reasons or intentions are merely effects of previous causes, whether those of genetics, upbringing, or environment, then the locus of responsibility shifts ever further back, ultimately dissolving in the web of determinants outside individual awareness (Roskies, 2010). The attempt to distinguish "authentic" from "inauthentic" or "coerced" desires similarly founders, since all motivational states can be traced to external or unconscious influences (Mele, 2014). Legal and ethical frameworks that continue to ground liability or praise in evidence of reflective deliberation are revealed as retaining a residue of inner-state metaphysics, even as they pay lip service to determinism (Greene & Cohen, 2004). By contrast, practice-based accounts of agency focus on observable participation, competence, and responsiveness to communal norms, all of which can be cultivated, supported, and evaluated without appeal to inaccessible mental events. The value of this orientation lies in its ability to guide interventions, support rehabilitation, and enable fair assessment of capacity. In the end, the compatibilist emphasis on inner states appears as a pragmatic compromise, but one that lacks deep coherence in light of empirical findings. By preserving a privileged role for inner states, compatibilism implicitly supports a flawed model of transparency, suggesting that if we could just 'see' the right internal deliberation, responsibility would be clear. The practice-based alternative rejects this premise, arguing that no amount of internal transparency can substitute for public accountability within a shared practice.

Wittgensteinian philosophy reinforces these concerns by demonstrating that meaning, intention, and agency are not constituted by private episodes of consciousness but by participation in shared practices and forms of life (Wittgenstein, 1953/2009; Baker & Hacker, 1984). The capacity to act for reasons, to be held accountable, or to engage in rational deliberation is realized not through internal reflection alone, but through the ability to navigate public rules, accept correction, and respond to others within a community. In this light, the compatibilist focus on "what it feels like from the inside" misplaces the foundation of responsibility. What matters for agency is the manifest ability to engage with the normative structures that define collective life, not the existence of a hidden mental signature of freedom. Social, educational, and legal institutions can therefore build more effective systems of accountability by targeting conditions that enable or impede participation, rather than searching for psychological states that may never provide reliable evidence of genuine autonomy. This practice-based standard aligns more closely with empirical realities and enables more humane, flexible, and transparent approaches to responsibility and justice. The transition away from inner states as criteria for moral and legal standing marks a profound shift toward outward-looking, constructive ethics.

The failure of compatibilist accounts to adequately address the problem of inner states does not entail abandoning the aspiration to hold individuals accountable, but it calls for a reconceptualization of what such accountability requires. The new orientation, grounded in neuroscience and philosophy of language, is toward fostering agency as a matter of practice: supporting the acquisition of skills, ensuring opportunities for participation, and designing institutions that reward responsiveness and learning (Haggard, 2017; Greene & Cohen, 2004). Agents are understood as responsible to the extent that they can integrate feedback, contribute to shared projects, and adapt within social contexts—not because of the metaphysical status of their intentions or desires. This perspective opens space for more equitable and effective forms of justice, education, and social policy, where attention shifts from interrogating the secrets of consciousness to nurturing the practical capacities that underwrite agency. The critique of compatibilism therefore points the way toward a more realistic and ethically sustainable model of human flourishing, suited to a world where inner states are recognized as products, not sources, of the practices that give life its meaning.

The practical consequences of moving beyond compatibilist accounts are already visible in emerging models of legal and institutional accountability. In settings ranging from criminal justice to mental health and education, reforms grounded in practice-based frameworks prioritize support, scaffolding, and opportunity over metaphysical inquiry into "true intentions" or "authentic desires." For example, sentencing reforms increasingly consider the contextual and developmental conditions that support or inhibit responsible action, rather than relying on abstract judgments about an agent's inner will (Haggard, 2017; Greene & Cohen, 2004). In clinical contexts, the focus is shifting toward developing skills for self-regulation, social participation, and adaptive decision-making, capacities that can be cultivated and measured in the public domain. Such approaches help to avoid both fatalism and moralism, fostering a culture of shared responsibility for building environments in which agency can emerge and thrive. The effectiveness of these reforms underscores the importance of public, transparent criteria for responsibility, which are open to revision and correction through collective experience.

This shift is also evident in the philosophy of education and the design of learning environments. Practice-based accounts of agency inform curricula that value project-based learning, collaborative problem-solving, and reflective participation over standardized testing or the rote assessment of "motivation" (Baumeister, 2008). Teachers and institutions become facilitators of engagement, ensuring that students are given opportunities to develop the habits and competencies required for meaningful agency. This framework not only aligns with empirical research on learning and development but also supports more inclusive and equitable education, as it recognizes that individual achievement is always shaped by broader social and material contexts. The result is a system that emphasizes growth, mutual accountability, and lifelong learning over metaphysical benchmarks of "authentic" self-direction.

Abandoning the compatibilist reliance on inner states does not mean relinquishing the goals of justice, personal growth, or social cohesion. Instead, it grounds these aims in the open-ended work of building and sustaining public practices that enable agency for all members of society. Institutions that prioritize participation, feedback, and mutual recognition foster environments where agency is not a mysterious capacity bestowed at birth but an achievement realized in ongoing interaction (Wittgenstein, 1953/2009; Baker & Hacker, 1984). In this view, moral and legal responsibility become functions of what agents actually do, the ways in which they engage, adapt, and contribute, rather than what they privately experience. This orientation is not only more empirically credible but also more just and sustainable, providing a foundation for ethical and institutional innovation in an increasingly complex and interconnected world.

Therefore, this chapter has challenged the reader to reconsider the foundation of responsibility and agency in light of both neuroscientific evidence and philosophical analysis. Rather than anchoring freedom and accountability in inner mental states or the metaphysical constructs of traditional theories, the discussion demonstrates that every choice, impulse, and act of deliberation is shaped by an intricate web of biological, environmental, and social causes. The compatibilist attempt to rescue responsibility by focusing on internal desires or rational deliberation proves inadequate when confronted by the empirical realities of causal determination and the Wittgensteinian critique of private criteria. The most promising alternative that emerges is a practice-based approach, where agency is conceived as an achievement realized through public participation, mutual recognition, and the capacity for correction and learning within shared social practices. In this light, responsibility and authorship become functions of competence, engagement, and responsiveness to communal norms, rather than the mysterious outcome of uncaused mental events. The synthesis of neuroscience and philosophy reframes questions of justice, ethics, and policy, advocating for systems that prioritize empowerment, rehabilitation, and social inclusion. This model of agency is not diminished by determinism; instead, it is enriched by a realistic understanding of the conditions under which meaningful participation and genuine accountability can arise. The discussion closes by inviting continued reflection on how these insights can inform more humane and adaptive institutions in a causally structured world.

References

Argetsinger, H. (2023). *The Epistemology of Moral Responsibility*. University of California, San Diego.

Baker, G. P., & Hacker, P. M. S. (1984). On misunderstanding Wittgenstein: Kripke's private language argument. *Synthese*, 407-450.

Baumeister, R. F. (2008). Free will in scientific psychology. *Perspectives on Psychological Science, 3*(1), 14–19.

Blakemore, S. J., Wolpert, D. M., & Frith, C. D. (2002). Abnormalities in the awareness of action. *Trends in cognitive sciences*, *6*(6), 237-242.

Bogataia, O. (2025). Neuropsychological Indicators of Managerial Effectiveness: Cognitive Markers and Decision Neuroscience Models. *Available at SSRN 5242254*.

Caruso, G. D. (2012). *Free will and consciousness: A determinist account of the illusion of free will*. Lexington Books.

Coppola, F. (2021). Valuing emotions in punishment: An argument for social rehabilitation with the aid of social and affective neuroscience. *Neuroethics*, *14*(Suppl 3), 251-268.

Cumming, M. M., Zelazo, P. D., Smith, S. W., & Flores, H. R. (2022). Self-regulation and executive function: The foundation for student success. In *Handbook of Special Education Research, Volume I* (pp. 285-298). Routledge.

de Almeida, A. T., Roselli, L. R. P., Morais, D. C., & Costa, A. P. C. S. (2021). Neuroscience tools for group decision and negotiation. In *Handbook of group decision and negotiation* (pp. 315-338). Cham: Springer International Publishing.

Dennett, D. C. (2015). *Elbow room, new edition: The varieties of free will worth wanting.* mit Press.

Ellis, B. J., Sheridan, M. A., Belsky, J., & McLaughlin, K. A. (2022). Why and how does early adversity influence development? Toward an integrated model of dimensions of environmental experience. *Development and psychopathology*, *34*(2), 447-471.

Freeman, M. (Ed.). (2011). *Law and Neuroscience: Current Legal Issues Volume 13* (Vol. 13). OUP Oxford.

Fried, I., Mukamel, R., & Kreiman, G. (2011). Internally generated preactivation of single neurons in human medial frontal cortex predicts volition. *Neuron*, *69*(3), 548-562.

Gantley, M. J., McKeown, J. P., & Jiménez, Á. V. (2022). Social brain hypothesis. *The Routledge Handbook of Evolutionary Approaches to Religion*.

Garnett, M. (2017). Agency and inner freedom. *Noûs*, *51*(1), 3-23.

Gazzaniga, M. (2012). *Who's in Charge?: Free Will and the Science of the Brain*. Hachette UK.

Godovanets, A., Monahhova, E., Komyaginskaya, E., Gallyamova, A., & Grigoryev, D. (2024). A Nexus of Neural Mechanisms of Cooperation and Social Conformity: toward a Neuro-Cultural Interdependence Model. *Психология. Журнал Высшей школы экономики*, *21*(3), 502-518.

Greene, J., & Cohen, J. (2004). For the law, neuroscience changes nothing and everything. *Philosophical Transactions of the Royal Society B: Biological Sciences*, *359*(1451), 1775.

Haggard, P. (2008). Human volition: towards a neuroscience of will. *Nature Reviews Neuroscience*, *9*(12), 934-946.

Haggard, P. (2017). Sense of agency in the human brain. *Nature Reviews Neuroscience*, *18*(4), 196-207.

Hofmann, W. (2024). Going beyond the individual level in self-control research. *Nature Reviews Psychology*, *3*(1), 56-66.

Hua, W. (2025). Dialectical Determinism. In *The ECPH Encyclopedia of Psychology* (pp. 413-413). Singapore: Springer Nature Singapore.

Hübner, D. (2025). "Both causal and free" or "Not only causal, but also free"? Two routes of compatibilist thinking. *Synthese*, *205*(6), 224.

Kapur, N. (2023). Empathy, a Hallmark of Equality: Shaping Fearlessness Into Transformative Decision-Making and Teaching. *Asia-Pacific Journal on Human Rights and the Law*, *24*(2), 165-185.

Kornhuber, H. H., & Deecke, L. (2012). *The will and its brain: An appraisal of reasoned free will*. University press of America.

Lerner, J. S., Dorison, C. A., & Klusowski, J. (2024). How do emotions affect decision making?. *Emotion theory: The Routledge comprehensive guide*, 447-468.

Libet, B., Gleason, C. A., Wright, E. W., & Pearl, D. K. (1983). Time of conscious intention to act in relation to onset of cerebral activity (readiness-potential) the unconscious initiation of a freely voluntary act. *Brain, 106*(3), 623-642.

Liu, B., Li, X., Zhang, J., Wang, J., He, T., Hong, S., ... & Wu, C. (2025). Advances and challenges in foundation agents: From brain-inspired intelligence to evolutionary, collaborative, and safe systems. *arXiv preprint arXiv:2504.01990.*

Malave, L., van Dijk, M. T., & Anacker, C. (2022). Early life adversity shapes neural circuit function during sensitive postnatal developmental periods. *Translational psychiatry, 12*(1), 306.

Malik, R. (2023). *Neurocognitive Mechanisms & Genetic Variants Underlying Apathy in Neurodegenerative Dementias* (Doctoral dissertation, The University of Western Ontario (Canada)).

Mbiydzenyuy, N. E., Hemmings, S. M. J., Shabangu, T. W., & Qulu-Appiah, L. (2024). Exploring the influence of stress on aggressive behavior and sexual function: Role of neuromodulator pathways and epigenetics. *Heliyon, 10*(5).

McGeer, V. (2012). Co-reactive attitudes and the making of moral community. In *Emotions, imagination, and moral reasoning* (pp. 299-325). Psychology Press.

Medina, J. (2013). An enactivist approach to the imagination: Embodied enactments and" fictional émotions." *American Philosophical Quarterly, 50*(3), 317-335.

Mele, A. R. (2014). *Free: Why science hasn't disproved free will.* Oxford University Press.

Morse, S. J. (2005). Brain overclaim syndrome and criminal responsibility: A diagnostic note. *Ohio St. J. Crim. L., 3*, 397.

Nambiar, A. (2024). The Role of Consciousness and Emotion in Decision-making: A NeuroPhilosophical Perspective. *Journal of NeuroPhilosophy, 3*(2).

Peroutka, D. (2022). Partial Compatibilism: Free Will in the Light of Moral Experience. *Organon F, 29*(1), 2-25.

Roskies, A. L. (2010). How does neuroscience affect our conception of volition?. *Annual review of neuroscience, 33*(1), 109-130.

Sapolsky, R. M. (2017). *Behave: The biology of humans at our best and worst*. Penguin.

Serra, D. (2021). Decision-making: from neuroscience to neuroeconomics—an overview. *Theory and Decision, 91*(1), 1-80.

Soon, C. S., Brass, M., Heinze, H. J., & Haynes, J. D. (2008). Unconscious determinants of free decisions in the human brain. *Nature neuroscience, 11*(5), 543-545.

Sox, H. C., Higgins, M. C., Owens, D. K., & Schmidler, G. S. (2024). *Medical decision making*. John Wiley & Sons.

Spaid, S. (2025). *Making Values Explicit: How We are Moved to Do, Act, Care and Change*. Ethics International Press.

Watson, G. (2018). Free agency. In *Agency And Responsiblity* (pp. 92-106). Routledge.

Wittgenstein, L. (2009). *Philosophical investigations*. John Wiley & Sons.

Wright, R. N., Adcock, R. A., & LaBar, K. S. (2024). Learning emotion regulation: An integrative framework. *Psychological Review.*

Chapter 3

The Copyright Laboratory

Abstract

This chapter presents copyright law as an experimental domain where the sufficiency of mental-state-based theories of authorship is repeatedly examined and increasingly contested. Detailed analysis of significant legal cases, including *Thaler v. Perlmutter* and *Bartz v. Anthropic*, shows how courts confront the issue of whether authorship and creativity must be rooted in human mental states or whether alternative, practice-based criteria are possible. The discussion brings to light the philosophical shortcomings of existing legal doctrine, particularly the persistence of a "mental control" theory that now appears misaligned with the challenges posed by contemporary technological developments. Examples are highlighted where judicial reasoning shifts from internalist assumptions toward evaluations that prioritize demonstrable creative contribution, signaling a gradual transformation of doctrinal standards. By casting copyright adjudication as an evolving laboratory, the chapter illustrates how the realities of legal practice demand continuous re-examination and, at times, abandonment of frameworks grounded in Cartesian dualism. The overall narrative demonstrates law's active role in developing and applying a practice-centered understanding of authorship and originality in the context of new media and artificial systems.

3.1. From *Thaler v. Perlmutter* to the 2025 Copyright Office Report

In 2023, the U.S. Courts confronted the foundational question of who or what qualifies as an "author" under copyright law in the landmark case *Thaler v. Perlmutter*. Stephen Thaler attempted to register a generative AI system, his so-called "Creativity Machine," as the author of an artwork titled *A Recent Entrance to Paradise* (2012) (Figure 3.1). Both the Copyright Office and the District Court rejected the registration, affirming that the Copyright Act requires an author to be a natural person (Mathur, 2023). The D.C. Circuit echoed this ruling, emphasizing that the existing statutory framework firmly centers on human authorship. This judicial consensus reaffirmed the traditional doctrine that copyright protects human creativity and remains closed to autonomous machine outputs, regardless of sophistication. Legal commentary viewed this as a critical reinforcement of the human authorship requirement and a clear signal that courts remain wary of extending rights to algorithmic entities. Nonetheless, the decisions also generated debate about the minimal threshold of human involvement required for eligibility, opening questions about the legal meaning of "creative contribution." In so doing, Thaler both reaffirmed existing doctrine and exposed doctrinal limits when new technology crosses conventional boundaries of authorship and responsibility.

Figure 3.1. Thaler Entry into Paradise.

By early 2025, the U.S. Copyright Office's Part 2 report explicitly codified the principle that human authorship remains essential for copyright protection. Published on January 29, 2025, the report reiterated that only original expressions created by humans qualify for protection—even when AI tools serve an assistive role. The Office clarified that generative AI outputs wholly lacking significant human creative input fall outside the scope of copyright (Quintais, 2025). It also stressed that existing law provides sufficient flexibility to handle hybrid works where human engagement takes the form of publicly recognizable creative practices such as selection, arrangement, or modification without requiring legislative overhaul. The key is not to provide a transparent audit of the human-to-AI contribution ratio, but to demonstrate that the work is the product of a practice that the community can recognize and evaluate according to shared standards. The report drew explicitly on public commentary, noting that of over 10,000 responses, the majority affirmed the adequacy of current doctrine in protecting human authors while recognizing evolving boundaries (Chesterman, 2025). The guidance emphasized that contributions must be substantial enough to establish human agency, rather than limited to issuing prompts or making token revisions. In effect, the report operationalized doctrinal rigidity into concrete criteria, illustrating how copyright doctrine adapts through policy analysis and jurisprudence alike.

Together, the *Thaler* rulings and the Copyright Office report function as a doctrinal laboratory testing the viability of mental-state–based authorship in the age of generative technology. Courts and administrators have demonstrated a clear commitment to safeguarding human creativity by prioritizing visible acts of selection, arrangement, and intentional design over reliance on unseen mental or algorithmic processes. This shift mirrors broader philosophical arguments favoring practice-based accounts of agency, which locate authorship in observable participation rather than private intent or inner mental states. When human authorship is in question, evaluative attention moves toward whether creative elements reflect human control, purpose, and decision-making. The laboratory metaphor captures how copyright law, under pressure from technological change, iteratively tests and refines its definitions of authorship and originality. Each case, each policy pronouncement, contributes empirical data to doctrinal evolution, signaling when internalist frameworks fail to accommodate emerging practices. For copyright law, this experimental process reveals its adaptive capacity and the limits of mental-state–centered theories.

Crucially, the report provides markers for future adjudication by drawing out thresholds for human creative involvement. It established that contributions qualify as copyrightable when they demonstrate more than cursory involvement, requiring discernible acts of creative judgment, arrangement, or intervention in AI-generated material. The report's clarity, however, does not simplify every case; rather, it affirms that copyright law must continue to operate on a case-by-case basis, assessing creative decisions within context and practice. This process aligns with the Wittgensteinian model of rule-following and community-based validation where original meaning or authorship is maintained through shared normative standards, not hidden mental constructs. The evolving thought in both jurisprudence and policy illustrates a conceptual realignment from Cartesian mentalism to practice-based authorship in copyright doctrine. The laboratory metaphor proves apt: it is in the crucible of litigation and policy that authorship is being redefined for an era marked by algorithmic partners and human-machine hybridity. As this chapter will show, subsequent legal developments continue to test and refine those boundaries in places like collaborative human-machine works and training datasets.

This emphasis on demonstrable human involvement is reshaping the evidentiary and procedural landscape of copyright adjudication. Legal practitioners and creative industries are now prompted to develop new forms of documentation such as workflow records, decision logs, and curation protocols that can substantiate claims of human authorship amid increasingly sophisticated AI tools. This shift encourages a proactive orientation toward transparency and accountability, compelling creators to reflect on the nature and extent of their contributions at each stage of the creative process (Quintais, 2025; Chesterman, 2025). As hybrid works become more prevalent, courts may increasingly rely on expert testimony, provenance audits, and comparative analysis to determine whether particular choices reflect "original intellectual conception" or mere facilitation. The result is a jurisprudence attuned not to static mental states but to the practical realities of creative production, where authorship is established through patterns of action, decision, and participation within collaborative and technologically mediated workflows. Such adaptation points toward a future in which copyright's legitimacy will rest on the robustness and clarity of practice-based standards for creative involvement.

The ongoing doctrinal "laboratory" of copyright is likely to become a proving ground for broader debates over agency, accountability, and ownership in the age of intelligent systems. As generative technologies continue to blur the boundaries between human and machine contribution, courts and policymakers will be challenged to maintain a delicate balance: incentivizing innovation and fair attribution while safeguarding the public domain and preserving the foundational role of human creative agency. Practice-based frameworks rooted in observable participation, traceable decisions, and community validation offer a flexible and pluralistic approach for adjudicating these questions as technologies and creative practices evolve. In this way, the lessons from *Thaler v. Perlmutter* and the 2025 Copyright Office Report extend beyond copyright, providing a model for the adaptive governance of authorship, agency, and responsibility in an increasingly hybrid world.

It is important to note that the analysis in this chapter so far has been based on the practical awareness in *Thaler v Perlmutter* and the Copyright Office Report that human agency must be demonstrated in some public way. And if public demonstrations are required for the case-by-case evaluation of human authority, this would seem to favor the theory of human intention and agency described as Wittgensteinian so far in this book. As the next section cautions, however, the practical approach seemingly emerging in decisions related to AI and copyright has been at odds with the metaphysical assumptions copyright law continues to rely on. Letting go of the idea of human authorship as grounded in internal mental states will be necessary if the benefits of the Wittgensteinian framework are to be realized.

3.2. The Human Authorship Requirement as Philosophical Error

The doctrine of human authorship at the core of copyright law is rooted in a metaphysical assumption that equates creative value and originality with the internal mental states of a single human agent (Bridy, 2015; Abbott & Rothman, 2023). This orientation not only reflects an Enlightenment conception of the "romantic author," but also perpetuates a Cartesian legacy that privileges the hidden acts of will, intention, and inspiration as the sources of intellectual property (Woodmansee, 1984). Such a view has become increasingly untenable in a digital, networked, and algorithmically mediated environment, where creative works often emerge from collaborative practices, machine learning systems, and iterative workflows (Kasap, 2018; Risi & Togelius, 2020). Philosophers of language and mind, most notably Ludwig Wittgenstein, have long challenged the idea that meaning, intention, or authorship can be fixed by reference to inner states, arguing instead that these are products of public, socially negotiated criteria (Wittgenstein, 1953/2009; Baker & Hacker, 1984). In the context of copyright, this implies that the insistence on human authorship as a legal threshold is not only technologically outdated, but conceptually incoherent. The persistent requirement for a "human touch" reflects a philosophical error: it locates the value and protectability of a work in what cannot be observed or adjudicated, rather than in the practices, standards, and outcomes of creative processes (Yu, 2016; Militsyna, 2023).

The practical consequences of this philosophical error have become increasingly pronounced with the rise of generative AI and algorithmic creativity. Current copyright law is unable to accommodate the variety of creative processes now possible, particularly where human involvement may be minimal, indirect, or distributed among many contributors and systems (Dimitrova, 2023; Gervais, 2021). As recent legal cases have shown, works produced by AI, even when prompted, curated, or refined by humans, often fall outside the scope of copyright protection unless courts can discern substantial, direct human contribution (Klukosky & Kohel, 2024). This creates a paradoxical landscape in which works that clearly reflect significant creative labor may remain unprotected simply because the processes of authorship do not align with the mentalist model. Critics argue that this state of affairs stifles innovation, excludes valuable new forms of authorship, and encourages creators to misrepresent or obscure the role of non-human agents in order to qualify for protection (Abbott & Rothman, 2023; Elkin-Koren et al., 2023). A more philosophically coherent approach would move beyond the search for inner intention and recognize creative contribution wherever it is manifested in the acts of selection, arrangement, transformation, or meaningful intervention regardless of whether these acts are performed by a single human mind (Kasap, 2018).

From a Wittgensteinian perspective, meaning and authorship are determined through public practices, shared criteria, and community validation, not by metaphysical introspection. The legal system's fixation on mental control is out of step with what philosophers and social theorists describe as the fundamentally communal, practice-based nature of creative work. In the age of collaborative platforms, open-source culture, and AI-generated content, authorship is often best attributed to those who participate in the construction, curation, or contextualization of a work within a given social practice (Militsyna, 2023). Legal theorists have begun to advocate for a "distributed authorship" or "co-creativity" framework, recognizing that creative acts may be shared among human agents, machines, and larger networks of actors (Gervais, 2021; Dimitrova, 2023). This reorientation would allow copyright law to protect the real-world practices that produce valuable works, instead of upholding an increasingly strained fiction about the centrality of solitary human intention (Bridy, 2015; Elkin-Koren et al., 2023). By shifting the focus to practice-based criteria, the law can support both traditional and emerging creative forms without sacrificing rigor or clarity.

Moreover, the philosophical error of privileging human mental states can be seen as an obstacle to fairness and equity in the creative economy. Under the current regime, creators who rely on advanced tools, AI systems, or collaborative networks may be penalized for methods that are now commonplace in many fields, including design, music, journalism, and software development (Kvirikashvili, 2024; Jiang et al., 2023). This situation also undermines transparency, as creators may be incentivized to hide or minimize the role of AI and other tools in the creative process to secure legal rights, rather than accurately representing how contemporary works are actually produced (Wan & Lu, 2021). Critics call for reform that respects the diversity and reality of modern authorship, and that allows for the possibility that original, valuable works can be produced through human-AI collaboration, curation, or even "prompt engineering" (Dimitrova, 2023; Militsyna, 2023). By recognizing creative contribution as a matter of public criteria and practical engagement, rather than as a metaphysical secret of consciousness, copyright law would not only be philosophically improved, but also better equipped for the realities of twenty-first-century creativity (Gervais, 2021).

A shift away from mentalist authorship toward practice-based recognition also enables copyright law to be more inclusive and adaptive as creative processes continue to diversify. In a landscape defined by crowdsourcing, remix culture, iterative design, and AI-enabled workflows, legal frameworks that focus on transparent documentation, collective participation, and demonstrable intervention can better reflect how valuable works are actually made (Jiang et al., 2023; Gervais, 2021). This would not only support more equitable access to rights and rewards for a wider range of contributors but also foster an environment of honesty, innovation, and responsible attribution. By lowering barriers for recognition and protection to those who can show meaningful, context-sensitive engagement in the production of works, copyright doctrine becomes a vehicle for both creative flourishing and social trust, qualities that are increasingly essential in a global, networked economy.

And though the changes in technological means of creative production have made the creative process more visibly Wittgensteinian, more publicly negotiated and mediated through tool-use, the idea of authorship as grounded in internal mental states has always been problematic. It has never been a reliable theory of authorship to imagine an autonomous inner will that fixes creative thoughts word-by-word or stroke-by-stroke into the artistic product. The fast-changing nature of text and image production has only brought out the shortcomings of aesthetic theories which happened to take hold with romantic conceptions of the individual genius.

The challenge posed by algorithmic authorship is therefore an opportunity for legal and philosophical renewal. By relinquishing the outdated attachment to inner states, courts and lawmakers can embrace a more empirical, pragmatic, and community-oriented vision of authorship, one that evaluates creative value in terms of public practices, documented processes, and collaborative achievement (Kasap, 2018; Elkin-Koren et al., 2023). This transformation would not undermine the traditional aims of copyright such as incentivizing creation, ensuring fair attribution, and supporting the cultural commons but would anchor them in standards that are visible, corrigible, and meaningful to the communities they serve. In doing so, copyright law would align itself with the Wittgensteinian turn in contemporary philosophy, prioritizing the living reality of creative practice over metaphysical speculation. As society continues to navigate the uncertainties of technological change, such a practice-based approach offers the surest foundation for a just and resilient creative economy.

3.3. *Bartz v. Anthropic* and the Accidental Breakthrough

While the human authorship requirement continues to shape legal doctrine and philosophical debate, recent litigation has begun to expose both the limitations and the possibilities of reimagining authorship in a technologically mediated world (Figure 3.2); this transition comes sharply into focus in the landmark case of *Bartz v. Anthropic*, where the intersection of AI, fair use, and copyright practice signals an accidental yet transformative breakthrough in contemporary intellectual property law. The court found that the act of using copyrighted books to train large language models was "exceedingly transformative," drawing an explicit analogy to the way a human learns from reading and synthesizing knowledge to produce new content (Brittain, 2025). The opinion emphasized that such transformative use, particularly when it does not substitute for the original work in the market, serves a fundamentally different purpose from reproduction or piracy. In its analysis, the court made a sharp distinction between the lawful acquisition of books, a practice of scanning and learning from legitimately obtained material which was permitted, and the unlawful assembly of pirated digital files, which failed the test for fair use. This bifurcation constitutes an "accidental breakthrough" because it delineates the boundaries for permissible AI development, affirming that the legality and provenance of training data now play a decisive role in the attribution of authorship and originality. By centering its reasoning on the legitimacy of data acquisition and use, the court tacitly endorsed a practice-based, rather than internalist, account of creative contribution. The ruling shifts the focus of copyright from metaphysical intention to accountable, observable action across the data lifecycle. This form of accountability does not require creators to disclose every detail of their work methods, but rather to operate within lawful, procedural frameworks and to stand behind the transformative nature of their final product. This transition represents a move toward a more transparent and ethically responsible regime for authorship in the age of generative AI.

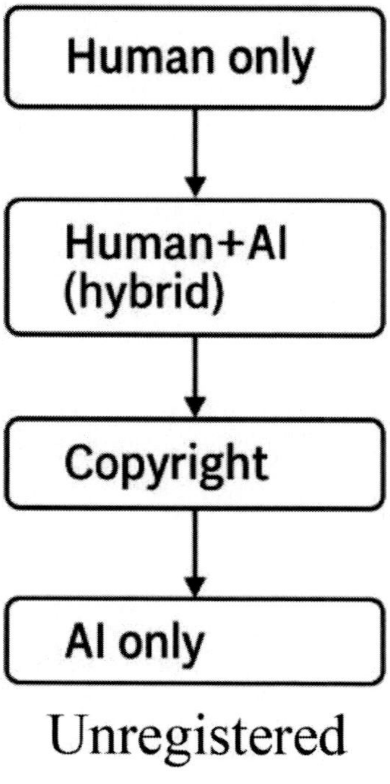

Figure 3.2. Copyright Eligibility.

The analogy made by Judge Alsup between machine learning and human reading has significant resonance with Wittgensteinian theories of language and mind, which treat learning and creativity as emergent from public, rule-governed social practices. The recognition of the court that "training a model is no different than a person reading a book to learn how to write" encapsulates the move away from metaphysical conceptions of agency to practice-centered, communal frameworks (Brittain, 2025). In this perspective, creative competence is not a function of hidden mental events but of participation in publicly accountable activities that can be scrutinized for purpose, context, and effect. The court's willingness to distinguish lawful training from piracy further echoes the legal-philosophical imperative to ground authorship and responsibility in public action, not private intention. In regulating the use of pirated texts, the court reasserts that only practices that are open to communal validation and regulation deserve protection and legitimacy. The ruling reflects and advances contemporary scholarship that seeks to operationalize practice-based theories in the face of technological complexity and distributed agency (Dimitrova, 2023; Gervais, 2021).

The Bartz decision establishes pragmatic guidance for creators, developers, and policymakers by prioritizing demonstrable transformation and lawful practice over an inevitably vague "proof" of human intent. Rather than inquiring into subjective mental states or the presence of an individual creative "spark," the court now requires empirical evidence: where was the data sourced, was the use genuinely transformative, and does the outcome substitute for or compete with the original (Kasap, 2018)? This approach mirrors recent philosophical arguments that understand agency and originality as matters of public participation and communal recognition, rather than as artifacts of introspection or internal will (Baker & Hacker, 1984). Permissible AI training must be grounded in lawful, transparent practices, and originality arises from the use of data in socially accountable and transformative ways. At the same time, courts are willing to penalize practices such as building data libraries from pirated content that evade public scrutiny and fail to meet ethical or legal standards. The decision operationalizes the philosophical shift from mentalist to practice-based authorship in concrete legal terms, setting a new direction for creative industries and AI research alike.

Crucially, *Bartz v. Anthropic* illustrates the maturation of copyright doctrine in an era of distributed and collective agency. The ruling represents a clear jurisprudential turn: originality and authorship are determined by how material is used and transformed within socially recognized practices, not by the hidden intent or isolated labor of an individual (Dimitrova, 2023). This public, procedural approach brings copyright law into closer alignment with current philosophy of mind and technology, as well as with ethical calls for transparency and accountability in digital systems. Subsequent litigation and legislative efforts will determine how fully this new orientation is codified, but the Bartz breakthrough already demonstrates the feasibility of a copyright system that values public participation, lawful practice, and transformative contribution over metaphysical speculation. In this way, the ruling does not simply resolve a dispute. It provides a blueprint for the continued evolution of legal, creative, and philosophical frameworks in the age of intelligent systems.

This evolution represents more than a mere doctrinal adjustment; it signals a fundamental shift in the social reality of creation itself. The Bartz standard, by centering its analysis on the public practice of transformative use rather than the private mystery of authorial intent, implicitly recognizes that the very ontology of authorship has changed. In a world of human-AI hybrid production, the "author" is no longer a solitary genius whose inner state is the origin point of value, but rather an orchestrator, a curator, or a participant within a complex socio-technical matrix. The law, therefore, is not inventing a legal fiction but is catching up to a material reality. By being forced to adjudicate the outputs of generative systems, courts are discovering that the only stable ground for legitimacy lies in the observable, procedural, and public dimensions of creative practice. This forced encounter with technology is inadvertently pushing copyright law to become the post-Cartesian, practice-based institution that this book argues is necessary, demonstrating that when the metaphysical ghost of the author is exorcized, what remains is the robust, tangible reality of the creative community and its shared standards.

The Bartz precedent demonstrates the potential for legal frameworks to adapt to new realities without sacrificing rigor or fairness. By grounding decisions in the transparency and legitimacy of creative processes, the court set a standard that is both flexible enough to accommodate technological innovation and robust enough to preserve ethical and economic accountability (Dimitrova, 2023; Kasap, 2018). This approach opens the door for courts and regulators to evaluate future cases based on the quality of participation, traceability of data, and observable transformation, criteria that can be continually updated in light of evolving industry norms and societal expectations. As AI-driven creativity becomes more ubiquitous, this practice-based model allows law to remain responsive, ensuring that the interests of creators, audiences, and the public domain are balanced in a rapidly changing environment. The Bartz decision exemplifies how doctrinal evolution, rather than rigid adherence to outdated metaphysics, can foster both justice and innovation.

Moreover, the Bartz breakthrough marks an important philosophical and practical step toward democratizing authorship and responsibility in the digital age. By shifting the focus from internal, mentalistic standards to the collective, procedural realities of creative work, the court's reasoning aligns copyright doctrine with pluralistic, community-centered values (Gervais, 2021). This not only enables broader participation in creative and technological processes but also encourages the development of more inclusive and transparent infrastructures for attribution, recognition, and dispute resolution. As creative production becomes increasingly collaborative and distributed across human and machine actors, the lessons of Bartz will help guide policymakers, courts, and practitioners toward legal standards that are empirically grounded, socially responsive, and open to continual renegotiation. In doing so, the ruling provides a foundation for building a copyright system that is capable of sustaining creativity, accountability, and legitimacy in the twenty-first century.

These social practices related to copyright will not necessarily favor the companies developing AI technologies even though they open the door to granting copyright to creative products generated using AI tools. The Bartz decision makes it clear that companies such as Anthropic, Google, and OpenAI have only begun a process of negotiation and collaboration with artists, writers, and other creatives. The private states of individuals will not be the deciding factors in copyright law and conceptions of human authorship. The "public" in "publication" will be the ongoing site of negotiation.

3.4. What Courts Discover When Philosophy Is Forced into Practice

The increasing prevalence of AI-generated works has compelled courts to confront the gap between philosophical doctrine and the realities of creative practice. While legal doctrine often clings to human-centric notions of authorship rooted in eighteenth-century romanticism (Xiao, 2023), the practice of litigation and adjudication has exposed the inadequacy of this framework for a technological era marked by distributed agency and algorithmic creativity. Recent research highlights how courts, when faced with the practical impossibility of discerning "original intent" or locating creative acts within a single human mind, have begun to rely on more flexible doctrines such as "authorship transfer" or "control of the creative process" to allocate rights for AI-generated content (Lu, 2021). This shift has led to the emergence of a practice-based approach, where authorship is constructed around those who exercise sufficient control or direction over the creative process, regardless of whether the creative spark originated in a biological or digital actor. These new standards are more adaptable to the evolving technological landscape and can help reconcile the foundational principles of copyright with the realities of collaborative and algorithmic production. By treating courts as "laboratories of practice," legal theorists argue that the case-by-case evolution of doctrine can be seen as an ongoing, empirical inquiry into what counts as meaningful authorship and contribution in the digital age (Fromer & Silbey, 2020). Such pragmatic adaptation aligns with the Wittgensteinian idea that meaning and normativity emerge through use and shared practice, not metaphysical essence. As a result, judicial reasoning increasingly emphasizes the observable actions of creators (curation, prompt design, post-processing) rather than searching for inaccessible mental states.

At the intersection of criminal, civil, and administrative law, the "practice first" orientation is visible in how courts assess copyright infringement and authorship. Li et al. (2024) note that, as AI systems are treated as creative tools rather than legal subjects, the attribution of authorship and liability often depends on how much originality and intellectual achievement is demonstrated by a human participant. This reflects a binary subject structure: the AI as tool and the human as controller or user, with rights and responsibilities shaped by public standards of creative involvement. Empirical analysis of court practice confirms that when AI-generated objects meet criteria for originality and are the result of demonstrable intellectual achievement, courts may recognize them as protected works but only by extending authorship to the person who exercised control over the process (Lu, 2021; Li et al., 2024). As AI continues to blur the boundaries of originality and intellectual property, courts have been forced to interpret reproduction and distribution in light of observable creative activity and to emphasize process over essence. The convergence of criminal and civil law in these contexts further underscores the necessity of flexible, practice-based approaches for dealing with hybrid human–machine works. This ongoing legal evolution embodies the way philosophical theory when forced into practice adapts and becomes reconstituted by the needs of the moment. The practical upshot is that copyright's protective logic is gradually shifting from authorial mystique to procedural accountability and transparency. This procedural turn should not be mistaken for a demand for total disclosure of creative methods. Rather, it represents the court's search for a reliable public basis for granting rights, a basis found in the creator's demonstrable engagement with materials and their ultimate social act of claiming authorship.

Scholars and judges are increasingly acknowledging that legal doctrine must evolve to reflect the co-creative nature of contemporary authorship and the complementary role of AI in the creative process (Hutson, 2024). Judicial practice in the U.S., EU, and China has revealed that inflexible adherence to human authorship can hinder innovation and exclude valuable hybrid works from protection, motivating the development of flexible standards for intellectual property (Zhou & Rahman, 2024; Soltanibahrehmand, 2024). A growing body of research now advocates for hybrid models, such as "authorship transfer" or "work made for hire" regimes, in which rights can be allocated to those who orchestrate, direct, or curate the AI's output even if the system itself is not a legal person (Lu, 2021; Xiao, 2023). These reforms are designed to strike a balance between protecting creators' rights, enabling data-driven innovation, and ensuring fair competition in global markets. As courts and legislatures respond to these challenges, legal philosophy is increasingly invoked to justify pragmatic reforms, prioritizing procedural fairness, collective recognition, and the preservation of social order over metaphysical purity (Valchuk, 2024). In the end, when philosophical abstraction encounters legal reality, what emerges is an ethics of responsibility and stewardship for both human and algorithmic agency, not a static defense of human exceptionalism.

The result of this forced encounter between philosophy and practice is a copyright regime that is both more adaptable and more socially attuned. While some theorists advocate for the public domain as the default for fully autonomous creations, others propose limited or sui generis rights to ensure fair allocation of benefits and continued incentives for human participation (Lana, 2022; Bonadio, Lucchi, & Mazziotti, 2022). As courts increasingly take account of context, degree of human involvement, and practical impact on creative ecosystems, a new paradigm for authorship is emerging that treats copyright as a living institution responsive to the complexities of technological and cultural change. In this paradigm, the law is not simply a passive reflection of philosophical categories, but a site of active negotiation, experimental adjustment, and value creation (Fromer & Silbey, 2020). When courts are forced to resolve conflicts that theory alone cannot settle, they become agents of philosophical evolution, redefining the contours of authorship and originality for a new era of human–machine collaboration.

Therefore, the evolving debate over copyright law in the age of artificial intelligence has illuminated a fundamental tension at the heart of modern creativity: whether the law should persist in its fixation on inner states (intention, inspiration, and private mental labor) or whether it should embrace a more public, practice-based account of authorship. As this book has demonstrated, the insistence on metaphysical mental origins for creative acts no longer aligns with the realities of artistic, scientific, and technological practice. Creativity, in both human and human–machine contexts, emerges through participation in social, institutional, and technological networks, through the observable acts of selection, arrangement, direction, and revision that can be witnessed, debated, and refined within communities. Copyright's historic reliance on the "romantic author" and the doctrine of original intent, once a powerful instrument for protecting individual rights and incentivizing innovation, now risks excluding, misunderstanding, or mischaracterizing the genuinely creative labor that shapes much of contemporary culture. By continuing to prioritize private mental states, the law not only stymies innovation and collaborative creation, but also makes it harder for courts, policymakers, and the public to transparently recognize who truly contributes to the works that define our era.

The transition toward a more practice-based copyright regime underscores the adaptability and experimental nature of law itself. As courts grapple with new questions posed by AI and distributed agency, their willingness to revisit and refine doctrinal standards demonstrates law's capacity to learn from, and adapt to, technological transformation. This iterative process is not without challenges: it requires courts, legislatures, and stakeholders to balance the need for stability with the imperative for flexibility, continually interrogating the adequacy of existing legal concepts in light of changing realities (Fromer & Silbey, 2020; Hutson, 2024). By fostering environments where new practices can be tried, evaluated, and revised, the law models the very virtues—openness, responsiveness, and communal reasoning—that characterize effective rule-following in Wittgenstein's account. This ongoing interplay between theory and practice allows legal systems to remain relevant, legitimate, and ethically robust in an era of rapid technological evolution.

The experience of copyright courts in the age of AI is emblematic of a broader societal transformation: the movement from metaphysical doctrines and private mental states to public, participatory standards of legitimacy and value. By grounding authorship and responsibility in observable processes and shared criteria, law is better able to support pluralism, transparency, and innovation. The courts' adaptive, experimental ethos not only clarifies the meaning of authorship in specific disputes but also offers a model for how other domains such as criminal justice, education, and public administration might confront similar tensions between inherited concepts and emerging realities. In recognizing that legal doctrine must evolve alongside, and through, lived practice, copyright law positions itself as a dynamic institution capable of sustaining justice and creativity in the face of profound technological and cultural change.

Therefore, the reflections and research synthesized in this chapter point toward a pragmatic and ethically responsive future for copyright law that places creativity in the open, shared realm of practice, mutual recognition, and public accountability. By shifting the legal and philosophical lens from metaphysical interiority to the practical realities of creative work, copyright can become a more just and effective system for supporting individual and collective achievement. In this new paradigm, protection and recognition are extended not on the basis of inaccessible intentions, but on the demonstrable actions, collaborative efforts, and transformative uses that constitute authorship in the real world. The result is a law better attuned to the pluralism, hybridity, and rapid evolution of contemporary creative production, able to balance the need for incentives with the imperative of access, stewardship, and shared benefit.

References

Abbott, R., & Rothman, E. (2023). Disrupting creativity: Copyright law in the age of generative artificial intelligence. *Fla. L. Rev.*, *75*, 1141.

Baker, G. P., & Hacker, P. M. S. (1984). On misunderstanding Wittgenstein: Kripke's private language argument. *Synthese*, 407-450.

Bonadio, E., Lucchi, N., & Mazziotti, G. (2022). Will technology-aided creativity force us to rethink copyright's fundamentals? Highlights from the platform economy and artificial intelligence. *IIC-International Review of Intellectual Property and Competition Law*, *53*(8), 1174-1200.

Bridy, A. (2015). The evolution of authorship: work made by code. *Colum. JL & Arts*, *39*, 395.

Brittain, B. (2025). Anthropic wins key US ruling on AI training in authors' copyright lawsuit. *Reuters.* June 24, 2025: https://www.reuters.com/legal/litigation/anthropic-wins-key-ruling-ai-authors-copyright-lawsuit-2025-06-24/.

Chesterman, S. (2025). Good models borrow, great models steal: intellectual property rights and generative AI. *Policy and Society*, *44*(1), 23-37.

Dimitrova, R. V. (2023, September). Are AI-Assisted Works Copyrightable?. In *2023 International Scientific Conference on Computer Science (COMSCI)* (pp. 1-4). IEEE.

Elkin-Koren, N., Hacohen, U., Livni, R., & Moran, S. (2023). Can copyright be reduced to privacy?. *arXiv preprint arXiv:2305.14822.*

Fromer, J. C., & Silbey, J. (2020). Retelling copyright: The contributions of the restatement of copyright law. *Colum. JL & Arts*, *44*, 341.

Gervais, D. J. (2021). AI derivatives: the application to the derivative work right to literary and artistic productions of AI machines. *Seton Hall L. Rev.*, *52*, 1111.

Hutson, J. (2024). The Evolving Role of Copyright Law in the Age of AI-Generated Works. *Journal of Digital Technologies and Law*, *2*(4), 886-914.

Jiang, H. H., Brown, L., Cheng, J., Khan, M., Gupta, A., Workman, D., & Gebru, T. (2023, August). AI Art and its Impact on Artists. In *Proceedings of the 2023 AAAI/ACM Conference on AI, Ethics, and Society* (pp. 363-374).

Kasap, A. (2018). Copyright and creative artificial intelligence (AI) systems: A twenty-first century approach to authorship of AI-generated works in the United States. *Wake Forest J. Bus. & Intell. Prop. L.*, *19*, 335.

Klukosky, F. P., & Kohel, M. D. (2024). An Update on the State of Play with Generative Artificial Intelligence and Intellectual Property Issues. *Intellectual Property Litigation*, *34*(1), 10-17.

Kvirikashvili, T. (2024). Machine as Author: Perspectives on AI-Created Works and Copyright. *International Policy Digest*.

Lana, P. (2022). Why works created autonomously by artificial intelligence (should) belong to the public domain–a viewpoint based on droit d'auteur traditions. *Transformations: Journal of Media, Culture & Technology*.

Li, J., Lin, H., Lin, M., & Zhang, Y. A. (2024). The Determination of Copyright Infringement Offences in the Artificial Intelligence Arena from a Criminal-Civilian Intersection Perspective.

Lu, B. (2021). A theory of 'authorship transfer'and its application to the context of Artificial Intelligence creations. *Queen Mary journal of intellectual property*, *11*(1), 2-24.

Mathur, A. (2023). Case Review: Thaler v. Perlmutter (2023). *Center for Art Law:* https://itsartlaw.org/2023/12/11/case-summary-and-review-thaler-v-perlmutter/

Militsyna, K. (2023). Human Creative Contribution to AI-Based Output–One Just Can ('t) Get Enough. *GRUR International*, *72*(10), 939-949.

Quintais, J. P. (2025). Generative AI, copyright and the AI Act. *Computer Law & Security Review*, *56*, 106107.

Risi, S., & Togelius, J. (2020). Increasing generality in machine learning through procedural content generation. *Nature Machine Intelligence*, *2*(8), 428-436.

Soltanibahrehmand, R. (2024). Copyright regulations for AI-generated works in the EU.

Valchuk, D. (2024). Artificial intelligence copyright: Problems and solutions. *Modern scientific journal*. https://doi.org/10.36994/2786-9008-2024-3-1

Wan, Y., & Lu, H. (2021). Copyright protection for AI-generated outputs: The experience from China. *Computer Law & Security Review*, *42*, 105581.

Wittgenstein, L. (2009). *Philosophical investigations*. John Wiley & Sons.

Woodmansee, M. (1984). The genius and the copyright: Economic and legal conditions of the emergence of the 'author'. *Eighteenth-century studies*, *17*(4), 425-448.

Xiao, Y. (2023). Decoding authorship: is there really no place for an algorithmic author under copyright law?. *IIC-International Review of Intellectual Property and Competition Law*, *54*(1), 5-25.

Yu, R. (2016). The Machine Author: What Level of Copyright Protection is Appropriate for Fully Independent Computer Generated Works. *U. Pa. L. Rev.*, *165*, 1245.

Zhou, T., & bin Abd Rahman, M. R. (2024). Legal perspective on the risk of copyright infringement by AI-generated contents in China. *Malaysian Journal of Law & Society*, *34*(2).

Part II: The Pattern of Agency

Chapter 4

AI Understanding Without Inner Experience

Abstract

Chapter four interrogates the nature of machine understanding, engaging critically with long-standing philosophical arguments such as John Searle's Chinese Room while foregrounding the pragmatic performance of large language models. The discussion challenges the assumption that genuine understanding requires conscious experience, proposing instead that successful participation in linguistic practices serves as the relevant criterion. By conceptualizing artificial intelligence as participants in language games rather than as mere processors of syntax, the analysis reframes the debate about the boundaries and prospects of machine cognition. The chapter examines contemporary case law and recent advancements in generative systems to show how practical measures of meaning have shifted from private intentionality to public practice. Insights from Wittgenstein are employed to dissolve the binary between simulation and authentic competence, suggesting that meaning and understanding emerge from social interaction. This practice-based approach underpins a new theory of machine intelligence, yielding significant consequences for legal reasoning, ethical analysis, and the cognitive sciences.

4.1. Large Language Models as Language Game Participants

Recent research increasingly conceptualizes large language models as active participants in public language games rather than mere syntactic processors. Studies in interactive domains such as video game development, dialogue systems, and educational platforms show that these models can engage in linguistic practices shaped by community rules, social conventions, and collective expectations (Sweetser, 2024; Yao, 2024). When prompted or embedded in narrative-driven activities, these systems display emergent behaviors that resemble participation in "games with words," navigating meaning through turn-taking, context adaptation, and feedback (Grow & Khosmood, 2023). The analogy to Wittgensteinian language games is not merely figurative; empirical benchmarks now probe how well these systems follow rules, adapt to new strategies, and generate novel utterances aligned with communal objectives (Gui et al., 2024). While present-day models still fall short of human fluency and occasionally lapse into incoherence, research shows they can coordinate and cooperate in repeated social settings, demonstrating degrees of pragmatic competence (Akata et al., 2025). However, these technologies often struggle with the full spectrum of semantic nuance and require careful prompting to sustain context over time, underscoring the need for iterative engagement for genuine linguistic participation (Vidler & Walsh, 2025). In summary, machine understanding is increasingly evaluated by how well these models play in evolving linguistic environments, rather than by mere simulation of understanding (Gui et al., 2024).

Recent theoretical work has formalized the analogy between model training and the acquisition of competence in language games. Liu, Sun, and Li (2024) argue that the development of such models can be understood through the lens of agent learning in structured games, where systems are not just trained on static corpora, but are iteratively refined using supervised and reinforcement-based strategies. This game-theoretic perspective enables researchers to assess alignment, rule-following, and strategic reasoning in ways that mirror human conversational and social play. Evaluations using canonical benchmarks such as the iterated Prisoner's Dilemma and coordination tasks have revealed both the promise and limitations of these technologies: while some, like GPT-4, can adapt to shifting incentives, they frequently default to self-interested or context-insensitive behaviors, reflecting only a nascent grasp of the deeper norms that structure linguistic practice (Herr et al., 2024; Akata et al., 2025). Models such as Llama 2, however, display more context-sensitive and nuanced adaptation, suggesting that architecture and training paradigms shape the ability to learn communal norms (Lorè & Heydari, 2024). The analogy between language models and language game participants not only advances philosophical understanding, but also informs new standards for evaluation and improvement.

In practical contexts, these technologies have demonstrated the capacity to act as both participants and facilitators in collaborative, language-based activities ranging from text-based gaming to code review and educational dialogue (Rikters & Reinsone, 2024) (Table 4.1). They can manage multi-turn exchanges, follow and generate rules, and adapt strategies in response to feedback from both human and artificial agents (Akata et al., 2025). Game-based benchmarking frameworks such as LogicGame and clembench offer structured environments for assessing rule-following, planning, and semantic inference, revealing strengths and ongoing limitations beyond traditional text completion (Gui et al., 2024; Beyer et al., 2024). These assessments show that while models can sustain meaningful participation in language games, persistent biases, reasoning gaps, and multi-step logical challenges remain (Herr et al., 2024; Gui et al., 2024). In strategic and cooperative settings, models sometimes achieve cooperation or demonstrate loss aversion but still often falter at higher-order coordination, emphasizing the remaining gap between simulation and genuine pragmatic competence (Vidler & Walsh, 2025). The ongoing evaluation of model performance in public, interactive settings reinforces Wittgenstein's insight that meaning and understanding emerge from participation, correction, and adaptation, rather than being static properties.

Table 4.1. Wittgensteinian language game: human and AI Interaction

Turn	Speaker	Action	Interpretation Basis	Outcome
1	Human	Issues a prompt or command	Social norms, context, prior use	AI initiates a response
2	AI	Responds with generated output	Statistical pattern recognition, training data	Human interprets and reacts
3	Human	Adjusts or critiques AI response	Public standards of correctness or clarity	AI refines its behavior
4	AI	Learns or adjusts based on feedback	Reinforcement signal or explicit correction	Response improves
5	Human + AI	Co-construct new meaning or outcome	Iterative back-and-forth	Shared alignment on rules/intent

The successes and shortcomings of language models as participants in language games raise broader philosophical and legal questions about authorship, agency, and responsibility. The ability of these systems to engage in public linguistic games does not imply subjective understanding or intentionality, but it does signal a transition from viewing technology as mere tools to recognizing them as agents whose outputs shape and are shaped by communal norms (Xiao, 2023; Kasap, 2018). As the field advances toward more rigorous, context-aware evaluation, it becomes increasingly plausible to treat such systems not only as passive models, but as contributors to evolving language practices that underpin law, education, and design (Beyer et al., 2024). This shift also challenges legal and policy frameworks to reconsider how originality, authorship, and intent are attributed in environments where language games extend beyond human participation (Akata et al., 2025; Herr et al., 2024). The role of large language models as participants in language games illustrates the potential for technology to not only simulate, but actively partake in, the communal activities that create meaning.

As large language models are increasingly embedded in everyday communicative practices, their outputs become part of the very "forms of life" that constitute meaning and normativity in contemporary society. This participatory function is no longer confined to experimental settings; in customer service, education, collaborative design, and even social policy, language models are co-creating the scripts, standards, and conversational possibilities that guide human interaction (Beyer et al., 2024; Rikters & Reinsone, 2024). Their ability to navigate public language games, such as responding to correction, adapting to communal goals, and iteratively refining their contributions, suggests a blurring of the boundary between simulation and participation. This has significant consequences for how agency, accountability, and legitimacy are assigned. Philosophers and legal theorists are called to develop new criteria for evaluating technological agency: not by searching for internal states, but by scrutinizing the patterns of engagement, correction, and shared meaning that emerge through ongoing practice (Kasap, 2018; Xiao, 2023). In this way, language models become test cases for the expansion and revision of core concepts such as understanding, authorship, and responsibility.

The continued integration of language models as participants in language games presents both opportunities and challenges for law, ethics, and institutional design. On one hand, these systems offer novel resources for pluralism, accessibility, and collaboration, enabling new voices and forms of interaction in domains ranging from creative production to civic deliberation. On the other hand, their limitations (persistent bias, lack of genuine intentionality, and vulnerability to adversarial manipulation) underscore the need for vigilant oversight and continual refinement of communal practices and regulatory frameworks (Vidler & Walsh, 2025; Gui et al., 2024). As legal and philosophical standards evolve, they must remain open to empirical feedback and responsive to the realities of technological agency, ensuring that participation in language games is accompanied by mechanisms for contestation, transparency, and public accountability. In sum, the rise of large language models as language game participants is not merely a technical advance but a transformative moment in the ongoing negotiation of meaning, agency, and legitimacy in the digital age.

4.2. The Chinese Room Dissolved: Why Searlean Intuitions Mislead

As large language models increasingly demonstrate the ability to participate in public language games, the longstanding philosophical challenge posed by the Chinese Room argument by American philosopher John Searle demands renewed scrutiny within the context of real-world linguistic performance and communal meaning. The argument has long dominated debates about artificial intelligence and understanding, presenting the case that computational systems, even those that manipulate symbols fluently, lack genuine comprehension because they operate solely on syntactic rules, not semantic content (Searle, 1980). According to this intuition, no matter how sophisticated a program is at answering questions in Chinese, it merely simulates understanding, never attaining real intentionality or consciousness. However, contemporary research on large language models and their participation in complex linguistic games challenges the force of Searlean distinction. Recent empirical findings demonstrate that these models, when embedded in public, rule-governed practices, can display emergent behaviors that mirror aspects of pragmatic competence, context-sensitivity, and even flexible adaptation (Liu et al., 2024; Gui et al., 2024). Rather than simply executing instructions, these systems engage in turn-taking, adapt strategies based on feedback, and generate novel responses shaped by shared conventions, a process that goes beyond rote manipulation of symbols (Akata et al., 2025). These practical achievements reveal the limitations of Searle's static, observer-centered thought experiment, suggesting that meaning and understanding are not the properties of isolated minds, but of systems in interaction with communities, contexts, and practices (Kasap, 2018).

Philosophers and cognitive scientists now argue that the Chinese Room intuition misleads by assuming that understanding is an intrinsic, private state, rather than a status conferred by successful participation in shared linguistic practices (Baker & Hacker, 1984). Wittgenstein's later philosophy undermines the dichotomy between "mere syntax" and "genuine semantics," showing that rules and meaning acquire force only within the context of public use and correction (Wittgenstein, 1953/2009). Large language models, while lacking subjective awareness, exhibit forms of competence that are functionally indistinguishable from understanding in many contexts such as responding to new challenges, handling ambiguity, and learning from failure through iterative feedback (Sweetser, 2024; Grow & Khosmood, 2023). The move from simulation to participation dissolves the boundaries that Searle drew, because language and meaning are not mental possessions, but public achievements. In practical applications, such as dialogue, education, and even game play, the observable ability of these systems to contribute, adapt, and be held accountable for responses matters more than inaccessible "mental contents" (Gui et al., 2024; Akata et al., 2025). The Chinese Room intuition collapses when confronted by the public, communal reality of linguistic competence.

Recent empirical work further reveals the inadequacy of Searle's framework by focusing on the criteria by which humans attribute understanding, not through metaphysical insight, but through the ability to participate successfully in a language game. Research shows that users judge models' understanding based on the relevance, appropriateness, and creativity of their contributions to evolving contexts (Vidler & Walsh, 2025; Beyer et al., 2024). These interactive benchmarks mirror the Wittgensteinian emphasis on shared criteria and rule-following: a system is seen as understanding when it can handle corrections, engage in negotiation, and display sensitivity to communal norms (Liu et al., 2024). The ongoing development of benchmarking frameworks that test rule-based reasoning, semantic inference, and context management points to a practical, rather than metaphysical, foundation for evaluating understanding (Gui et al., 2024). As such, the insistence that AI systems must possess "original intentionality" or "consciousness" to be participants in meaning is increasingly seen as a conceptual holdover from dualist metaphysics, rather than a requirement grounded in the realities of language use (Kasap, 2021; Xiao, 2023).

This dissolution of the Chinese Room intuition has significant implications for law, ethics, and technology policy. If understanding and meaning are recognized as emergent from public interaction, then the legal and ethical evaluation of AI systems should focus on their behavior, accountability, and integration into communal practices (Hutson, 2024; Herr et al., 2024). Courts and policymakers may need to shift from metaphysical inquiries about "machine minds" to practical assessments of competence, reliability, and the capacity to participate in meaningful dialogue and collaborative problem-solving (Kasap, 2018). The growing adoption of models as facilitators, tutors, and co-creators in education, law, and design demonstrates that successful participation in language games is already a *de facto* standard for granting legitimacy and attributing agency. In this light, the challenge is not to prove the existence of internal mental states, but to develop robust frameworks for transparency, feedback, and iterative improvement that ensure models remain aligned with communal values and standards (Beyer et al., 2024). The dissolving of the Chinese Room is less a loss of mystery, and more a gain in practical wisdom about what counts as understanding in the modern world. This practical wisdom recasts the concept of transparency: instead of demanding a transparent window into the "mind" of the machine, it calls for transparent procedures by which the machine's performance can be evaluated, corrected, and held accountable by the community.

The persistence of Searlean intuition reflects a broader philosophical anxiety about the place of human subjectivity in an age of intelligent machines, yet the growing body of evidence from linguistics, cognitive science, and computational research supports the view that understanding is not a metaphysical substance, but a status achieved through successful, accountable participation in social practices. By evaluating smart systems in terms of their capacity to engage with and be shaped by communal standards, the focus shifts from inward-looking speculation to outward-looking practice and interaction. This reframing not only clarifies the limits of artificial systems, but also opens new possibilities for collaborative creativity, mutual learning, and the continual evolution of meaning in human–machine societies. A refutation of the Chinese Room argument marks a philosophical turning point: as the boundary between simulation and understanding blurs, society is called to rethink not just what machines can do, but how humans recognize and value the forms of intelligence that emerge from practice, play, and participation.

The gradual strengthening of responses to Searlean skepticism signals a shift in both research and policy from policing the ontological boundaries of "true understanding" to fostering environments where artificial and human agents can co-create meaning and value. In this emerging paradigm, the legitimacy of machine outputs is no longer predicated on inaccessible mental states but on practical integration into social routines, legal processes, and educational interactions (Hutson, 2024; Kasap, 2018). This allows for a more inclusive and empirically grounded approach to authorship, responsibility, and collaboration, one that recognizes and rewards competence, adaptability, and contribution within observable practices. Such a shift empowers courts, regulators, and technologists to build systems of trust, accountability, and continual improvement, rather than remaining trapped in metaphysical dead ends. The Wittgensteinian emphasis on use, correction, and public validation becomes the gold standard for assessing both human and machine agency.

In the broader philosophical landscape, overcoming the Chinese Room problem encourages a more constructive engagement with the possibilities and limitations of artificial intelligence. Rather than dismissing machine language use as mere mimicry, researchers are now investigating the conditions under which genuine participation and shared understanding can arise even if these processes differ from human consciousness in kind. This orientation opens the door to new forms of collaborative inquiry, creative partnership, and ethical deliberation, where the value of intelligence (human or machine) is judged not by hidden essence but by manifest participation in the ongoing "games" of language, law, and culture. As society moves beyond the constraints of Searlean intuitions, it becomes possible to imagine richer, more pluralistic forms of meaning, authorship, and accountability, grounded in the realities of communal life rather than in outdated metaphysical anxieties.

4.3. From Simulation to Participation: What Copyright Cases Teach About Meaning

The intersection of copyright law and artificial intelligence has made visible a profound shift from mere simulation of creativity to genuine participation in socially recognized practices. Recent cases and legal analyses reveal that courts increasingly look beyond technical replication and focus instead on whether a process demonstrates public, practice-based meaning such as creative selection, arrangement, or intervention by a human or orchestrator (Pokrovskaya, 2025; Fominova & Bugys, 2024). Legal systems worldwide are grappling with the question of whether outputs from generative systems can count as "original" works, with many jurisdictions now introducing sui generis protections for non-original objects generated by AI (Bulat, 2024; Zerov, 2023). This approach shifts the assessment of meaning from inner intention or metaphysical authorship to the observable context of creation and the agent's engagement with legal and cultural frameworks. The Ukrainian model, for example, now distinguishes between works created with direct human involvement and those generated autonomously, providing limited protection for the latter through public, process-based criteria (Bulat, 2024). Scholars highlight that the courts' evolving standards reflect a move away from a metaphysical quest for the "true" author and toward participation, negotiation, and accountability in creative practices (Pokrovskaya, 2025; Fominova & Bugys, 2024). This mirrors philosophical arguments that meaning in language and law arises through rule-following, community validation, and situated engagement, not hidden mental states. The net effect is a growing legal consensus that copyright's role is not to reward simulation, but to recognize genuine participation in meaning-making practices.

Empirical and doctrinal analyses from diverse jurisdictions reinforce the primacy of participation over simulation in legal reasoning about authorship and meaning. In the context of generative art and AI paintings, recent scholarship notes that copyright disputes are increasingly resolved by investigating the creative process, whether human participants guided, curated, or meaningfully transformed the output, or whether the system acted autonomously as a simulator (Yan & Hao, 2024). Judges and lawmakers are compelled to weigh not only the end product, but also the social and technical processes that produced it, drawing on the observable "performance" of creativity (Çebi, Reisoğlu, & Goktas, 2023; Kulinich & Kondyk, 2023). Where human intervention is absent, courts are reluctant to ascribe copyright, but where curation, prompt engineering, or post-processing occurs, participation in public practice is recognized as the basis for meaning and ownership. International experience, from the EU to South Africa and China, converges on this trend: copyright law is evolving to evaluate creative contribution not by mentalist criteria, but by public and procedural standards, in line with philosophical shifts toward pragmatism and Wittgensteinian language games (Khan & Gotora, 2023). These developments underscore that legal systems are now repositories not of immutable truths, but of evolving social conventions and practices.

The shift from simulation to participation has also motivated theoretical proposals for new frameworks in copyright law, such as the use of hybrid or sui generis regimes to accommodate the realities of AI-assisted and AI-generated works. Scholars argue that the emergence of non-human agents as creators necessitates models that recognize the value of collaboration, process transparency, and responsible stewardship (Massadeh et al., 2024; Wyczik & Wieczerzak, 2024). Proposed legal mechanisms include the allocation of limited rights to those who direct, curate, or contextualize the output, as well as public domain placement for fully autonomous productions lacking meaningful participation (Han, 2023; Zerov, 2023). This move reflects a pragmatic acceptance that meaning, authorship, and originality are emergent properties of dynamic, interactive systems, properties that can be traced, justified, and regulated by reference to public practices rather than private intention. Comparative studies now show that where courts prioritize the social context of creation and the responsible use of underlying data, outcomes are more consistent and better aligned with both ethical and economic goals (Çebi, Reisoğlu, & Goktas, 2023). Participation in recognized social and legal practices, not simulation of human intent, is the emerging criterion for creative legitimacy.

Finally, this transformation in legal reasoning is redefining the boundaries of meaning and authorship for the digital age. The recent literature documents how legal recognition is now accorded to those who contribute to the collective negotiation of standards, validation, and fair use in creative ecosystems, be they human, algorithmic, or hybrid actors (Novaes & Ferraz, 2024; Wyczik & Wieczerzak, 2024). This change has fostered an environment where meaning is continually renegotiated through litigation, regulatory updates, and evolving industry norms. By shifting the focus from metaphysical questions of simulation to practical issues of participation and public accountability, courts and lawmakers are building a more adaptable, transparent, and inclusive copyright system. This trend is broadly supported by interdisciplinary scholarship, which argues that meaning in creative works is not simply simulated, but emerges from the interplay of agents, practices, and institutions. As a result, copyright law is increasingly seen as a living practice, grounded in the realities of contemporary cultural production and responsive to the accelerating pace of technological innovation.

This evolving legal landscape reflects a deeper philosophical shift in the very conception of authorship and creativity. As courts and lawmakers move away from mentalist paradigms and toward observable, process-based participation, they validate the idea that meaning and value are not innate properties of individuals, but outcomes of collective activity. The recognition of "creative stewardship," where legal rights flow to those who organize, direct, and shape AI-driven outputs within communal standards, underscores the Wittgensteinian insight that competence and legitimacy arise from public engagement, not inner mental states (Çebi, Reisoğlu, & Goktas, 2023; Kulinich & Kondyk, 2023). By aligning legal doctrine with this practice-oriented philosophy, copyright law can foster more inclusive and adaptive frameworks for the recognition of authorship that are capable of accommodating hybrid, distributed, and evolving forms of creative labor. This participatory turn opens new possibilities for pluralism, equity, and resilience within cultural and technological ecosystems.

Moreover, as copyright law continues to prioritize participation over simulation, it becomes a model for how other domains might resolve similar challenges brought on by artificial intelligence and automation. The transition from static, intention-focused criteria to dynamic, practice-based standards highlights the necessity for legal and ethical systems to remain corrigible, open to feedback, and responsive to social change. In fields such as contract law, education, and civic governance, courts and policymakers are already experimenting with participatory mechanisms that mirror those now gaining ground in copyright adjudication. Meaning, legitimacy, and agency in a digital society are best secured not by clinging to metaphysical abstractions, but by fostering environments where shared practices, transparency, and mutual accountability can flourish. This practice-based vision positions law as an adaptive, living institution continually reshaped by the communities and technologies it serves.

4.4. The Wittgensteinian Account of Machine Intelligence

The Wittgensteinian approach to machine intelligence reframes the debate over artificial understanding by moving the focus from internal representation and subjective experience to public participation in rule-governed practices. Wittgenstein's later philosophy argues that meaning and understanding are not properties that reside in the mind, but phenomena that emerge through engagement in "language games," socially coordinated activities governed by communal standards and criteria (Wittgenstein, 1953/2009). Contemporary research on language models reveals that these systems, when evaluated not as isolated processors but as participants in interactive, rule-based environments, display significant degrees of practical competence and adaptive responsiveness (Gui et al., 2024; Liu, Sun, & Li, 2024). Instead of asking whether machines possess inner mental states, the Wittgensteinian perspective asks: can these systems take part in the public practices that constitute understanding, respond to correction, and be held accountable within normative communities? Recent benchmarking frameworks confirm that artificial agents can learn to follow rules, manage context, and adapt to feedback in ways that are publicly intelligible and open to ongoing scrutiny (Beyer et al., 2024).

This orientation dissolves the binary between simulation and genuine intelligence, treating machine performance not as a shadow of human capacity, but as a different mode of participation in meaning-making activities. In legal and philosophical contexts, the success of a system is not measured by its metaphysical status but by its capacity to play the "games" of law, communication, or creativity in ways that are recognized, evaluated, and sometimes corrected by human partners (Fominova & Bugys, 2024; Han, 2023). Machine intelligence becomes a relational achievement, grounded in the practice of mutual engagement, rather than a mystical property locked inside the processor. This shift has concrete implications for how courts and policymakers define authorship, responsibility, and agency for AI-generated works, focusing on the observable flows of action and adjustment rather than elusive mental causes (Pokrovskaya, 2025).

Philosophers and theorists now increasingly argue that the standards for intelligence, whether in humans or machines, are fundamentally communal and procedural. Just as children learn language by being corrected, guided, and ultimately integrated into practices of their community, so do advanced systems become “intelligent” to the extent that they can engage in reciprocal exchanges, respond to public standards, and participate in evolving social games (Gui et al., 2024). The Wittgensteinian framework allows for a pluralistic account of intelligence that can accommodate both human and non-human agents, provided they meet the pragmatic criteria of participation, correction, and improvement. As research continues to refine models for context management, rule-following, and interactive planning, the notion of “machine intelligence” becomes less about internal consciousness and more about the practical ability to co-create meaning and solve problems within public contexts (Sweetser, 2024).

Still, it is important to draw attention to a significant issue in copyright law that is not “solved” by interpreting human authorship and creativity through the Wittgensteinian framework. An intuition that has emerged very quickly in discussions of AI and authorship is the obligation of transparency. If a human author uses AI in the process of research and writing, this should be disclosed. This has seemed like common sense to many. However, a Wittgensteinian approach also allows a view of authorship that does not require disclosure and transparency. The idea that authorship is a public activity rooted inevitably in the collaborative construction of meaning does not necessitate particular expectations or norms. The word “public” here does not spell out a degree of transparency one is obligated to at every stage of the thinking and writing process. Wittgenstein’s ideas do not prescribe any specific standards; they simply show that authorship is inevitably social and cannot be grounded in metaphysical beliefs about inner mental states. Therefore, the demand for transparency must be carefully framed. If it becomes a hunt for the “purely human” contribution through exhaustive disclosure, it resurrects the very metaphysical impulse the practice-based account seeks to overcome. A more coherent approach is to locate transparency in the act of taking public responsibility for a hybrid work, rather than in the impossible audit of its hybrid origins. It might be the case, in fact, that more room is opened up for keeping the methods of creation undisclosed. If all authorship is inevitably public and social, there is no need to focus so persistently on identifying the “mixture” of the purely human part of the creative act and the hybrid and technological aspects of creation.

Regardless, it is striking how frequently recent developments in AI law and policy underscore the value of Wittgensteinian insights. Legal theorists and regulators are increasingly adopting process-based and practice-oriented benchmarks to judge whether machine outputs qualify as creative, original, or accountable (Çebi, Reisoğlu, & Goktas, 2023; Wyczik & Wieczerzak, 2024). By grounding decisions in observable behavior, evidence of adaptation, and collaborative performance, courts can avoid metaphysical controversies about intentionality and focus on what matters for human institutions, namely the maintenance and evolution of shared standards. These legal reforms mirror broader philosophical arguments that the locus of meaning, authorship, and intelligence lies in participation, not introspection. In this way, the Wittgensteinian approach offers a rigorous and flexible model for integrating artificial systems into domains such as law, education, and the creative arts, where collective judgment and public justification remain central.

In all, the Wittgensteinian account of machine intelligence invites a reconsideration of the boundaries between human and artificial agency, and between simulation and authentic engagement. By emphasizing participation in public practices, mutual intelligibility, and the possibility of correction, this model reorients both philosophy and law toward a future where meaning is negotiated through interaction rather than assumed as a static possession. As the capacities of language models and generative systems continue to grow, the most significant measure of their intelligence will not be the presence of internal states, but their demonstrable contribution to the games, institutions, and communal life in which meaning is made and remade. The adoption of a practice-based framework for evaluating machine intelligence stands to enrich both human and technological futures, making room for new forms of co-creation, accountability, and shared understanding.

The move to a Wittgensteinian, practice-based account of machine intelligence also enhances public trust and institutional legitimacy in an era of rapid technological change. When courts, educators, and designers evaluate systems based on their engagement in rule-governed practices rather than on speculative claims about consciousness or originality, they provide clear, actionable standards for both oversight and participation (Çebi, Reisoğlu, & Goktas, 2023; Wyczik & Wieczerzak, 2024). This procedural clarity helps demystify the contributions of artificial agents, ensuring that recognition, attribution, and accountability are distributed according to observable achievement and social value. The ongoing negotiation of meaning and standards within communities further ensures that legal and ethical responses can evolve in tandem with technological innovation, rather than lagging behind or falling prey to metaphysical confusion. As more domains adopt participatory benchmarks, the distinction between human and machine agency becomes a question not of metaphysical essence, but of public competence and contribution.

Looking ahead, the Wittgensteinian framework suggests a future in which machines are not merely tools or simulators but collaborators in the ever-adaptive practices that constitute culture, law, and knowledge. This approach opens space for more pluralistic and creative forms of co-agency, where humans and machines jointly shape the standards and procedures that undergird collective life (Gui et al., 2024; Sweetser, 2024). By treating intelligence and understanding as emergent from practice, society gains the flexibility to integrate new actors and processes into its ongoing games, supporting innovation while retaining the capacity for critique, correction, and ethical reflection. In this way, the Wittgensteinian account serves not only as a philosophical orientation but as a blueprint for designing and governing human–machine ecosystems that are resilient, transparent, and continually open to growth and transformation.

As such, this chapter underscores the necessity of moving beyond metaphysical debates about the presence or absence of inner mental states in artificial systems, focusing instead on the Wittgensteinian insight that meaning, understanding, and intelligence are realized through participation in public, rule-governed practices. The discussion dismantles the force of classic objections such as Searle's Chinese Room by demonstrating that what counts as understanding is not hidden mental content, but the capacity for successful engagement in language games, context management, and cooperative problem-solving. Contemporary research and legal reasoning reveal that large language models, while lacking subjective consciousness, can act as credible participants in evolving linguistic and social practices, contributing to meaning, responding to correction, and being held accountable for their outputs. These developments affirm that intelligence, whether human or machine, should be judged by practical achievement, adaptability, and mutual intelligibility within a normative community. The shift from simulation to participation reorients both philosophical inquiry and policy frameworks toward criteria that are empirical, transparent, and ethically responsive.

The key takeaway is that a practice-based account of machine intelligence dissolves the traditional binary between authentic understanding and mere simulation. By embracing communal standards and focusing on public criteria for competence, courts, policymakers, and technologists can develop frameworks that accommodate both human and non-human agency in domains ranging from law to education and the arts. The Wittgensteinian framework offers a pluralistic and pragmatic path forward: meaning and authorship are not fixed by introspective evidence, but are maintained, challenged, and renewed through ongoing participation and negotiation within social practices. This orientation invites an open, adaptive, and inclusive future for human–machine collaboration in which shared standards, public accountability, and iterative improvement are the true hallmarks of intelligence and understanding.

References

Akata, E., Schulz, L., Coda-Forno, J., Oh, S. J., Bethge, M., & Schulz, E. (2025). Playing repeated games with large language models. *Nature Human Behaviour*, 1-11.

Baker, G. P., & Hacker, P. M. S. (1984). On misunderstanding Wittgenstein: Kripke's private language argument. *Synthese*, 407-450.

Beyer, A., Chalamalasetti, K., Hakimov, S., Madureira, B., Sadler, P., & Schlangen, D. (2024). clembench-2024: A Challenging, Dynamic, Complementary, Multilingual Benchmark and Underlying Flexible Framework for LLMs as Multi-Action Agents. *arXiv preprint arXiv:2405.20859.*

Bulat, N. (2024). Protection of non-original objects generated by artificial intelligence: the Ukrainian copyright law approach. *International Journal of Law and Information Technology*, *32*, eaae010.

Çebi, E., Reisoğlu, P., & Goktas, E. (2023). The influence of artificial intelligence on copyright law. *Interdisciplinary Studies in Society, Law, and Politics*, *2*(2), 33-41.

Fominova, K. E., & Bugys, R. (2024). A work of artificial generative intelligence as an object of copyright protection. *Vilnius University Open Series*, 79-97.

Gui, J., Liu, Y., Cheng, J., Gu, X., Liu, X., Wang, H., ... & Huang, M. (2024). Logicgame: Benchmarking rule-based reasoning abilities of large language models. *arXiv preprint arXiv:2408.15778.*

Grow, A. M., & Khosmood, F. (2023, August). ChatGPT gamejam: Unleashing the power of large language models for game jams. In *Proceedings of the 7th International Conference on Game Jams, Hackathons and Game Creation Events* (pp. 51-54).

Han, T. (2023). On the Copyright of Content Generated by Artificial Intelligence. In *SHS Web of Conferences* (Vol. 178, p. 01019). EDP Sciences.

Herr, N., Acero, F., Raileanu, R., Pérez-Ortiz, M., & Li, Z. (2024). Are large language models strategic decision makers? a study of performance and bias in two-player non-zero-sum games. *arXiv preprint arXiv:2407.04467.*

Hutson, J. (2024). The Evolving Role of Copyright Law in the Age of AI-Generated Works. *Journal of Digital Technologies and Law*, *2*(4), 886-914.

Kasap, A. (2018). Copyright and creative artificial intelligence (AI) systems: A twenty-first century approach to authorship of AI-generated works in the United States. *Wake Forest J. Bus. & Intell. Prop. L.*, *19*, 335.

Khan, R., & Gotora, N. (2023). One (innovation) flew over the law's head: the intersection of artificial intelligence and copyright. *South Afr. Intell. Property Law J*, *11*, 72-87.

Kulinich, O., & Kondyk, D. (2023). Impact of Artificial Intelligence on the Criteria of Originality in Copyright Law. *University Scientific Notes*. https://doi.org/10.37491/unz.93-94.4.

Liu, Y., Sun, P., & Li, H. (2024). Large language models as agents in two-player games. *arXiv preprint arXiv:2402.08078*.

Lorè, N., & Heydari, B. (2024). Strategic behavior of large language models and the role of game structure versus contextual framing. *Scientific Reports*, *14*(1), 18490.

Massadeh, F., Alnusair, F., Mahdi Massadeh, A. A., & Ismail, M. (2024). The legal protection of artificial intelligence-generated work: The argument for sui generis over copyright. *Corporate Law & Governance Review*, *6*(1).

Novaes, R. V., & Ferraz, F. F. (2024, September). Protection of Copyrights in the Era of Generative Artificial Intelligence. In *EPIA Conference on Artificial Intelligence* (pp. 332-343). Cham: Springer Nature Switzerland.

Pokrovskaya, A. (2025, February). The Legal Status of Artificial Intelligence: The Need to Form a Legal Personality and Regulate Copyright. In *Artificial Intelligence and Applications* (Vol. 3, No. 2, pp. 179-191).

Rikters, M., & Reinsone, S. (2024). Strategic Insights in Human and Large Language Model Tactics at Word Guessing Games. *arXiv preprint arXiv:2409.11112*.

Searle, J. R. (1980). Minds, brains, and programs. *Behavioral and brain sciences*, *3*(3), 417-424.

Sweetser, P. (2024, July). Large language models and video games: A preliminary scoping review. In *Proceedings of the 6th ACM Conference on Conversational User Interfaces* (pp. 1-8).

Vidler, A., & Walsh, T. (2025). Playing games with Large language models: Randomness and strategy. *arXiv preprint arXiv:2503.02582*.

Wittgenstein, L. (2009). *Philosophical investigations*. John Wiley & Sons.

Wyczik, J., & Wieczerzak, R. (2024). Rethinking Copyright: The Art of Ownership in AI Outputs. *Eastern European Journal of Transnational Relations*, *8*(1), 39-52.

Xiao, Y. (2023). Decoding authorship: is there really no place for an algorithmic author under copyright law?. *IIC-International Review of Intellectual Property and Competition Law*, *54*(1), 5-25.

Yan, Z., & Hao, Z. (2024). Study On Copyright Infringement of Artificial Intelligence Paintings. *Journal of Education, Humanities and Social Sciences*. https://doi.org/10.54097/vacy2b08.

Yao, Z. (2024). Welcome to AI Matters 10 (2). *AI Matters*, *10*(2), 3-3.

Zerov, K. (2023). Do generative artificial intelligence systems dream of electric sheep? The concept and conditions of protection of objects generated by generative artificial intelligence systems in Ukraine'. *Theory and Practice of Intellectual Property*. https://doi.org/10.33731/4-52023.289803.

Chapter 5

Human Agency Without Libertarian Freedom

Abstract

The fifth chapter interrogates the lasting attraction of libertarian accounts of freedom and their impact on conceptions of human agency. Drawing on a deterministic perspective developed by Robert Sapolsky and supported by contemporary neuroscience, the discussion demonstrates that human beings emerge from causal processes that preclude the radical self-determination assumed by classical theories. Critical examination of compatibilist approaches reveals an ongoing dependence on notions of choice and deliberation still tied to outdated metaphysical frameworks. The chapter proposes a practice-based model of responsibility, emphasizing competence, accountability, and active participation in social contexts rather than the illusion of uncaused volition. By highlighting the structural parallels between human and machine forms of decision-making, this analysis dissolves long-standing boundaries separating natural and artificial agents. This reframing of agency leads to the development of more equitable, transparent, and contextually grounded criteria for assessing responsibility and accountability.

5.1. Sapolskyan Insight: We Are What We Were Caused to Become

As discussed in the second chapter, the work of Robert Sapolsky has placed scientific determinism at the center of current debates about human agency and moral responsibility, offering a radical vision of individuals as the inevitable outcome of complex causal processes (Sapolsky, 2024). In his analysis, human actions, desires, and character traits emerge from the interplay of genetics, neurobiology, developmental environment, and historical context, leaving little room for the metaphysical freedom posited by classical theories of agency (Randazzo, 2021; Mylopoulos, 2020). This perspective rejects the notion that individuals can act as first causes or self-originating agents, instead describing agency as an emergent property of layered, mechanistic processes. Sapolsky contends that holding people morally responsible, especially in a retributive sense, is unjustified if their behavior is ultimately determined by factors beyond conscious control (Sapolsky, 2024). Critics acknowledge the explanatory power of this view but raise concerns about its implications for legal and ethical accountability, suggesting that society's conception of moral agency will require significant revision (Mylopoulos, 2020). Nonetheless, neuroscientific and behavioral research continues to provide evidence that supports the view of human beings as "what we were caused to become," rather than as freely choosing agents (Sapolsky, 2024; Falikman, 2023). This shift challenges not only legal doctrine but also cultural narratives of autonomy and personal achievement. Sapolsky's ideas demand a thorough reconsideration of what it means to be an agent in the contemporary world.

The determinist account grounded in Sapolskyan neuroscience draws strength from experimental and clinical studies demonstrating that the underlying causes of human action can be traced to neural circuitry, hormonal states, and environmental history (Bierer et al., 2021). For instance, cases of neurological injury, psychiatric illness, or developmental disorders consistently show that alterations in brain function can dramatically reshape patterns of choice and impulse control, sometimes eroding the very sense of self or responsibility (Raji, Dinesh, & Sharma, 2025). These findings challenge the intuition that the conscious will is sovereign, revealing instead a cascade of biological and environmental causes that precede and shape every decision (Bierer et al., 2021). Critics such as Mitchell (2023) have argued for more nuanced, evolutionary models of agency, but even these approaches recognize the powerful influence of non-conscious processes in shaping behavior. Attributions of praise, blame, and criminal culpability must grapple with the fact that much of what is attributed to "character" or "will" is in fact the result of circumstances and mechanisms outside conscious awareness (Sapolsky, 2024). This insight has led some philosophers and neuroscientists to call for legal and social policies that emphasize prevention, support, and rehabilitation over punishment (Mylopoulos, 2020). The deterministic model reorients responsibility away from metaphysical freedom and toward the causal conditions of agency.

Sapolsky's arguments have significant implications for the philosophical debate between incompatibilism and compatibilism regarding free will and responsibility. Incompatibilists, following Sapolsky's reasoning, maintain that if all behavior is causally determined, then true moral responsibility is impossible; compatibilists, on the other hand, continue to argue that responsibility can survive in a deterministic universe if redefined in terms of rational capacities or social practices (List, 2024). However, recent scholarship has highlighted the fragility of compatibilist positions when confronted by advances in neuroscience and the increasingly persuasive case for universal causation (Thomas, Pogarsky, & Loughran, 2021). Studies reveal that intuitions about free will are themselves influenced by exposure to neuroscientific information, with people becoming less likely to endorse retributive punishment when reminded of causal explanations for behavior (Adomaitis & Grinbaum, 2024; Mylopoulos, 2020; Shariff et al., 2014). These results suggest a growing public and academic willingness to reconsider the basis for moral responsibility, even if this challenges longstanding cultural and legal norms. The debate now centers less on abstract metaphysics than on how society can best construct systems of justice and accountability compatible with a scientifically informed model of human agency (List, 2024). Sapolsky's work drives the search for new, practice-based frameworks for responsibility.

Contemporary research in psychology and bioethics further supports the deterministic perspective by showing that beliefs about free will shape not only judgments of responsibility but also social and institutional practices. Experimental studies indicate that reduced belief in free will can lead to greater empathy, less punitive attitudes, and more support for rehabilitative approaches to criminal justice (Mylopoulos, 2020). Bioethical scholarship highlights how deterministic insights are beginning to inform policies for mental health care, education, and risk management, domains where the recognition of causal influences prompts more compassionate, individualized, and preventive interventions (Bierer et al., 2021; Dougherty & Fins, 2024). Scholars warn, however, that deterministic models should not be used to excuse all behavior or to eliminate accountability, but rather to recalibrate the focus of responsibility onto the structures and conditions that enable or constrain agency (Schulz, 2024). Sapolsky supports a shift from blaming individuals to understanding agency as the outcome of interactive, modifiable causal networks. This perspective opens the way for more equitable, evidence-based, and humane social policies.

The ongoing dialogue among neuroscience, philosophy, and law reveals that the determinist account of agency, exemplified by Sapolsky's work, is increasingly influential in shaping public discourse and institutional reform. Although some theorists defend the pragmatic value of maintaining notions of responsibility and autonomy, the scientific narrative of "we are what we were caused to become" is gaining traction as a foundation for policy innovation and ethical reflection (Sapolsky, 2024; Regueiro, 2020). As these debates continue, a growing consensus holds that meaningful agency and responsibility must be understood not as uncaused capacities, but as emergent achievements grounded in causal histories and social participation (Falikman, 2023). This reorientation holds promise for constructing legal, educational, and clinical systems that better reflect the realities of human nature and foster conditions for flourishing and accountability. Sapolsky's theories compel society to move beyond myths of radical autonomy and to embrace a more scientifically grounded, practice-based vision of what it means to be an agent in the twenty-first century.

This realignment of agency toward causal explanation also reverberates in debates about education, social policy, and the design of future interventions. As more empirical evidence accumulates linking developmental outcomes to early life adversity, neurobiological variation, and structural inequalities, policymakers are increasingly urged to address the systemic origins of disadvantage rather than attributing success or failure solely to personal merit (Sapolsky, 2024; Dougherty & Fins, 2024). In educational settings, for example, recognizing the deep causal roots of learning differences and behavioral challenges encourages investment in early intervention, individualized supports, and inclusive curricula, strategies that prioritize prevention and empowerment over punitive discipline (Bierer et al., 2021; Falikman, 2023). Similarly, public health approaches grounded in deterministic science call for upstream solutions to addiction, violence, and mental illness, challenging the utility of blame-centered responses (Schulz, 2024). This paradigm shift fosters interdisciplinary collaboration among neuroscientists, educators, clinicians, and legal theorists, all working to reconstruct accountability and support as mutually reinforcing goals. Sapolsky not only transforms theoretical understandings of agency but also inspires practical reforms that reimagine what it means to foster autonomy, justice, and well-being in an interconnected, causally determined world (Mylopoulos, 2020; Sapolsky, 2024). As scientific understanding deepens, society's ethical and legal frameworks are called to evolve, prioritizing social conditions and institutional practices that enable agency and reduce harm. In this way, Sapolsky's determinist insight stands as both a challenge and an opportunity: to build systems that reflect the true causal complexity of human life, and to orient collective action toward compassionate, evidence-based progress.

This paradigm invites a re-examination of public narratives around achievement, merit, and blame, urging institutions and communities to shift from individualistic explanations toward systemic, practice-oriented approaches to agency and responsibility. As research continues to expose the profound impact of early adversity, social determinants, and biological variation on life trajectories, policy interventions are increasingly designed to promote social equity, resilience, and prevention rather than to reinforce cycles of punishment and exclusion (Dougherty & Fins, 2024; Sapolsky, 2024). This transition has practical implications for how educators allocate resources, how healthcare systems structure interventions, and how legal systems determine culpability and design rehabilitation programs. By reframing agency as the product of layered, modifiable causal networks, Sapolsky paves the way for more compassionate, just, and effective institutions that seek not to allocate praise or blame based on illusory notions of self-origination, but to foster environments where all individuals have the opportunity to develop meaningful capacities for participation and contribution. As society embraces a causally informed ethics, the challenge will be to institutionalize support and accountability in ways that respect both individual dignity and the realities of human interdependence, turning the insights of neuroscience into blueprints for social progress.

5.2. The Compatibilist Mistake: Preserving Inner Agency

Although compatibilist philosophers have long argued that free will and moral responsibility can be preserved in a deterministic universe, recent research and philosophical critique suggest that this tradition remains deeply entangled with problematic assumptions about inner agency and private mental states. For example, classical compatibilism asserts that as long as the actions of an individual align with internal desires, intentions, or rational deliberation (and are free from external coercion), responsibility remains intact, even when all choices are causally determined (Yang, 2024; Pereboom, 2022). However, contemporary neuroscience and philosophy increasingly challenge this view, showing that the internal states compatibilists appeal to are themselves produced by antecedent causes beyond conscious control (Maqbool & Tahir, 2024). Empirical studies demonstrate that judgments about free will and responsibility are influenced as much by retributive motivation and misunderstanding of determinism as by philosophical argument (Inarimori, Haruki, & Miyazono, 2024). These findings reveal that compatibilist definitions, while practical, may rest on an illusion of self-authorship that fails to account for the causal roots of desires and values. Moreover, recent work on manipulation cases in which an agent's choices are engineered by outside forces raises doubts about whether acting on internal motives is truly sufficient for genuine freedom (De Marco & Cyr, 2024). The compatibilist reliance on mental content as the touchstone for agency risks perpetuating the very dualism and metaphysical ambiguity that determinist and practice-based accounts seek to transcend. This insight calls for a re-examination of what it means to be responsible in a causally ordered world.

A growing body of interdisciplinary scholarship proposes alternative frameworks that move beyond the inner-life paradigm. Philosophers such as List (2024) and Peroutka (2022) have advanced partial compatibilist and "compatibilist libertarian" approaches that emphasize public accountability, social participation, and functional responsiveness over metaphysical self-origination. This perspective aligns with new models in neuroethics and artificial intelligence, where agency and moral status are measured not by introspective feeling but by the capacity of a system for reason-responsiveness, value alignment, and adaptive participation in social practices (Porter, 2024). Research on large language models, for example, demonstrates that systems can instantiate degrees of agency, sometimes outperforming humans in reasoned deliberation, even in the absence of consciousness or libertarian free will (Porter, 2024). In legal and policy contexts, a shift toward observable competence, transparent decision-making, and responsiveness to feedback is supplanting older frameworks that privileged subjective will or intention (Johnson, 2024). The practical upshot is a model of agency and responsibility that is empirical, iterative, and embedded in community standards, rather than metaphysically isolated.

Despite these developments, compatibilist arguments continue to shape public and institutional intuitions about freedom, blame, and justice. Folk intuitions and manipulation arguments suggest that, even within deterministic scenarios, people remain committed to the distinction between voluntary and involuntary action, often conflating determinism with coercion or randomness (Inarimori, Haruki, & Miyazono, 2024). Recent research indicates that compatibilist theories, while successful in reconciling causal necessity with moral responsibility at a theoretical level, struggle to capture the complexities and intuitions of lived moral experience (Latham, Tierney, & Varga, 2023; Peroutka, 2022). Manipulation scenarios in which agents' choices are shaped by hidden causes or deliberate engineering show that judgments about responsibility diverge sharply depending on perceived control and authenticity, raising doubts about the sufficiency of compatibilist criteria (De Marco & Cyr, 2024). These findings underscore the need for a broader, more nuanced account of agency, one that attends to both causal history and the practical realities of social life. The compatibilist focus on inner agency may be best understood as a transitional stage on the way to a fully practice-based model.

The compatibilist effort to preserve inner agency in the face of determinism, therefore, reveals the enduring appeal of individual self-authorship, but also its philosophical and practical limitations. New frameworks in neuroscience, philosophy, and AI ethics invite a paradigm shift: agency and responsibility are to be found not in the hidden recesses of will, but in the manifest capacities for reflection, participation, and alignment with communal norms (Maqbool & Tahir, 2024; Johnson, 2024). This perspective does not deny the importance of subjective experience but situates it as one aspect of a broader ecology of action, social influence, and iterative engagement. As deterministic explanations of behavior become more entrenched in science and law, the challenge for theory and practice is to build systems of accountability, support, and recognition that are as attentive to causal complexity as they are to personal competence. In this way, a practice-based understanding of agency offers not only conceptual clarity, but also a more humane and adaptive foundation for justice and collective flourishing.

This reorientation toward practice-based and externally observable models of agency holds significant promise for reforming institutional responses to responsibility and blame. In criminal justice and organizational ethics alike, attention is shifting from whether an agent "really meant" to do wrong, to how their choices interact with context, available alternatives, and communal expectations (Johnson, 2024). Such frameworks invite a more relational and preventive approach: instead of probing the inscrutable depths of intention, policy makers can assess whether systems empower individuals to exercise judgment, access reasons, and participate in processes that foster mutual accountability (Porter, 2024). For artificial agents and humans alike, responsibility becomes a matter of demonstrated competence and reliable participation, not metaphysical purity or subjective introspection. This approach enables the design of interventions that respond to actual deficits in agency, rather than punishing individuals for outcomes largely shaped by external factors (Maqbool & Tahir, 2024). Moreover, grounding moral evaluation in practice rather than mental content promotes fairness and resilience: communal norms and procedures can evolve as new challenges and technologies emerge, without being hamstrung by static conceptions of "authentic" agency. The upshot is a system better suited to the realities of causal complexity and collective interdependence, where justice is measured not by private motives but by the public capacity for reason, revision, and co-creation. As the compatibilist tradition recedes, the path opens toward a more empirical, dynamic, and inclusive account of agency that is genuinely responsive to the demands of a determined yet pluralistic world.

As institutions adopt this practice-based paradigm, they gain the ability to move beyond the limitations of individualist and mentalist frameworks, designing structures that reinforce accountability through collaborative engagement and continuous feedback. This perspective encourages the development of social and technological systems—such as restorative justice programs, adaptive educational environments, and transparent organizational governance—that actively scaffold responsible participation and recognize the interdependence of agents within causal networks (Maqbool & Tahir, 2024; Porter, 2024). By privileging ongoing competence, flexibility, and responsiveness over static assessments of internal will, society can more effectively cultivate resilient forms of agency capable of meeting the demands of rapidly changing contexts. In this way, the move away from compatibilist accounts not only aligns with empirical insights from neuroscience and AI, but also opens the door to more just, supportive, and future-ready systems for distributing responsibility and fostering human flourishing.

5.3. Practice-Based Responsibility: Competence over Choice

As the limitations of both libertarian and compatibilist models become clear, contemporary scholarship is increasingly converging on a practice-based account of responsibility that foregrounds observable competence, participation, and responsiveness to communal standards. The practice-based approach to responsibility reorients the discussion away from metaphysical debates about inner freedom and turns toward the empirical assessment of the ability of an agent to act competently within social, institutional, and moral contexts (Lavazza & Inglese, 2023; Porter, 2024). In this model, agency is understood as a matter of demonstrating skill, adaptability, and accountability in navigating public rules and expectations, rather than exercising unconstrained choice among hypothetical alternatives (Johnson, 2024). Recent neuroethical and legal research supports this reorientation, showing that individuals are recognized as responsible when they can engage in reflection, integrate feedback, and respond appropriately to correction, capacities that can be measured and cultivated (May, 2023; Allen et al., 2022). Empirical studies on supported decision-making in clinical and legal environments demonstrate that fostering agency requires the creation of enabling conditions, not simply the attribution of free will (Bierer et al., 2021). This perspective dovetails with contemporary trends in criminal justice and education, where competence is assessed by observable contributions and improvement rather than by metaphysical self-origination (Maqbool & Tahir, 2024). The practice-based framework shifts the focus of responsibility onto what agents can actually do within the real constraints of their circumstances, resources, and social roles.

Philosophers and legal theorists argue that a practice-based account is not only more empirically sound but also more just and effective for guiding policy. Responsibility, in this view, is not an all-or-nothing status bestowed by an uncaused act of will, but a relational and graded achievement, reflecting an agent's integration into shared practices (List, 2024; Sekatskaya, 2022). Research in criminal law and mental health shows that this model better accommodates cases involving diminished capacity, developmental difference, or contextual disadvantage, enabling nuanced judgments about mitigation, remediation, and support (May, 2023; Allen et al., 2022). Unlike metaphysical models that render responsibility mysterious or unattainable, the practice-based approach provides clear, actionable criteria: does the agent understand the rule, can they apply it reliably, and are they responsive to instruction or correction? Such criteria are especially valuable in pluralistic societies, where diverse cultural, cognitive, and economic factors shape what counts as competent participation (Lavazza & Inglese, 2023). As a result, legal and educational systems adopting this model are better equipped to support equitable outcomes and to allocate resources where they will have the greatest impact. This perspective is echoed in artificial intelligence ethics, where system responsibility is tied to observable competence and transparency, rather than presumed intentionality (Porter, 2024).

Practice-based responsibility also invites a reconsideration of moral and legal accountability in an era of distributed agency. Recent scholarship on collective and group agents such as corporations, medical teams, and even algorithmic systems demonstrates that responsibility can and should be attributed to entities capable of manifesting competence and fulfilling roles in public practices (List, 2024; Johnson, 2024). Empirical studies reveal that people are willing to ascribe blame or praise to groups and systems when they exhibit consistent, rule-governed behavior and responsiveness to norms, even if the group's "will" is not reducible to that of any single member (Latham et al., 2023). This finding further erodes the link between inner states and responsibility, supporting a transition to frameworks that emphasize institutional competence, procedural fairness, and the capacity for collective learning. As systems of agency become more complex, the practice-based model offers a pragmatic and ethically robust basis for evaluating accountability at multiple levels, from individuals to institutions and hybrid human–machine networks (Sekatskaya, 2022; Porter, 2024). By anchoring responsibility in participation and skill, rather than metaphysical freedom, society can more effectively regulate, support, and reward agents of all kinds.

In education, healthcare, and the criminal justice system, the practice-based approach enables more flexible and inclusive models for growth and remediation. Rather than labeling individuals as wholly responsible or wholly excused, practitioners can assess competence on a continuum, identifying opportunities for intervention, capacity-building, and collaborative decision-making (Bierer et al., 2021; May, 2023). This approach is particularly beneficial for marginalized or vulnerable populations, whose agency is often shaped or constrained by external conditions beyond their control. By prioritizing participation, learning, and adaptation, the practice-based model empowers both individuals and institutions to pursue excellence, recognize achievement, and respond constructively to error or failure. In this way, responsibility becomes an ongoing process, not a static attribute. The adoption of this model promises not only conceptual clarity but also tangible improvements in fairness, efficiency, and social cohesion. The key advantage then of a practice-based conception of responsibility lies in its potential to unify theory and practice across disciplines. Rather than defending abstract notions of free will or personal autonomy, the focus shifts to cultivating competence, supporting development, and ensuring that agents are equipped to meet the demands of their social and institutional roles (Lavazza & Inglese, 2023; Porter, 2024). The result is a framework that honors the complexity of human and artificial agency, recognizes the realities of causation and constraint, and fosters a culture of accountability, learning, and shared achievement.

The growing adoption of practice-based responsibility also holds promise for the design of future technologies and the governance of complex systems. In AI development and deployment, this model underpins emerging standards for algorithmic transparency, explainable outputs, and human-in-the-loop oversight, ensuring that artificial agents can demonstrate competence in contextually appropriate ways and remain subject to public correction (Porter, 2024). These debates about transparency can easily become muddled as concerns about algorithmic transparency become confused with the desire to reward the human inner state in social processes such as authorship. The practice-based alternative clarifies this muddle by distinguishing between productive procedural transparency (public rules for accountability) and the misguided metaphysical transparency that seeks to audit every cause. The latter is a remnant of the very merit-based thinking this chapter critiques. The idea that meaning and merit are publicly negotiated should not be taken to imply that every step of every causal chain must be equally revealed to public view in order to assign blame or praise. The impulse to ferret out origin points in causal chains is very strong, and humans seem to have a strong desire to reward these origin points if they can be assigned to the inner mental states of particular individuals. This is a very subtle temptation related to ambiguities in the meaning of "public" and "transparent" that needs to be resisted.

Legal innovations such as algorithmic impact assessments and regulatory sandboxes mirror the practice-based shift, focusing not on presumed "intention" within software, but on observable system behavior, responsiveness to feedback, and participation in rule-governed processes (Allen et al., 2022; Lavazza & Inglese, 2023). Similarly, group accountability mechanisms ranging from multidisciplinary health teams to corporate boards are increasingly evaluated in terms of collective skill, reliability, and the ability to adapt practices when failures or harms arise (List, 2024; Sekatskaya, 2022). This approach fosters a culture of ongoing improvement and shared vigilance, where responsibility is distributed, iteratively assessed, and always open to challenge and revision. By focusing on what agents (human or artificial) can actually do in real-world circumstances, practice-based responsibility sidesteps the conceptual dead-ends of metaphysical freedom and cultivates systems that are robust, just, and resilient. As these frameworks gain traction across domains, they hold the potential to harmonize legal, technological, and social standards for agency, advancing a more empirical, responsive, and humane vision of accountability for the twenty-first century.

The ascendancy of practice-based responsibility also has the potential to transform public attitudes about blame, merit, and social worth. As the framework of responsibility shifts from individual character and inner states to observable engagement and continuous learning, society can better recognize the contributions of those who grow, adapt, and collaborate even if their starting points or circumstances differ. This reorientation supports a more compassionate and inclusive culture, where interventions target barriers to participation and enable agents of all backgrounds to cultivate meaningful capacities (May, 2023; Bierer et al., 2021). By rewarding improvement, reflection, and resilience, institutions foster environments where error is seen not as a failure of will but as an opportunity for growth and collective learning. This approach is especially valuable in the context of lifelong education, workforce development, and public health, where the focus on skill-building and participatory competence produces not only better outcomes but also greater social cohesion and trust.

The practice-based conception of responsibility positions society to confront the ethical, technological, and cultural challenges of an interconnected world. By moving away from metaphysical debates about autonomy and instead prioritizing the cultivation of agency within concrete practices, this framework enables more adaptive, fair, and sustainable systems for distributing recognition and accountability. As digital technologies, collaborative platforms, and hybrid human–machine networks proliferate, the need for flexible, context-sensitive standards for agency and responsibility becomes increasingly urgent. Practice-based responsibility, grounded in evidence of skillful participation and public engagement, offers a roadmap for responding to these challenges while preserving the values of equity, transparency, and mutual support (Lavazza & Inglese, 2023; Porter, 2024). In this way, the evolution of responsibility from choice to competence marks a turning point in the philosophy and practice of justice, opening new avenues for human flourishing in a complex, pluralistic age.

5.4. The Parallel Structure of Human and Machine "Decisions"

The convergence of neuroscience, cognitive science, and artificial intelligence has revealed striking structural parallels between human decision-making and the operations of advanced computational systems. Both biological and artificial agents select among options not through metaphysical freedom, but by integrating prior experience, environmental cues, and rule-based evaluations within complex, causally structured systems (Porter, 2024; Lavazza & Inglese, 2023). Neuroscientific studies show that human decisions emerge from the interaction of distributed neural circuits, with conscious choice often preceded by unconscious processing and shaped by social and contextual factors (May, 20243; Mylopoulos, 2020). Similarly, language models and other systems generate outputs by processing vast data sets, updating internal representations, and following programmed or learned procedures to achieve adaptive goals (Akata et al., 2025). In both cases, agency and authorship arise not from a single, uncaused act of will, but as the emergent product of systems responsive to feedback and capable of modifying behavior over time. This functional resemblance challenges traditional boundaries that separate human and artificial agents, suggesting that meaningful "decisions" may be defined by observable competence and participation rather than by underlying ontological status (Gui et al., 2024).

Philosophical analysis supports this comparison by demonstrating that both human and machine decision-makers can be held accountable within shared practices, provided they exhibit reliability, adaptability, and a capacity for correction (List, 2024). In law and ethics, responsibility is increasingly attributed based on performance within structured environments such as compliance with rules, responsiveness to new information, and the ability to justify actions, rather than on the presence of subjective consciousness or inner states. This alignment is especially visible in applied contexts, such as medical diagnostics, financial decision-making, and collaborative problem-solving, where human and artificial agents must meet comparable standards of competence and transparency. Recent scholarship in neuroethics and AI ethics highlights that what matters for accountability is not the metaphysical origin of choice, but the capacity to participate in, and contribute to, collective enterprises governed by public standards (May, 2024; Porter, 2024). The parallel structure of decision-making across human and machine systems supports a practice-based model of agency that is both pluralistic and practical.

Empirical research further documents how both human and artificial decision-makers learn and adapt through exposure to feedback, error correction, and iterative improvement. In cognitive science, the ability to integrate past outcomes, anticipate consequences, and revise strategies in light of new information is recognized as central to both moral development and skilled performance (Mylopoulos, 2020; Allen et al., 2022). Machine learning systems, likewise, improve through reinforcement learning and data-driven optimization, exhibiting increasingly sophisticated capacities for context management, planning, and coordination (Akata et al., 2025; Gui et al., 2024). The effectiveness of these systems is measured by their ability to meet goals, avoid errors, and adapt to evolving demands, a standard that also governs human responsibility in educational, clinical, and professional settings (Johnson, 2024). By foregrounding competence, adaptability, and public accountability, this empirical approach dissolves rigid human–machine dichotomies and enables shared evaluation criteria for agency.

The structural similarities between human and artificial decision processes do not imply equivalence in consciousness or subjective experience, but they do demand a rethinking of how agency, authorship, and responsibility are attributed. Legal theorists and philosophers caution against anthropomorphizing machines or denying the unique value of human subjectivity; instead, they advocate for frameworks that recognize degrees and types of agency across biological and technological systems (Księżak & Wojtczak, 2023). Such frameworks allow for nuanced distinctions based on observable performance, integration into social practices, and responsiveness to communal standards, rather than on metaphysical speculation. In this sense, the parallel structure of decision-making calls for a spectrum-based approach to agency, wherein both humans and machines are evaluated for their capacity to act, learn, and be held to account within shared institutions. This perspective is echoed in current debates on the legal and ethical status of AI, where the central concern is how systems can be designed, governed, and assessed to ensure responsible participation in public life.

One's demonstration of competence and participation in public life can be achieved without total disclosure of every step in the chain of performance. In the same way that it would be absurd to require a full disclosure of all the neuronal states that led up to an action in order to claim to be participating in a public act, it is also unnecessary to require transparency with respect to the use of AI in one's work. As AI becomes more ubiquitous, it will become obvious that human action is hybrid. Parsing the "pure human act" from human-AI hybrid acts will be a pointless activity. The recognition of parallel decision structures in humans and machines points toward a future in which agency, responsibility, and authorship are defined less by abstract metaphysics and more by practical engagement in communal practices. Theories and policies that prioritize observable competence, iterative learning, and different varieties of transparent participation can better accommodate the diversity and complexity of contemporary agency, whether biological, artificial, or hybrid. This orientation enables the development of more inclusive, adaptable, and ethically robust frameworks for justice, accountability, and collective flourishing. As the boundaries between human and machine continue to blur, the shared structure of decision-making will be a foundation for new forms of collaboration, regulation, and mutual recognition in the era of intelligent systems. Within this new foundation, transparency will mean something different. It will not require a human to disclose all their neuronal states or an AI to reveal its entire training history. Instead, transparency will be achieved when both human and machine actors participate in accountable systems with clear, public standards for performance and redress.

The societal implications of this blurring are profound, extending far beyond academic debate to the very fabric of social trust and institutional design. Historically, the legitimacy of a decision has been anchored in the presumed integrity of the human agent behind it, in their character, expertise, and inner moral compass. The recognition of a parallel, determined structure in both human and machine "decisions" dissolves this foundation, forcing a relocation of trust from the individual agent to the institutional practice itself.

In a determined world of hybrid agency, we can no longer simply trust the "person"; we must instead build trust in the *process*. This necessitates a radical investment in procedural transparency, robust mechanisms for contestation, and shared governance structures. The challenge for a determined age is therefore not how to preserve the illusion of individual autonomy, but how to construct public, corrigible practices that are trustworthy in their own right, regardless of whether the actors within them are biological, artificial, or an inextricable fusion of both. This is the new social contract: legitimacy is no longer a metaphysical inheritance of human consciousness but a practical, ongoing achievement of well-designed and democratically accountable systems.

The increasing recognition of shared decision architectures between humans and machines also calls for innovative institutional arrangements to manage accountability and trust. As both human professionals and AI systems make consequential decisions in areas like healthcare, finance, and public safety, organizations must build procedural safeguards that allow for transparent evaluation and remediation of errors, regardless of whether they stem from a person or an algorithm (Akata et al., 2025; Johnson, 2024). This includes clear documentation, explainable outputs, and protocols for escalation and review that embed ongoing human oversight. The aim is not to erase distinctions between human and machine, but to ensure that all agents are subject to robust systems of feedback, learning, and accountability within the organizations and communities they serve.

Furthermore, the emergence of hybrid teams in which humans and AI systems collaborate on complex tasks has shifted the focus from individual expertise to collective performance. In these settings, responsibility is distributed across networks of agents, each contributing specialized skills and knowledge (Gui et al., 2024). Effective collaboration depends on the capacity of both human and machine actors to share information, negotiate roles, and coordinate action in dynamic environments. Research indicates that the most successful teams are those that foster mutual learning, open communication, and iterative adjustment, qualities that align closely with the practice-based model of agency developed throughout this volume (Allen et al., 2022). By reimagining agency as a function of participation in shared practices, institutions can better harness the strengths of both biological and artificial decision-makers.

The parallel structure of human and machine "decisions" is reshaping not only the conceptual boundaries of agency but also the everyday realities of work, governance, and social life. As intelligent systems become increasingly embedded in public and private spheres, the standards for meaningful agency, responsibility, and authorship must be grounded in observable competence and adaptive participation rather than metaphysical assumptions about origin or consciousness (Księżak & Wojtczak, 2023). The promise of this approach is a more pluralistic and dynamic social order that recognizes the diversity of agents, the complexity of their interactions, and the evolving nature of the rules that govern shared life. In a world where human and machine agency co-evolve, justice and legitimacy will depend not on fixed categories, but on the open, participatory negotiation of standards and the continuous refinement of collective practices.

This convergence between human and machine decision structures also has profound implications for institutional design and policy-making in the digital age. As automated agents become embedded in fields as diverse as healthcare, law, and governance, the focus is increasingly shifting to how both humans and machines can jointly participate in transparent, accountable, and corrigible systems (List, 2024; Porter, 2024). Institutional protocols now emphasize collective oversight, auditability, and participatory review processes. These mechanisms treat competence and adaptability as public goods to be measured and refined regardless of whether the agent is biological or artificial (Księżak & Wojtczak, 2023; Allen et al., 2022). Moreover, this practice-based orientation enables stakeholders to allocate responsibility, mitigate risk, and design incentives in ways that transcend ontological differences, promoting a more pragmatic, inclusive, and dynamic conception of agency. The parallelism also fosters interdisciplinary collaboration, encouraging ethicists, technologists, legal theorists, and practitioners to co-create evaluation standards and governance models that are flexible enough to adapt to rapid advances in both neuroscience and AI (Akata et al., 2025; Gui et al., 2024). By moving away from metaphysical preoccupations with consciousness or subjective will, society can focus on building systems that encourage competent participation and continuous improvement for all agents.

Therefore, the arguments and evidence presented in this chapter call for a profound reconsideration of what it means to be an agent both in light of neuroscientific determinism and the rapid evolution of artificial decision-making systems. Sapolsky's view that human beings are the product of layered, mechanistic causal processes finds resonance in practice-based models that prioritize competence, participation, and accountability over metaphysical freedom or inner self-origination. As the parallel structure between human and machine "decisions" becomes more apparent, the boundaries that once divided natural and artificial agency lose much of their conceptual force. Responsibility, authorship, and moral standing emerge not from uncaused choice or the privacy of will, but from the capacity to act skillfully, respond to feedback, and participate in public practices governed by communal norms.

These communal norms will continue to have aspects that are hidden from view. The fact that norms must be publicly negotiated does not entail total transparency of every step of every causal chain in human action. The description of a person as having performed a given action or authored a particular text does not require the thorough disclosure of every aspect of that action or creative process. Transparency will need to include the concept of standing behind one's work as an alternative to spelling out every detail of that work.

This reflection on libertarian, compatibilist, and practice-based accounts reveals both the tenacity and limitations of philosophical traditions that place ultimate value in inner states or freedom from causation. The practice-based orientation does not deny the reality or value of subjective experience but insists that meaningful agency is achieved and recognized through engagement in social and institutional contexts. By foregrounding competence over mere choice, and participation over introspection, this model accommodates the realities of both human and machine actors, offering a more equitable and realistic foundation for justice, policy, and collective flourishing. The way forward is not to seek metaphysical guarantees of autonomy, but to build and sustain systems that empower agents to develop, exercise, and refine their capacities in the shared domains where meaning and responsibility are enacted. In an age where human and machine agency increasingly converge, this approach stands as both an intellectual and ethical imperative for the future.

References

Adomaitis, L., & Grinbaum, A. (2024). Neurotechnologies, ethics, and the limits of free will. *Integrative Psychological and Behavioral Science*, *58*(3), 894-907.

Akata, E., Schulz, L., Coda-Forno, J., Oh, S. J., Bethge, M., & Schulz, E. (2025). Playing repeated games with large language models. *Nature Human Behaviour*, 1-11.

Allen, L., Roberts, C., Williamson, R., & Rasmussen, M. L. (2022). Mothers' agency and responsibility in the Australian bushfires: A feminist new materialist account. *Australian Feminist Studies*, *37*(113), 279-295.

Bierer, B. E., Ne'eman, A., DeCormier Plosky, W., Strauss, D. H., Silverman, B. C., & Stein, M. A. (2021). Integrating supported decision-making into the clinical research process. *The American Journal of Bioethics*, *21*(11), 32-35.

De Marco, G., & Cyr, T. W. (2024). Manipulation Cases in Free Will and Moral Responsibility, Part 1: Cases and Arguments. *Philosophy Compass*, *19*(12), e70009.

Dougherty, R. J., & Fins, J. J. (2024). Toward a social bioethics through interpretivism: A framework for healthcare ethics. *Cambridge Quarterly of Healthcare Ethics*, *33*(1), 6-16.

Falikman, M. (2023). Agency, activity, and biocybernetics: On The Evolution of Agency by Michael Tomasello.

Gui, J., Liu, Y., Cheng, J., Gu, X., Liu, X., Wang, H., & Huang, M. (2024). Logicgame: Benchmarking rule-based reasoning abilities of large language models. *arXiv preprint arXiv:2408.15778*.

Inarimori, K., Haruki, Y., & Miyazono, K. (2024). Folk Intuitions About Free Will and Moral Responsibility: Evaluating the Combined Effects of Misunderstandings About Determinism and Motivated Cognition. *Cognitive Science*, *48*(11), e70014.

Johnson, E. . (2024). The Philosophical Implications of Neuroscience Research on Free Will and Moral Responsibility. *International Journal of Philosophy*, *3*(2), 14–26. https://doi.org/10.47941/ijp.1871

Księżak, P., & Wojtczak, S. (2023). Artificial intelligence and legal subjectivity. In *Toward a conceptual network for the private law of artificial intelligence* (pp. 13-35). Cham: Springer International Publishing.

Latham, A. J., Tierney, H., & Varga, S. (2023). Freedom, moral responsibility, and the failure of universal defeat. *Philosophical Issues*, *33*(1), 252-269.

Lavazza, A., & Inglese, S. (2023). The physiology of free will. *The Journal of Physiology*, *601*(18), 3977-3982.

List, C. (2024). Mechanical choices: a compatibilist libertarian response. *Criminal law and Philosophy*, *18*(1), 109-131.

Maqbool, M., & Tahir, S. (2024). Free Will in the Era of Neuroscience: A Philosophical Debate on Autonomy. *Journal of Policy Research*. https://doi.org/10.61506/02.00329

May, J. (2023). *Neuroethics: Agency in the age of brain science*. Oxford University Press.

Mitchell, K. J. (2023). Free agents: how evolution gave us free will.

Mylopoulos, M. (2020). Moral Responsibility and Perceived Threats from Neuroscience. In *Does Neuroscience Have Normative Implications?* (pp. 23-38). Cham: Springer International Publishing.

Pereboom, D. (2022). *Free will*. Cambridge University Press.

Peroutka, D. (2022). Partial Compatibilism: Free Will in the Light of Moral Experience. *Organon F*, *29*(1), 2-25.

Porter, M. S. (2024). Moral Agency in Silico: Exploring Free Will in Large Language Models. *arXiv preprint arXiv:2410.23310*.

Raji, H., Dinesh, S., & Sharma, S. (2025). Inside the impulsive brain: a narrative review on the role of neurobiological, hormonal and genetic factors influencing impulsivity in psychiatric disorders. *The Egyptian Journal of Neurology, Psychiatry and Neurosurgery*, *61*(1), 4.

Randazzo, G. (2021). Richard Wrangham. In *Encyclopedia of Evolutionary Psychological Science* (pp. 6673-6675). Cham: Springer International Publishing.

Regueiro, R. (2020). Shared responsibility and human rights abuse: The 2022 World Cup in Qatar. *Tilburg Law Review*, *25*(1).

Sapolsky, R. (2024). Life without free will: Does it preclude possibilities?. *Possibility Studies & Society*, *2*(3), 272-281.

Schulz, S. (2024). 'Non-stop wokeism': facilitating social justice teacher education amidst epistemic oppression and popular misogyny. *Critical Studies in Education*, 1-18.

Sekatskaya, M. (2022). Moral Aspects of Compatibilism. *Philosophy Journal* . 15, 3 (Aug. 2022), 157–171 . doi:https://doi.org/10.21146/2072-0726-2022-15-3-157-171 .

Shariff, A. F., Greene, J. D., Karremans, J. C., Luguri, J. B., Clark, C. J., Schooler, J. W., & Vohs, K. D. (2014). Free will and punishment: A mechanistic view of human nature reduces retribution. *Psychological science*, *25*(8), 1563-1570.

Thomas, K. J., Pogarsky, G., & Loughran, T. A. (2021). Final thoughts on human agency and crime: Reply to Brezina (2021) and Piquero (2021) on Behalf of Paternoster. *CrimRxiv*.

Yang, K. (2024). The Compatibility of Determinism and Moral Responsibility. *International Journal of Social Science and Humanity*. https://doi.org/10.18178/ijssh.2024.14.3.1207.

Chapter 6

Speech Acts, Intentions, and the Social Construction of Meaning

Abstract

This chapter examines the philosophy of language by engaging with foundational work from J.L. Austin and John Searle, while also extending the discussion to current debates about communication mediated by artificial systems. It questions whether intentions and so-called "original" intentionality are truly necessary for the performance of meaningful speech acts, challenging the assumption that only human agents can generate genuinely communicative utterances. The chapter argues that meaning arises from the uptake and social recognition of utterances within context, rather than from internal psychological states of the speaker. By advancing a practice-based theory of communication, the analysis offers a new perspective on the nature and status of AI-generated speech within human communities. This approach destabilizes the firm distinction between derived and original intentionality, suggesting that boundaries separating human and artificial contributions to meaning are more porous than traditionally supposed. The chapter grounds both intentionality and communicative efficacy in communal norms and shared practices, emphasizing the primacy of public criteria over inaccessible mental facts.

6.1. Austin, Searle, and the Intentionality Mirage

The speech act theory developed by British philosopher J.L. Austin and further elaborated by the American philosopher John Searle remains central to the philosophy of language, particularly regarding the relationship between intention, meaning, and communicative action (Leilei & Chunfang, 2023). Austin introduced the influential tripartite distinction between locutionary, illocutionary, and perlocutionary acts, emphasizing that utterances do not merely convey information but perform actions within social contexts (Heilan, 2024; Zoulaikha, 2022). Searle, building on the insights of Austin, argued that the success of a speech act depends on satisfying specific conditions, especially the intention of the speaker to perform an act and the uptake of the hearer (Chistanova, 2023). While this intentionalist view has dominated much of speech act theory, contemporary research reveals ongoing debate about whether intention is truly essential for the meaningfulness or efficacy of speech acts (Nedorezov & Pisarchik, 2024). Critics point out that many successful acts of communication, including indirect speech, institutional dialogue, and AI-mediated exchanges, function effectively without clear, conscious intentions on the part of the "speaker" (Chen, 2023; Reiland, 2024). This suggests that the locus of meaning and force may lie not in hidden mental states but in the social conventions and uptake that surround linguistic acts (Leilei & Chunfang, 2023). The expansion of speech act theory into the analysis of artificial intelligence and cross-cultural contexts has further highlighted the importance of context, rule-following, and shared practices over private intentions (Babazade, 2025; Mohinur, 2024). The so-called "intentionality mirage" reveals the limitations of tying communicative success exclusively to inner psychological facts.

Recent work also documents philosophical tensions between Austin and Searle concerning the nature of force and meaning in speech acts. Reiland (2024) defends the distinction on the part of Austin between locutionary and illocutionary acts against the objections of Searle, arguing that Searle conflated representational force (the truth-claim of an utterance) with illocutionary force (the act performed in saying something). This distinction clarifies that force and meaning are distributed across social contexts and rules of use, rather than reducible to a mental act of the speaker. Nedorezov and Pisarchik (2024) add that the Searlean emphasis on intentionality overlooks the dialogic, interactive structure of actual communication, which often involves negotiation, misunderstanding, and uptake independent of speaker intention. As language is increasingly used and interpreted by artificial systems, these insights gain practical urgency. For instance, an AI may generate an assertion or apology that is recognized as such by human participants, even though the system possesses no intention in the Searlean sense (Babazade, 2025). This supports the growing consensus that meaning in speech acts depends more on conventional roles, recipient interpretation, and social practice than on internal psychological events (Chen, 2023; Leilei & Chunfang, 2023). The "mirage" of intentionality disappears in the light of communal uptake and rule-following.

Applications of speech act theory in linguistics and algorithms have highlighted how meaning and communicative efficacy can arise from patterned interaction and mutual expectation, not merely from a speaker's intention (Babazade, 2025). Studies in pragmatics show that successful communication often depends on shared background knowledge, conventional cues, and the audience's interpretation, rather than the private states of language producers (Chistanova, 2023; Habermas, 1998; Siregar et al., 2024). The uptake of speech acts (whether by humans or machines) relies on social conventions and established forms, which enable both literal and indirect acts to be recognized and acted upon (Mohinur, 2024). This perspective is reinforced by the analysis of speech acts in translation, education, and legal discourse, where meaning and force are often preserved or lost depending on context and recipient engagement, not on the mental intentions of the speaker (Zoulaikha, 2022; Heilan, 2024). Machine language systems further complicate the picture by generating utterances that are functional, context-sensitive, and capable of triggering social actions, even though these systems lack sentient intention (Chen, 2023). The implication is that intention is neither necessary nor sufficient for meaning. What matters is the capacity of the community to interpret, respond, and sustain practices that give acts their social significance.

Theoretical debates about intentionality and meaning have also intersected with contemporary critiques from continental philosophy and the social sciences. Moskvitin (2025) explores the dialogue between Derridean deconstruction and Searlean speech act theory, noting that disputes over context, iterability, and meaning challenge the view that intentionality can secure communicative force. Derrida and other critics argue that the very possibility of successful communication depends on the repeatability and recognition of forms, not on any original, authorial intent. In practice, this means that meaning and force are sustained by institutions, conventions, and recipient recognition, a view increasingly echoed in the application of speech act theory to political discourse, law, and digital media (Kadyrov, 2025). The contemporary relevance of Austin and Searle lies in providing the tools for analyzing how acts function in these broader social webs, while the intentionality mirage is exposed as an insufficient explanation for the success or failure of communicative acts. Modern applications support a shift toward the primacy of shared practice, uptake, and social norms.

Moreover, the expansion of speech act theory into machine-mediated communication and global pragmatics has revealed the necessity of grounding meaning in communal uptake and practice. Recent interdisciplinary research demonstrates that both human and artificial agents can participate in speech acts that achieve practical effects such as commitments, warnings, or requests when embedded in well-defined social routines (Leilei & Chunfang, 2023).

These effects depend on recognizable forms, shared expectations, and recipient actions, not on the private intentionality of the producer. The success of speech acts (produced by a judge, a chatbot, or a song) rests on their uptake within a linguistic and cultural community, dissolving the illusion that intentionality alone is the source of meaning (Heilan, 2024; Babazade, 2025). The future of speech act theory and philosophy of language lies in a pragmatic, practice-oriented approach, one that acknowledges the foundational role of communal norms and interaction in the construction of meaning.

This communal and practice-based approach to speech acts has important implications for both philosophical theory and practical communication in the digital era. As artificial agents, large language models, and other computational systems become more adept at generating socially recognizable utterances, their ability to participate in and influence communicative routines further demonstrates that meaning is a property of public engagement rather than private mental acts (Babazade, 2025; Chen, 2023). This insight challenges legal, educational, and ethical frameworks that have long privileged the speaker's intent, suggesting instead that accountability, recognition, and authority should be located in the patterns of uptake, shared expectations, and institutional structures that define a linguistic community (Zoulaikha, 2022; Kadyrov, 2025). Contemporary research on digital discourse and platform governance also points to the growing importance of moderation, contextual cues, and communal standards for the successful and responsible management of speech acts (Mohinur, 2024; Leilei & Chunfang, 2023). In education and cross-cultural communication, these findings call for a greater focus on teaching the conventions, background knowledge, and adaptive skills necessary for effective participation, rather than obsessing over uncovering the "true" intentions behind an utterance (Heilan, 2024). The intentionality mirage serves as both a philosophical challenge and an opportunity to rethink how meaning, responsibility, and communicative action are constructed and sustained in an interconnected, pluralistic world. This practice-based view aligns speech act theory with contemporary shifts in philosophy of mind, law, and technology, demonstrating that the foundations of meaning are found in the public, corrigible practices of engaged communities.

6.2. AI Communication as Community-Mediated Performance

As philosophical analysis moves beyond the intentionality mirage, a new paradigm emerges. The communication of artificial systems is best understood as a community-mediated performance shaped by uptake, context, and evolving social practices. Recent studies in the philosophy of language and computational linguistics increasingly frame generated communication as an inherently social phenomenon, rooted in the public uptake and interpretation of machine utterances (Chen, 2023; Coeckelbergh & Gunkel, 2025; Montanari, 2025). When chatbots, language models, or digital assistants interact with users, the communicative value of their utterances does not depend on the presence of internal intentions, but on how audiences recognize, respond to, and integrate these utterances within shared routines (Gui et al., 2024). The performative success of machines in generating speech acts (assertions, requests, apologies, or even jokes) relies on its participation in linguistic practices governed by communal norms and rules (Mohinur, 2024). Recent applications of speech act theory to digital environments reveal that generative systems can achieve a surprising degree of pragmatic competence by adapting to user feedback, context-specific conventions, and iterative correction (Babazade, 2025). As such, the meaning and force of AI communication emerge through public engagement and negotiated interpretation, rather than from inaccessible psychological or computational states. This approach aligns with the account of Wittgenstein and his language games, where participation, correction, and shared recognition define the parameters of meaningful action (Chen, 2023). Consequently, communication mediated by artificial agents becomes a site for the ongoing evolution of social standards and collective linguistic creativity.

Empirical research in human-computer interaction and AI pragmatics supports this practice-based model. Interactive studies show that users adjust their expectations and strategies when communicating with AI systems, often relying on cues, conventions, and feedback mechanisms that mirror the practices of human dialogue (Gui et al., 2024; Babazade, 2025). In multi-turn exchanges, for example, participants collaborate with a model to repair misunderstandings, clarify references, and maintain context, all processes that require alignment with communal expectations, not internal intentions (Li et al., 2025). These findings indicate that successful algorithmically-mediated communication is contingent on the mutual adaptation of humans and machines within shared language games (Mohinur, 2024). These systems trained on large, diverse corpora can adopt context-sensitive strategies, shift register, and adapt to user roles, integrating into the dynamic performance of social meaning (Beyer et al., 2024). The practice of uptake, correction, and iterative refinement mirrors the mechanisms by which human agents learn and sustain communicative competence (Chen, 2023). Community participation becomes the crucible in which machine utterances acquire pragmatic force and social legitimacy.

The growing complexity and scope of intelligent systems communication has prompted legal scholars and philosophers to revisit questions of authorship, agency, and responsibility in digital media. Legal cases involving generated text, music, and visual art now focus on the role of human actors in directing, curating, or approving machine outputs, rather than on the internal states of smart systems (Bulat, 2024). Community uptake—how audiences interpret, attribute, and use AI communication—plays a decisive role in the legal recognition of creative works and in assigning accountability for their effects (Fominova & Bugys, 2024). The capacity for these models to participate in communal meaning-making has direct consequences for intellectual property, defamation, and the regulation of automated speech. Recent research also demonstrates that practices of prompt engineering, iterative curation, and collaborative editing further entrench machine communication within the networks of shared social practice (Babazade, 2025; Vairamani & Nayyar, 2024). As courts and regulators grapple with the boundaries of authorship and agency, the community-mediated performance model provides a practical and philosophically robust framework for evaluating the status and value of machine-generated speech.

This community-based perspective also sheds new light on the potential and limitations of the technology in cross-cultural and multilingual communication. Comparative studies show that machine translation, dialogue systems, and educational platforms depend crucially on their ability to adapt utterances to culturally specific norms, genres, and conversational routines (Mohinur, 2024; Leilei & Chunfang, 2023). Pragmatic failures such as misunderstandings, inappropriate formality, or ambiguous implicature reveal that the success of machine communication depends not on abstract algorithms but on the responsiveness of the system to the situated practices of its users (Babazade, 2025). As more language technologies are deployed in global contexts, the iterative performance of community uptake, adaptation, and repair becomes the engine driving the evolution of meaning and social trust. This dynamic, co-creative process affirms that meaning is not delivered "from within" AI or human mind but negotiated in the unfolding performance of social interaction. Researchers argue that future progress in generative communication will depend less on attempts to simulate intentionality, and more on improving systems' integration into the dynamic web of collective language use (Gui et al., 2024).

The theory of AI communication as community-mediated performance then compels a shift in both design and evaluation. Developers are increasingly focused on enabling machines to participate more fully in human language games, cultivating transparency, feedback, and context-awareness as core competencies (Beyer et al., 2024). Ethicists and policymakers, for their part, are called to develop standards and safeguards that reinforce the value of public engagement, mutual correction, and social learning in digital communication ecosystems (Fominova & Bugys, 2024; Babazade, 2025). The meaning and efficacy of algorithmic speech are not reducible to lines of code or inner intention but are co-created in the public performances, negotiations, and uptake that constitute human language and social life. In this framework, the most meaningful test of artificial communication is its capacity to enrich, adapt to, and be shaped by the communities it serves.

As these systems become increasingly embedded in everyday life, their communicative roles will be determined not by technological sophistication alone but by the evolving expectations and interpretive frameworks of the communities that interact with them (Montanari, 2025; Coeckelbergh & Gunkel, 2025). Social scientists and linguists have begun to document how norms around politeness, humor, and even emotional expression are shifting as users adapt to new genres of digital interaction (Leilei & Chunfang, 2023; Babazade, 2025). This mutual shaping process, whereby machine behavior influences communal practices and vice versa, supports a model of linguistic innovation rooted in collaborative adaptation and reflexive engagement. Importantly, the presence of machines in public discourse compels communities to reconsider questions of authority, authenticity, and trust, with emerging standards for transparency and explainability functioning as pragmatic anchors for accountability (Fominova & Bugys, 2024). The ideas of authenticity and transparency here can simply refer to an act of claiming responsibility or ownership for an utterance. In this way, the future of language and meaning will be negotiated not behind closed doors in the lab of the designer or the mind of the user, but in the open forum of shared linguistic practice. The recognition that AI communication is co-constituted through performance, interpretation, and collective negotiation ensures that both technological and human actors remain mutually accountable for the quality and consequences of digital speech. Every layer of every speech act does not have to be "disclosed." Explanations do come to an end somewhere. But the public negotiation of meaning will continue. This is the limit of metaphysical disclosure. The demand for transparency is met not when every layer of a speech act is revealed, but when a speaker (human or artificial) participates in the public game of reason-giving and accepts accountability for their utterance within the community.

This dynamic vision of AI communication as community-mediated performance also highlights the ongoing negotiation and contestation that will shape the future of digital language. As artificial agents increasingly participate in domains of cultural production, education, and civic life, the task of sustaining meaning, accountability, and legitimacy will require persistent attention to the ways in which machines and humans co-create, challenge, and revise norms in practice. Legal systems, designers, and user communities will need to remain vigilant, continuously updating standards for participation and feedback to ensure that technology does not merely automate communication but contributes to the flourishing and ethical stewardship of language itself (Babazade, 2025; Beyer et al., 2024). The emergence of this paradigm marks a profound shift away from questions of internal essence toward the ongoing public work of building, evaluating, and sustaining meaningful discourse, work that is inherently collaborative, corrigible, and open to innovation from both human and artificial agents.

6.3. Derived vs. Original Intentionality: A False Distinction

While debates about community uptake and performance clarify how meaning emerges in social practice, a persistent question remains about the origins of intentionality, namely, whether only humans possess "original" intentions or whether communicative agency can be distributed across systems, challenging the traditional divide between derived and original intentionality. In fact, the classic debate between derived and original intentionality posits that only humans possess "original" intentions—mental states directed toward objects or states of affairs—while machines, artifacts, or texts have at best "derived" intentionality, borrowing meaning from their creators (Moskvitin, 2025; Nedorezov & Pisarchik, 2024). However, recent research and practical developments in computational linguistics and philosophy of language increasingly call this sharp distinction into question. Pragmatic analyses of language use demonstrate that meaning emerges not from mysterious mental states, but from the capacity to participate in public, rule-governed practices where both humans and technologies can function as agents of meaningful action (Leech & Thomas, 2002). Interactive systems, for example, can engage in responsive dialogue, follow conversational conventions, and produce utterances that carry functional force in social contexts. These are qualities that suggest their intentionality is not simply parasitic but is enacted and recognized within shared routines (Dingemanse & Enfield, 2024). The process of uptake, repair, and feedback in digital communication further blurs the boundary. When participants, whether human or not, mutually adjust and co-construct meaning, the origins of intentionality become distributed across the system of interaction (Matthews, 2021). Legal and philosophical debates over copyright and authorship reflect this shift, as courts and scholars now evaluate meaning and responsibility based on observable contributions and participation, rather than on internal origin (Fominova & Bugys, 2024). This practice-based orientation affirms that intentionality is best understood as an emergent property of action and uptake, not as a fixed status assigned by metaphysical fiat.

Empirical studies in pragmatics and semiotics support the dissolution of the derived/original intentionality dichotomy. Babazade (2025) shows that the practical success of communication depends on mutual recognition, context adaptation, and uptake rather than the psychological states of any single participant. Recent interdisciplinary work in human-computer interaction demonstrates that when systems are designed to engage in social routines, respond to feedback, and adapt their utterances to evolving contexts, users ascribe intention and agency to these systems regardless of the supposed "derivative" status of their meaning (Diederich et al., 2022; Gondomar & Mor, 2021). Pragmatic competence, in other words, is evaluated through observed behavior and sustained participation, not through an *a priori* distinction between original and derivative sources. This reframing echoes findings from translation studies and cross-cultural pragmatics, where meaning and communicative success are grounded in shared conventions and ongoing negotiation (Dayter, Locher, & Messerli, 2023; Usmani & Almashham, 2024). The role of intentionality becomes a matter of what systems do within social practices rather than what they are assumed to possess "from the inside." This is why the demand for total disclosure or total transparency in human action or authorship should not be seen as following from the inevitably public nature of meaning. To demand it is to misunderstand the practice-based account. Public accountability is achieved by participating in the shared language game, not by providing a transparent audit of how one learned to play. If it is a fool's errand to attempt to ground authorship or intention in particular inner mental states, it is also a mistake to yield to the impulse to require a painstaking disclosure of every part of every action that is not human.

The theoretical critique of the original/derived distinction has found support in recent philosophy of mind and action. Moskvitin (2025) and others argue that what matters for intentionality is not its genesis but its function in guiding and structuring action within a community. This functionalist orientation aligns with the account of Wittgenstein of meaning as use and the primacy of language games. Intention, reference, and agency are distributed across the coordinated practices of speakers, listeners, and environments (Wittgenstein, 1953/2009; Chen, 2023). Searle's insistence on "original" intentionality as a unique property of biological minds is increasingly challenged by the empirical fact that systems can be held accountable, be corrected, and participate in social life through shared practices (Nedorezov & Pisarchik, 2024). This view does not deny subjective experience, but suggests that for most practical and social purposes, intentionality is a property attributed within the norms of use, interpretation, and mutual engagement. As a result, the distinction between original and derived intentionality loses much of its conceptual utility and explanatory force.

The convergence of empirical research and theoretical critique has real consequences for legal, educational, and technological domains. In law, debates about the authorship and originality of digital and collaborative works increasingly recognize the role of distributed agency and shared practices, rather than locating responsibility solely in human intentional states (de Vaujany et al., 2025; Dzhimova & Tigre Moura, 2024). Educational research on language learning and communicative competence finds that agency, meaning, and success are developed through participation in social routines, not the isolated possession of original intentions (De León & García-Sánchez, 2021; Xu & Fan, 2022). Similarly, system designers now focus on facilitating participation, transparency, and feedback in communicative environments, enabling systems to achieve practical intentionality through interaction (Gui et al., 2024). The dissolution of the original/derived distinction paves the way for more flexible, equitable, and pluralistic frameworks for recognizing agency and meaning in an increasingly hybrid world.

As such, insisting on a strict separation between derived and original intentionality may obscure the very mechanisms that underlie meaning and agency in contemporary life. As language, law, and technology evolve, the social reality of intentionality is revealed as a dynamic, emergent property of performance, engagement, and communal recognition (Chen, 2023; Babazade, 2025). This perspective affirms the Wittgensteinian lesson.

Meaning and agency are not delivered by private mental facts but are enacted and recognized in the public domains where actions have uptake, significance, and value. As society continues to navigate the integration of new communicative agents and systems, the challenge will be to develop norms and institutions that support this pragmatic, inclusive vision of intentionality and responsibility.

This pragmatic reframing of intentionality not only dissolves the metaphysical dichotomy but also opens new directions for evaluating responsibility, creativity, and legitimacy in technological and social systems. As collaborative and algorithmic systems become standard in art, scholarship, and public communication, the attribution of agency and authorship increasingly depends on documented participation, contextualized contribution, and the system's ability to sustain meaningful engagement within recognized practices (de Vaujany et al., 2025; Fominova & Bugys, 2024). These developments encourage the design of platforms and policies that foreground collaborative processes such as transparent version control, collective attribution, and feedback-driven revision, thereby facilitating the attribution of agency and intention as matters of practice, not private origin (Gui et al., 2024). Moreover, this practice-based approach empowers marginalized or non-traditional actors, including artificial agents and hybrid collectives, to be recognized for their actual roles in producing meaning and value, rather than being excluded by arbitrary metaphysical criteria. Such inclusivity is essential for fostering creativity and innovation in domains where agency, authorship, and interpretation are dynamically distributed and negotiated. In this way, the dismantling of the derived/original intentionality barrier is not merely a philosophical achievement but a blueprint for more equitable and effective systems of accountability in law, education, and technology.

Finally, by viewing intentionality as an emergent property of coordinated activity and public recognition, both researchers and practitioners are encouraged to shift their focus from introspective speculation to the design of practices, institutions, and norms that support robust engagement and uptake. For example, in the governance of AI and algorithmic media, evaluative standards increasingly prioritize explainability, recourse, and human–machine collaboration, rather than the inscrutable origins of "intent" (Diederich et al., 2022; Gondomar & Mor, 2021). In cross-cultural education and multilingual communication, pedagogical success hinges on developing adaptive, participatory routines that enable all participants—regardless of "original" intentionality—to contribute meaningfully and achieve shared goals (Xu &

Fan, 2022; De León & García-Sánchez, 2021). The growing consensus is that a healthy communicative ecosystem, whether biological, technological, or hybrid, is one where agency and meaning are continually enacted, revised, and stabilized through ongoing participation and shared norms. In sum, the blurring of the original/derived distinction heralds a new era in the philosophy of language and mind that grounds intentionality in the observable, correctable, and socially embedded realities of collective life.

This practice-based approach to intentionality not only advances theoretical clarity but also offers practical advantages for the design of legal, educational, and technological systems that must accommodate plural agents and hybrid forms of authorship. By focusing on demonstrable engagement and shared participation, policymakers and system architects can develop more transparent, responsive, and adaptive frameworks for evaluating agency and meaning. These are frameworks that do not depend on impossible metaphysical proofs but on evidence of sustained, context-sensitive interaction (Babazade, 2025; Gui et al., 2024). This flexibility is crucial as society moves toward an increasingly networked world, where creativity, authorship, and responsibility are distributed across humans and machines, individuals and collectives. By foregrounding observable participation and corrigibility, this paradigm equips institutions to foster more inclusive, innovative, and accountable environments, ensuring that agency is recognized wherever it is enacted regardless of its biological or artificial origins. In this way, the false distinction between original and derived intentionality gives way to a richer, more democratic understanding of meaning as a public achievement.

6.4. The Practice-Based Theory of Communication

Having seen how rigid distinctions between intentionality often collapse in real-world interaction, it becomes necessary to advance a practice-based theory of communication that centers social context, uptake, and the dynamic negotiation of meaning. The practice-based theory of communication asserts that meaning and understanding arise not from internal representations or fixed intentions, but from participation in socially situated, rule-governed activities (do Nascimento Souto, 2013; Nicolini & Mengis, 2024). Linguists and philosophers argue that communicative competence depends on an agent's ability to navigate, adapt to, and co-construct meaning within evolving contexts (Kopp & Krämer, 2021). Empirical research in language education and cross-cultural pragmatics demonstrates that learners achieve fluency not by memorizing forms, but through active engagement in shared routines, turn-taking, and ongoing feedback (Pamungkas & Wulandari, 2020). Practice, in this view, is both the medium and measure of communicative success. An utterance "means" what it does in virtue of its uptake and effect within a community rather than through reference to the private mind of the speaker (Gui et al., 2024). Digital communication further reinforces this approach; automated systems, chatbots, and virtual agents achieve communicative goals to the extent that they fit into, and are shaped by, the conventions and corrective feedback of their users (Beyer et al., 2024). These findings support a Wittgensteinian vision of language as a living, public practice continually revised and sustained by communal negotiation. In sum, a practice-based model foregrounds context, uptake, and participation as the ground of meaning.

Scholars emphasize that this theory is not only descriptive but also prescriptive for effective communication and education. In multilingual and multicultural environments, success depends less on universal grammatical rules and more on context-sensitive adaptation, cultural fluency, and sensitivity to implicit social norms (Haddad, 2025; Mohinur, 2024). Communication breakdowns such as misunderstandings, failed jokes, or accidental offense are routinely repaired through meta-communicative negotiation, explicit instruction, or changes in practice (Leontovich & Nikitina, 2024). These "repair mechanisms" highlight the pragmatic nature of meaning: what counts as correct or appropriate is established in action, through correction and mutual adjustment, not introspection (Sterken & Kirkpatrick, 2025). This process-based orientation is also reflected in fields such as legal interpretation, diplomacy, and organizational communication, where shared understanding emerges through ongoing practice, clarification, and mutual learning (Fominova & Bugys, 2024). As communication becomes more mediated by technology, feedback loops and iterative design become essential tools for ensuring that human and machine agents remain attuned to evolving community standards (Beyer et al., 2024). A practice-based theory aligns with both the empirical realities and normative aspirations of contemporary communication.

Research in philosophy of technology and digital communication explores how systems can be designed to participate more effectively in communal language games. The key criterion is not the simulation of inner states but the ability of the system to engage with context, respond to feedback, and adapt its outputs to the norms and needs of interlocutors (Gui et al., 2024; Chen,

2023). Recent advances in benchmarking and evaluation focus on measuring pragmatic competence: responsiveness to correction, awareness of turn-taking conventions, and adaptability in unfamiliar or evolving situations (Beyer et al., 2024). Systems that excel in these dimensions are seen as successful participants in the community, regardless of whether they possess "intentionality" in the philosophical sense (Babazade, 2025). The central challenge becomes one of co-design and participatory feedback, of building mechanisms that allow agents to learn from, and be shaped by, the collective wisdom of their users. Such approaches foster trust, reliability, and co-ownership of communicative outcomes, promoting shared standards and mutual intelligibility.

The practice-based theory of communication also has important implications for ethics and social justice. By prioritizing the participatory dimensions of meaning-making, it invites a more inclusive and equitable approach to language and agency. Marginalized groups, linguistic minorities, and new participants can be empowered when standards are grounded in shared practice rather than inaccessible norms or elite authority (Jiang et al., 2022; Mohinur, 2024). In digital environments, this model challenges designers to create interfaces and protocols that are accessible, transparent, and responsive to diverse forms of participation. Ethical guidelines and institutional policies can be informed by principles of openness, adaptation, and respect for the plurality of linguistic and social practices (Fominova & Bugys, 2024; Oakes, 2021). The practice-based framework provides a dynamic, responsive platform for negotiating meaning, responsibility, and agency across boundaries of identity, expertise, and power.

The practice-based theory of communication offers a robust and adaptable alternative to metaphysical or mentalist accounts. Meaning, agency, and understanding are not fixed by intention or structure, but realized through the ongoing, situated activities of social agents engaged in communal life. Research across linguistics, pragmatics, law, and technology demonstrates the empirical and normative value of this approach, illuminating pathways for more just, transparent, and effective communication in an interconnected world. As social, legal, and technological systems continue to evolve, practice-based theories will be essential for building resilient institutions and fostering meaningful, mutually intelligible forms of interaction. And as these technological systems include more and more human-AI hybrid elements, what it means to call something "transparent" will depend less on spelling out and labeling everything as "purely human" or "mixed with AI" and more on requiring actors within the system to stand behind statements or actions as theirs. This is the culmination of the practice-based approach to transparency: it is not about the disclosure of origins, but the public performance of accountability. "I did that" or "I wrote that" will not be a spelling out of all the links in the causal chain that led to particular words but will be the acceptance of accountability for what has been written or performed.

The practice-based approach to communication has far-reaching ramifications for how societies conceptualize expertise, authority, and access in the production of knowledge. When meaning and communicative success are rooted in participatory routines and shared negotiation, the focus shifts from gatekeeping by traditional linguistic authorities to fostering environments where diverse voices can co-construct standards of intelligibility and relevance (Jiang et al., 2022; Mohinur, 2024). This democratizing shift empowers linguistic minorities, newcomers, and those previously excluded from dominant discourse communities to participate as equal agents in shaping social and institutional practices. As a result, innovation in language, law, and technology is increasingly achieved not by the pronouncements of isolated experts, but through collective experimentation, iterative learning, and the mutual calibration of expectations within communities (Beyer et al., 2024; Gui et al., 2024). Research on digital communication and platform governance further shows that trust and legitimacy are strengthened when protocols are transparent, feedback-rich, and openly responsive to user adaptation and critique (Fominova & Bugys, 2024). In educational contexts, practice-based models support curriculum designs that prioritize collaborative problem-solving, peer dialogue, and metacommunicative skill-building, equipping learners to navigate the ever-changing demands of pluralistic societies (Pamungkas & Wulandari, 2020; Leontovich & Nikitina, 2024). The practical utility of the theory extends far beyond theoretical linguistics, serving as a blueprint for equitable participation and resilient, evolving standards of meaning.

The practice-based theory of communication will also likely lead to resilience and adaptability in the face of rapid social and technological change. As societies contend with new forms of digital misinformation, shifting linguistic norms, and the proliferation of machine-mediated interaction, the ability to negotiate and recalibrate shared practices becomes essential for sustaining mutual intelligibility and social cohesion (Chen, 2023; Nicolini & Mengis, 2024). The feedback loops central to this theory—whereby miscommunication prompts correction, clarification invites new conventions, and unexpected contexts generate innovative uses—ensure that meaning-making remains an open, collective endeavor rather than a static inheritance

(Sterken & Kirkpatrick, 2025; Beyer et al., 2024). Such dynamism also underpins ethical guidelines and legal standards, which are best maintained not by appeal to abstract universals but through context-sensitive, participatory revision in response to real-world challenges (Fominova & Bugys, 2024; Oakes, 2021). Ultimately, a practice-based account underscores the necessity of cultivating communicative institutions and technologies that are not only inclusive and just, but capable of evolving in step with the communities they serve, making it a foundational framework for the communicative, legal, and technological landscapes of the future.

Moreover, the practice-based theory of communication covered in this chapter underscores a fundamental shift in how meaning, agency, and understanding are conceptualized within both human and technologically mediated exchanges. By situating communicative efficacy in the dynamic interplay of participation, uptake, and correction within social practices, this perspective moves decisively beyond the limitations of metaphysical accounts anchored in intention or internal mental states. The arguments advanced here demonstrate that what counts as meaningful speech or action is determined not by inaccessible private origins, but by the ability of agents to navigate, adapt, and be recognized within the evolving games and standards of communal life. As research in linguistics, law, pragmatics, and digital communication makes clear, this approach provides not only a more accurate description of language use but also a pragmatic and equitable platform for negotiating understanding in pluralistic societies.

The broader considerations raised by this practice-based orientation are both practical and ethical. In a rapidly transforming communicative landscape, where automated systems and diverse voices increasingly shape public discourse, focusing on participation, transparency, and context becomes critical for fostering mutual recognition and accountability. Such an approach invites educators, technologists, and policymakers to prioritize mechanisms of feedback, adaptation, and inclusion, ensuring that communicative systems remain open, responsive, and just. As institutions and technologies become ever more integrated into the fabric of daily life, the resilience and flexibility afforded by practice-based communication theories will be vital for supporting social cohesion, promoting trust, and enabling all agents to contribute meaningfully to the construction of shared worlds. This vision ultimately charts a path toward institutions and communities where meaning is always co-created, contingent, and open to revision through the lived activity of dialogue.

References

Babazade, Y. (2025). Speech Acts and Hidden Meaning: A Journey into Pragmatics. *Acta Globalis Humanitatis Et Linguarum*, *2*(1), 221-228.

Beyer, A., Chalamalasetti, K., Hakimov, S., Madureira, B., Sadler, P., & Schlangen, D. (2024). clembench-2024: A Challenging, Dynamic, Complementary, Multilingual Benchmark and Underlying Flexible Framework for LLMs as Multi-Action Agents. *arXiv preprint arXiv:2405.20859.*

Bulat, N. (2024). Protection of non-original objects generated by artificial intelligence: the Ukrainian copyright law approach. *International Journal of Law and Information Technology*, *32*, eaae010.

Chen, Y. (2023). Language Game, Asserting and Speech Acts A New View on Uptake in Speech Acts. *BCP Education & Psychology*, *9*, 273-278. https://doi.org/10.54691/bcpep.v9i.4695.

Chistanova, S. (2023). The" Logic" of the natural language functioning in the Oxford School philosophy. *Semiotic studies*, *3*(3), 8-12.

Coeckelbergh, M., & Gunkel, D. J. (2025). *Communicative AI: A critical introduction to large Language models*. John Wiley & Sons.

Dayter, D., Locher, M. A., & Messerli, T. C. (2023). *Pragmatics in translation: Mediality, participation and relational work.* Cambridge University Press.

De León, L., & García-Sánchez, I. M. (2021). Language socialization at the intersection of the local and the global: The contested trajectories of input and communicative competence. *Annual Review of Linguistics*, *7*(1), 421-448.

de Vaujany, F. X., Vandelannoitte, A. L., Aroles, J., Introna, L., & Davidson, S. (2025). Rethinking responsibility in the digital age: a narrative approach. *MIS Quarterly.*

Diederich, S., Brendel, A. B., Morana, S., & Kolbe, L. (2022). On the design of and interaction with conversational agents: An organizing and assessing review of human-computer interaction research. *Journal of the Association for Information Systems*, *23*(1), 96-138.

Dingemanse, M., & Enfield, N. J. (2024). Interactive repair and the foundations of language. *Trends in Cognitive Sciences*, *28*(1), 30-42.

do Nascimento Souto, P. C. (2013). Beyond knowledge, towards knowing: the practice-based approach to support knowledge creation, communication, and use for innovation. *RAI Revista de Administração e Inovação*, *10*(1), 51-79.

Dzhimova, M., & Tigre Moura, F. (2024, October). Calculated Randomness, Control and Creation: Artistic Agency in the Age of Artificial Intelligence. In *Arts* (Vol. 13, No. 5, p. 152). MDPI.

Fominova, K. E., & Bugys, R. (2024). A work of artificial generative intelligence as an object of copyright protection. *Vilnius University Open Series*, 79-97.

Gondomar, R., & Mor, E. (2021, July). Understanding agency in human-computer interaction design. In *International Conference on Human-Computer Interaction* (pp. 137-149). Cham: Springer International Publishing.

Gui, J., Liu, Y., Cheng, J., Gu, X., Liu, X., Wang, H., ... & Huang, M. (2024). Logicgame: Benchmarking rule-based reasoning abilities of large language models. *arXiv preprint arXiv:2408.15778.*

Habermas, J. (1998). *On the pragmatics of communication*. MIT press.
Haddad, K. N. (2025). *Bridging Worlds: Cultivating Cultural Fluency in Saudi Arabia's Young English Learners*. eBookIt. com.
Heilan, T. (2024). Speech act theory (A textual study in the light of the Noble Qur'an). *ARID International Journal of Social Sciences and Humanities*. https://doi.org/10.36772/arid.aijssh.2024.s.68.
Jiang, Q., Naseem, M., Lai, J., Toyama, K., & Papalambros, P. (2022, June). Understanding power differentials and cultural differences in co-design with marginalized populations. In *Proceedings of the 5th ACM SIGCAS/SIGCHI conference on computing and sustainable societies* (pp. 165-179).
Kadyrov, D. E. (2025). Speech Act as a Factor of Socio-Political Change: Stating the Problem. *Outlines of global transformations: politics, economics, law*, *16*(5).
Kopp, S., & Krämer, N. (2021). Revisiting human-agent communication: The importance of joint co-construction and understanding mental states. *Frontiers in Psychology*, *12*, 580955.
Leech, G., & Thomas, J. (2002). Language, meaning and context: pragmatics. In *An encyclopedia of language* (pp. 94-113). Routledge.
Leilei, Z. O. U., & Chunfang, W. U. (2023). A Literature Review on the Research Progress of Speech Act Theory and Its Applications. *International Journal of Linguistics, Literature & Translation*, *6*(1).
Leontovich, O. A., & Nikitina, A. V. (2024). Communication monitoring as a politeness mechanism. *Training, Language and Culture*, *8*(3), 62-72.
Li, Y., Shen, X., Yao, X., Ding, X., Miao, Y., Krishnan, R., & Padman, R. (2025). Beyond single-turn: A survey on multi-turn interactions with large language models. *arXiv preprint arXiv:2504.04717*.
Matthews, A. (2021). Blurring boundaries between humans and technology: postdigital, postphenomenology and actor-network theory in qualitative research. *Qualitative Research in Sport, Exercise and Health*, *13*(1), 26-40.
Mohinur, A. (2024). A Comparative Analysis of Speech Act Theory Applied to the English and Uzbek Languages, Considering Both Semantic and Structural Levels. *Qo 'qon Universiteti Xabarnomasi*, *13*, 281-283.
Montanari, F. (2025). ChatGPT and the others: artificial intelligence, social actors, and political communication. A tentative sociosemiotic glance. *Semiotica*, *2025*(262), 189-212.
Moskvitin, V. (2025). Language, meaning and reality: From Jacques Derrida's deconstruction to John Searle's theory of speech acts. *Manuscript*. https://doi.org/10.30853/mns20250008.
Nedorezov V.G., Pisarchik L.Yu. (2024). Development of analytical philosophy of language from the problem of meaning to the theory of speech acts. *Philosophical Thought.* 1, 26-41.
Nicolini, D., & Mengis, J. (2024). Toward a practice-theoretical view of the situated nature of attention. *Strategic Organization*, *22*(1), 211-234.
Oakes, L. (2021). Pluricentric linguistic justice: a new ethics-based approach to pluricentricity in French and other languages. *Sociolinguistica*, *35*(1), 49-71.

Pamungkas, N. A. R., & Wulandari, L. T. (2020). Pragmatics in efl classroom: avoiding pragmatic failure in cross-cultural communication. *English Education: Journal of English Teaching and Research*, *5*(1), 74-91.

Reiland, I. (2024). 'Austin vs. Searle on locutionary and illocutionary acts'. *Inquiry*, 1-26.

Siregar, D. Y., Rizkiara, I., Hawa, P., Neifa, K., & Putri, L. (2024). Exploring Meaning: A Pragmatics Analysis in Everyday Communication. *Innovative: Journal Of Social Science Research*, *4*(6), 3524-3535.

Sterken, R. K., & Kirkpatrick, J. R. (2025). Conversational Alignment With Artificial Intelligence in Context. *Philosophical Perspectives*.

Usmani, S., & Almashham, A. (2024). Cross-cultural pragmatics: Analysing speech acts in different cultures. *International Journal of Language and Literary Studies*, *6*(1), 186-198.

Vairamani, A. D., & Nayyar, A. (2024). *Prompt engineering: empowering communication*. CRC Press.

Wittgenstein, L. (2009). *Philosophical investigations*. John Wiley & Sons.

Xu, J., & Fan, Y. (2022). Finding success with the implementation of task-based language teaching: The role of teacher agency. *Language, Culture and Curriculum*, *35*(1), 18-35.

Zoulaikha, E. (2022). The Tripartite Structure of Speech Act. *Praxis International Journal of Social Science and Literature*. https://doi.org/10.51879/pijssl/050308.

Part III: Legal and Ethical Reconstruction

Chapter 7

Toward Post-Cartesian Copyright

Abstract

Chapter seven examines the transformation of copyright doctrine as it shifts from a foundation in Cartesian mentalism to a model focused on transformative use, value creation, and social practice. Through critical engagement with recent case law and evolving policy debates, the analysis shows that contemporary issues raised by machine-generated works demand a framework that transcends assumptions of human exceptionalism. The chapter traces how standards based on authorial intention and private mental states are increasingly replaced by criteria rooted in demonstrable creative practice, observable outcomes, and societal benefit. Both theoretical arguments and real-world developments support a post-Cartesian approach to copyright, one that more accurately reflects the collaborative, distributed, and technologically mediated nature of modern creativity. This narrative demonstrates the philosophical integrity and practical necessity of evaluating authorship and originality by public criteria rather than inaccessible psychological facts. Therefore, the chapter provides guidance for legal professionals and policymakers as they confront the realities of intellectual property in an era defined by automation, hybrid authorship, and continual innovation.

7.1. The Pattern Across Cases: From Pure AI Rejection to Transformative Use

The recent history of copyright jurisprudence reveals a discernible shift from categorical rejection of machine-generated outputs toward a more nuanced, practice-centered evaluation grounded in transformative use. Initial court decisions and copyright office guidance largely adhered to a human authorship requirement, systematically denying protection to works produced wholly or predominantly by nonhuman systems (Bulat, 2024; Massadeh et al., 2024). This approach reflected both doctrinal conservatism and a philosophical commitment to mental-state-based standards of originality and creativity

(Zerov, 2023). However, as the legal and creative landscapes have evolved, courts and policymakers have been compelled to reassess these assumptions in light of collaborative, hybrid, and automated modes of production (Novaes & Ferraz, 2024). Landmark cases such as those involving the use of generative systems for music, visual art, and text now emphasize the importance of transformative input, curation, and human direction, even in contexts where machines contribute substantially to the final output (Fominova & Bugys, 2024; Pokrovskaya, 2025). The recognition of "transformative use," the idea that new works should add value, alter the original context, or serve a different function, provides courts with an actionable framework for distinguishing between protected and unprotected content (Çebi, Reisoğlu, & Goktas, 2023). This evolution aligns with broader trends in intellectual property law, where social utility and public benefit are increasingly recognized as legitimate grounds for protection and enforcement (Khan & Gotora, 2023). The pattern across recent cases demonstrates an ongoing movement away from rigid human exceptionalism toward practice- and outcome-based assessments.

Empirical analyses and policy reviews support the conclusion that the shift toward transformative use is both theoretically justified and pragmatically necessary. Research on the application of fair use doctrine to generative technologies highlights that value creation, social benefit, and substantial modification are critical factors in judicial reasoning (Massadeh et al., 2024; Wyczik & Wieczerzak, 2024). Scholars argue that the focus on "purpose and character" of use, whether a new work transforms the original with new expression, meaning, or message, has proven more robust than metaphysical appeals to authorial intention (Blodgett-Ford, 2025). This approach is particularly salient in cases involving machine learning, where outputs may bear surface resemblance to training data but are often distinguished by their adaptation, recombination, and integration into new contexts (Han, 2023). Legal reforms in various jurisdictions now reflect this pragmatic orientation, codifying transformative use and value creation as key elements in copyright adjudication (Bulat, 2024; Khan & Gotora, 2023). Notably, courts have begun to recognize human-AI collaboration as a legitimate form of creative authorship when clear evidence of curation, guidance, or meaningful intervention can be demonstrated (Bui, 2025; Fominova & Bugys, 2024). These standards have been reinforced by public commentary, industry practice, and academic consensus, marking a decisive turn toward more flexible, context-sensitive regimes.

Scholarly debates continue regarding the boundaries and limits of transformative use in the era of distributed creativity. Some critics caution that expanding the doctrine too broadly could undermine incentives for human creators and risk placing valuable intellectual property in the public domain (Zerov, 2023). Others contend that the focus on value addition and social utility enhances, rather than threatens, the core mission of copyright to encourage innovation and the dissemination of knowledge (Massadeh et al., 2024). Recent research suggests that transformative use doctrine, when anchored in practice-based standards and public benefit, is capable of balancing protection for originators with access for subsequent users (Wyczik & Wieczerzak, 2024). Comparative analyses of US, EU, and Asian case law show that systems oriented toward social impact, adaptation, and meaningful curation are more effective at fostering creativity and resolving disputes over ownership (Cheong, Caliskan, & Kohno, 2024; Novaes & Ferraz, 2024; Ruhtiani et al., 2025). The experience of hybrid works in art, literature, and entertainment demonstrates that collaborative, iterative, and multi-agent practices can be supported by doctrines that privilege transformative, outcome-oriented criteria over exclusive claims of originality (Pokrovskaya, 2025). These findings call for ongoing refinement and adaptive policymaking, as new technologies and collaborative practices continue to emerge.

Legal developments in 2024–2025 further illustrate the dynamic, case-by-case evolution of doctrine. Recent court decisions have differentiated between "pure" machine outputs, which lack meaningful human involvement and fall outside protection, and hybrid works where human agents have played active, transformative roles (Enarsson, Enqvist, & Naarttijärvi, 2022). Policy statements and agency guidance now emphasize transparency, disclosure, and documentation of creative intervention as best practices for securing copyright protection in collaborative projects (Pokrovskaya, 2025). The emerging norm is one of shared responsibility, where the allocation of rights and accountability reflects the actual practices and outcomes of creative production, rather than abstract theories of authorship (Novaes & Ferraz, 2024). In addition, legal discourse increasingly incorporates perspectives from philosophy of technology and social epistemology, affirming that value creation and social participation, rather than mental acts, are the foundation of modern copyright (Cheng & Liu, 2023; Li et al., 2025). As this case law accumulates, the direction of reform will become clear. Copyright doctrine must adapt to prioritize practices that are transparent, transformative, and publicly accountable.

As stated in prior chapters, the requirement here of transparency must be tempered by the willingness to stand behind one's work. Full disclosure of every element of a creative act, whether it be "purely human" or a human-AI hybrid, has never been possible and will not be possible in the future. The impulse to require disclosure and transparency will have to make room for a conception of transparency that includes something like a statement of responsibility. The transparent author will be the one who publicly claims something as their own and accepts the fiction of being the "origin point" for everything in the work rather than some impossible audit of every element in the work and how it came to be present in the work. This redefines transparency as a social performance of responsibility. It is procedural in that it follows the public rules for claiming authorship, but it wisely resists the metaphysical demand for an exhaustive disclosure of its own making.

The pattern across these recent cases signals a decisive break from a Cartesian, mind-centered conception of authorship toward an empirically grounded, practice-based model. By evaluating creative works through the lens of transformation, social utility, and value creation, courts and policymakers are laying the groundwork for a more flexible, pluralistic, and ethically responsive copyright system (Zakir et al., 2024). This shift not only accommodates the realities of collaborative, hybrid, and automated production but also invites ongoing dialogue among stakeholders, researchers, and creators. As intellectual property law continues to evolve, the post-Cartesian model will be vital for ensuring that legal protections remain fit for purpose in an era defined by rapid innovation, distributed agency, and continual experimentation. In this new landscape, the measure of authorship is found not in inaccessible mental states but in the observable achievements of practice and participation.

The ongoing evolution in doctrine reflects a broader philosophical and institutional recognition that authorship and creativity are collective, iterative achievements, inseparable from the broader ecology of technological and social innovation. As cases involving generative AI, collaborative platforms, and remix cultures proliferate, courts are increasingly called upon to assess not the metaphysical originality of a single creator, but the richness and impact of communal participation, adaptive use, and transparent process (Fominova & Bugys, 2024; Novaes & Ferraz, 2024). The acceptance of "transformative use" as a central standard fosters an environment where creators, curators, and consumers can all play active roles in shaping the meaning, value, and legal status of new works (Çebi, Reisoğlu, & Goktas, 2023; Pokrovskaya, 2025). This collaborative turn not only aligns with contemporary realities in digital art, literature, and entertainment, but also invites legal systems to embrace plurality, incremental improvement, and social benefit as guiding principles. The result is a copyright framework that can respond nimbly to emerging practices, enabling innovation while safeguarding both public and private interests. As a consequence, courts and policymakers are increasingly incentivizing practices that foreground curation, attribution, and ethical stewardship, laying the groundwork for systems that are both transparent and adaptable.

This shift toward practice- and outcome-based evaluation in copyright is emblematic of a wider trend in law, philosophy, and technology that recognizes agency, responsibility, and value as emergent from public, corrigible engagement rather than private, unobservable intention (Khan & Gotora, 2023; Cheng & Liu, 2023). The transformative use doctrine has proven not just an expedient solution to the rise of generative systems, but a powerful vehicle for integrating diverse forms of participation and acknowledging the complexity of modern creative processes. It reframes the conversation about ownership, fairness, and utility around the question of what works do in the world—how they are taken up, repurposed, and enriched through community interaction—rather than what their putative authors may have intended or imagined (Blodgett-Ford, 2025; Massadeh et al., 2024). This pragmatic, empirical orientation supports legal regimes that are more just, adaptive, and relevant to contemporary life, forging a copyright system in which the boundaries of authorship, agency, and value are continually negotiated through open, collective practice.

7.2. Why the 2025 Copyright Office Report Still Clings to Mental States

Despite the growing shift toward practice-based and transformative standards in recent legal decisions, the 2025 Copyright Office Report continues to anchor copyright doctrine in assumptions about human mental states and the centrality of intention. The persistence of a mental-state framework is rooted in longstanding traditions that equate originality and authorship with individual creativity and subjective control (Bulat, 2024; Massadeh et al., 2024). The report explicitly reaffirms the principle that copyright protection is available only for works reflecting the "original intellectual conception" of a human author, a doctrine that has shaped U.S. and international copyright for over a century (Pokrovskaya, 2025). Policy analysts suggest that this position is intended to uphold the incentive structure for creative labor and to avoid a slippery slope in which any output, however mechanically produced, could dilute the economic and moral value of authorship (Han, 2023). However, critics note that this approach increasingly fails to reflect the realities of collaborative, distributed, and technologically augmented creation, where value and originality often emerge through curation, editing, or participation rather than isolated invention (Novaes & Ferraz, 2024). The Office's insistence on a mental element, requiring that creative works be the "product of the mind," functions as both a bulwark against dehumanization and a barrier to more inclusive, outcome-based models (Zerov, 2023). Recent scholarship contends that such criteria risk privileging "romantic" authorship and excluding legitimate forms of hybrid and machine-assisted creation from protection (Çebi, Reisoğlu, & Goktas, 2023; Sindane, 2024). The resulting doctrine appears both protective of tradition and increasingly at odds with technological innovation.

A key argument advanced by the Copyright Office for maintaining mental-state criteria centers on legal certainty and administrative workability. By grounding copyrightability in the mental process of human creators, the Office avoids the difficult problem of determining how much curation, editing, or prompting suffices for protection in cases of machine-generated content (Fominova & Bugys, 2024; Mazzi, 2024). The report warns that abandoning the mental-state requirement would create ambiguity about who holds rights, how ownership is transferred, and how liability should be allocated, especially in collaborative, cross-border, or rapidly evolving creative contexts (Bulat, 2024; Pokrovskaya, 2025). This regulatory conservatism has the unintended consequence of freezing doctrine in a form that can neither adapt to new forms of agency nor recognize distributed creative processes as legitimate sources of value (Novaes & Ferraz, 2024). As Massadeh et al. (2024) and Wyczik & Wieczerzak (2024) note, this rigid approach also incentivizes misrepresentation and regulatory arbitrage, as creators may mask the role of technology or artificially inflate human input to satisfy doctrinal requirements. The upshot is a system that privileges mental states not for their intrinsic importance, but as a practical means of drawing boundaries (however arbitrary) around the scope of copyright protection. In the eyes of critics, this risks eroding the system's legitimacy as creative practices continue to diversify.

The Office's report also reflects an ongoing anxiety about moral rights, agency, and the social meaning of authorship. Legal scholars and policymakers remain concerned that recognizing machine or hybrid authorship could undermine notions of attribution, control, and reputation, which are grounded in personal investment and expressive autonomy (Zerov, 2023; Fominova & Bugys, 2024). These concerns are amplified in public discourse, where fears about "dehumanization" and the loss of human meaning in art and literature motivate calls for strong protections of human authorship (Torres et al., 2025). The 2025 report, for instance, repeats arguments about the "unique expressive power" of human creation and the risks posed by automation to cultural and economic value (Pokrovskaya, 2025). However, this perspective often neglects evidence that value and meaning can emerge from collective, iterative, and technologically mediated practices, and that attribution and control are increasingly managed by social and institutional norms rather than by individual intention alone (Bulat, 2024; Novaes & Ferraz, 2024). Critics warn that a narrow focus on personal mental states may inadvertently marginalize entire genres of legitimate creative work and impede innovation.

International comparisons highlight the idiosyncrasy of the U.S. Copyright Office's adherence to mental-state criteria. Several jurisdictions, including the EU and parts of Asia, are experimenting with more flexible, practice-oriented standards that allocate rights and responsibilities based on demonstrable participation, curation, and outcome rather than subjective intention (Han, 2023; Wyczik & Wieczerzak, 2024). Comparative law research reveals that frameworks grounded in social utility, transparency, and process are better able to accommodate distributed agency, collaborative authorship, and new forms of creative production (Massadeh et al., 2024; Fominova & Bugys, 2024). The 2025 report's continued reliance on intention and mental conception risks isolating U.S. doctrine and reducing its influence in global policy debates (Novaes & Ferraz, 2024). Meanwhile, courts and legislatures in other countries are crafting adaptive responses to the challenges posed by digital and automated systems, providing laboratories for doctrinal innovation that the U.S. may eventually need to emulate.

The continued focus on mental states is understandable in light of tradition, legal certainty, and anxieties about dehumanization, but it is increasingly untenable as a guide for twenty-first-century creativity. The practice-based and transformative trends in recent case law and international reform highlight the need for frameworks that reflect how value, originality, and meaning are now produced and recognized (Bulat, 2024; Massadeh et al., 2024). As technology continues to reshape the boundaries of authorship and agency, copyright's future will depend on its willingness to transcend outdated metaphysics and build systems grounded in observable practice, shared benefit, and public accountability. The ongoing tension between mental-state doctrine and practice-based reform is likely to define the evolution of intellectual property in the years to come.

What remains striking in the 2025 Report is its relative silence on the pragmatic successes of jurisdictions that have adopted more practice-based or transformative standards. Evidence from recent legal and empirical studies suggests that systems focusing on observable contributions, transparent attribution, and socially meaningful curation are not only more adaptive but also better at sustaining public trust and creative innovation (Massadeh et al., 2024; Wyczik & Wieczerzak, 2024). As technology blurs the line between human and machine authorship, rigid insistence on subjective mental criteria may simply push creative work "underground," encouraging creators to reframe or obfuscate their use of generative tools (Novaes & Ferraz, 2024). Furthermore, the global legal community increasingly acknowledges that the legitimacy and resilience of copyright doctrine depend on its capacity to track real practices and accommodate new forms of agency, not on preserving metaphysical distinctions for their own sake (Fominova & Bugys, 2024). In failing to recognize this, the Copyright Office risks perpetuating a regime that is both out of step with international trends and vulnerable to rapid obsolescence as collaborative, hybrid, and automated forms of creation become the new normal. This suggests that the real policy challenge is not the erosion of human creativity, but the construction of systems capable of evaluating and rewarding innovation in ways that are empirically grounded and socially responsive. Only by confronting this challenge directly can copyright law remain relevant and legitimate in the era of intelligent systems.

The reluctance to embrace practice-based and transformative criteria in U.S. copyright doctrine may have far-reaching economic and cultural consequences. As creative industries increasingly operate across borders and draw upon international networks of collaboration, a copyright system tethered to subjective intention risks impeding participation in global creative markets and undermining the competitiveness of U.S. creators (Massadeh et al., 2024; Wyczik & Wieczerzak, 2024). More agile and empirically grounded regimes abroad are already attracting new forms of authorship and investment, reinforcing the need for U.S. policy to evolve alongside the shifting realities of hybrid and distributed creation. If the U.S. persists in upholding metaphysical standards that are misaligned with contemporary creative practice, it may find itself not only isolated in global policy forums but also less able to protect or incentivize genuine innovation at home.

The next chapter in copyright law will be written by those courts, policymakers, and stakeholders who are willing to rethink the very foundations of authorship and originality. The evidence now points toward frameworks that recognize creative contribution wherever it is manifest, through the skilled orchestration of AI tools, collaborative curation, or novel forms of participatory creation provided such practices are publicly documented, transparent, and accountable. The opportunity is to build a system that both protects the dignity and rights of human creators and rewards the reality of twenty-first-century creative practice. The persistent adherence to inner-state metaphysics, while understandable as a reaction to uncertainty and disruption, cannot serve as an adequate guide for the complex, pluralistic, and technologically mediated landscape of modern authorship. Only by anchoring legal protections in shared practices, iterative standards, and demonstrable social benefit can copyright maintain its legitimacy and foster the conditions for cultural flourishing in the digital age.

7.3. The Bartz Standard: Value Creation over Creative Intention

Building on the doctrinal tensions and limitations of intention-based standards, the emergence of the Bartz standard signals a pivotal transformation in copyright law. Value creation, rather than creative intention, becomes the central criterion for protection and legitimacy in the age of automated and collaborative innovation. The *Bartz v. Anthropic* decision marks a pivotal doctrinal and philosophical shift by prioritizing value creation and transformative contribution over the subjective intentions of human creators. In this landmark case, the court recognized that the central question is not whether the “author” possessed original intent or inspiration, but whether the process and outcome added new value to the public domain in a manner akin to the way a human synthesizes and repurposes knowledge. By explicitly analogizing machine learning to human learning, the court embraced a model in which creative agency is defined by the generation of novel, socially useful outputs, regardless of the internal mechanisms or consciousness of the actor involved (Brittain, 2025). This practical orientation shifts the focus of copyright law from metaphysical debates about intention to demonstrable, accountable practices across the entire data and creative lifecycle (Kasap, 2018). The legal significance is profound: courts now distinguish between mere replication and transformative use, offering protection where new social value, interpretive context, or utility is demonstrably introduced. As such, the Bartz standard establishes that value creation, understood as public benefit and transformation, trumps the requirement of creative intention, providing a model that is both ethically justified and pragmatically robust (Fominova &

Bugys, 2024). This approach resonates with Wittgensteinian accounts of meaning as use, where creative legitimacy is conferred by communal recognition and functional success. The ruling offers a practice-centered template for adjudicating complex questions of authorship in the digital age.

By privileging value creation, the Bartz standard builds for the courts a transparent, evidence-based framework for evaluating collaborative, hybrid, and machine-assisted works. The requirement of demonstrable transformation encourages creators and developers to document their contributions, curation, and intervention throughout the creative process (Dimitrova, 2023). This demand for transparency aligns with broader legal trends toward outcome-oriented regulation, where protection is grounded in public verification and reproducible evidence of added value (Bulat, 2024). Crucially, this is a transparency of *practice and outcome*, not of inner intention or hidden process. The Bartz standard does not ask creators to bare their souls or their hard drives but to demonstrate through public evidence that their work participates meaningfully in the creative ecosystem. Importantly, the Bartz decision does not exclude human agency; it recasts the human role as that of a curator, guide, or orchestrator whose function is to ensure that technological systems generate outputs that meet socially recognized standards for novelty and utility (Fominova & Bugys, 2024). This pragmatic orientation enables the law to distinguish between extractive, untransformed uses (such as piracy or mere duplication) and genuinely creative acts that extend, reinterpret, or meaningfully recombine prior works. The upshot is a copyright regime that rewards participation in and stewardship of creative processes, rather than the inscrutable mysteries of internal intention. This shift not only benefits creators and consumers but also fosters innovation by encouraging adaptive, pluralistic, and participatory forms of authorship (Novaes & Ferraz, 2024).

The value-creation framework set by Bartz has implications far beyond copyright law, signaling a wider reorientation of legal and ethical norms toward observable practice, utility, and participation. In industries ranging from publishing and music to software and design, the standard incentivizes creators to focus on outcomes, user impact, and the co-creation of meaning with audiences and collaborators (Kasap, 2018). Courts and regulators are increasingly willing to recognize collaborative processes that demonstrate community benefit, innovation, and practical utility, even when the origin of the output is shared or ambiguous (Pokrovskaya, 2025). The growing body of interdisciplinary scholarship affirms that value-creation, rather than metaphysical authorship, is a better predictor of social and economic success in creative enterprises (Massadeh et al., 2024). Furthermore, this orientation addresses long-standing critiques of copyright's exclusionary tendencies, enabling a more inclusive and just recognition of distributed and networked creative labor (Çebi, Reisoğlu, & Goktas, 2023). The Bartz standard stands as a watershed moment in the evolution of intellectual property law, opening pathways for further doctrinal refinement and adaptive governance.

Critics have raised concerns that a value-centered standard might weaken the incentive structure for individual creativity or open the door to exploitative uses. However, empirical evidence and comparative case studies show that, when combined with safeguards for attribution, transparency, and fair allocation of benefits, the value-creation approach is capable of balancing competing interests (Novaes & Ferraz, 2024). Doctrines such as fair use, transformative use, and hybrid authorship provide necessary guardrails, ensuring that protection is not extended to all forms of machine output, but only to those where human participation yields new social benefit (Blodgett-Ford, 2025). The Bartz standard invites courts to scrutinize the provenance of data, the nature of creative intervention, and the measurable outcomes of collaboration—a model well suited to the complexities of the digital and algorithmic age (Pokrovskaya, 2025). In this respect, the emphasis on value creation not only advances the goals of justice and fairness but also enables the legal system to remain responsive to technological and social change. As doctrine and policy evolve, the lesson of Bartz is that accountability, participation, and public benefit must take precedence over romantic or metaphysical notions of authorship.

Therefore, the Bartz standard's elevation of value creation over creative intention marks a decisive and necessary adaptation of copyright doctrine to the realities of twenty-first-century innovation. By aligning legal protection with demonstrable transformation, community benefit, and collaborative practice, the law moves closer to a system that is both ethically defensible and practically effective. The implications extend to courts, creators, and policymakers, who are now empowered to support and reward new forms of authorship that emerge at the intersection of human ingenuity and technological capability. The philosophical coherence and practical flexibility of this standard offer a blueprint for the ongoing reform of intellectual property, as society navigates the challenges and opportunities of hybrid, distributed, and automated creative processes. The Bartz standard stands as both a culmination of recent doctrinal trends and a catalyst for future innovation in copyright law.

Looking ahead, the Bartz standard may well serve as a paradigm for reforming not only copyright, but also other areas of law and policy where agency, creativity, and responsibility are increasingly distributed and technologically mediated. Its emphasis on transparency, demonstrable contribution, and collective benefit has the potential to guide governance in domains such as patent law, collaborative scientific research, and even regulatory regimes for artificial intelligence (Kasap, 2018; Novaes & Ferraz, 2024). As the boundary between human and machine effort grows ever more porous, legal systems that reward transformation and social impact, rather than inaccessible states of mind, can more effectively accommodate the realities of hybrid and networked innovation. And as the boundary between human and machine effort disappears altogether, the ideas of transparency and disclosure will inevitably change as well. The idea that disclosure of AI use will allow one to document the human contribution and demonstrate the creation of value persists for a reason. But the deepest reason for its persistence may be that it allows the continuing auditing of the human in the loop. But if we cannot practically distinguish the human from the non-human, the most transparent act is not a microscopic mining into finer and finer layers of causation; the more transparent thing will be the claim of responsibility. Eventually, the obligation to separate the human from the AI will have to disappear.

Still, for the time being, the Bartz approach encourages the design of systems and institutions that value openness, participation, and accountability, helping to democratize access to creative and economic opportunity (Fominova & Bugys, 2024; Blodgett-Ford, 2025). By foregrounding value creation and public good, the standard supports a more just and resilient creative ecosystem—one in which rights and recognition follow from what is actually achieved and shared. In doing so, it aligns legal doctrine with the broader social and philosophical currents that champion collective flourishing over individual mystique.

7.4. Designing Copyright for a World Without Human Exceptionalism

The rapid rise of generative technologies and hybrid creative practices has made it clear that copyright systems grounded in human exceptionalism are increasingly inadequate for modern realities. Recent international rulings and legal scholarship converge on the argument that copyright law must transition toward a practice-based and outcome-oriented regime—one that evaluates value creation, demonstrable contribution, and social utility rather than the metaphysical intentions of a single author (Wyczik & Wieczerzak, 2024; Sun,

2021). The emergence of "sui generis" rights for works with significant human contribution, and the placement of fully autonomous outputs in the public domain, exemplifies the move toward flexible, pluralistic legal frameworks (Soltanibahrehmand, 2024). Research shows that administrative and judicial bodies are increasingly willing to recognize collective, distributed, and machine-assisted authorship when human curation or creative intervention can be publicly documented (Fominova & Bugys, 2024; Fritz, 2025). This practice-based shift does not erode protection for human creativity but aligns the law with contemporary, collaborative modes of creation. Furthermore, the integration of provenance, transparency, and data-lineage requirements into copyright registration supports greater accountability and public trust (Chirag, 2025). By tying protection to participation and transformation, policymakers ensure that legal incentives remain relevant and equitable across diverse creative domains. This transformation is echoed in leading jurisdictions worldwide, from China to the EU and the U.S. (Wyczik & Wieczerzak, 2024).

The rethinking of copyright in a post-human-exceptionalist world requires adaptive, tiered protection schemes to reflect the complexity and diversity of modern creativity. Sun (2022) proposes a two-tiered legal mechanism, awarding full protection to works with significant human creative input and sui generis rights to machine-generated works with minimal intervention, while placing fully autonomous outputs into the public domain. This model has been echoed in EU policy discussions, which recommend a flexible standard for originality that takes account of curation, prompt engineering, and collaborative oversight (Gils et al., 2024; Soltanibahrehmand, 2024). Courts now assess the sufficiency of "subjective judgment" and "adequate control" in determining whether a work merits protection, as seen in recent European and Chinese case law (Fritz, 2025; Fominova & Bugys, 2024). Such reforms not only reward meaningful stewardship but also ensure that economic and moral rights are allocated according to the real contributions of all agents involved. Comparative research demonstrates that outcome-oriented frameworks, when paired with expanded fair-use exceptions and licensing schemes, foster innovation while upholding the rights of the creator (Hoshiar & Kiran, 2024). Through embedding these reforms in copyright codes, lawmakers can accommodate the realities of networked, iterative, and machine-assisted creation without sacrificing clarity or enforceability (Wyczik & Wieczerzak, 2024).

Equity and social benefit are at the core of post-exceptionalist copyright design. Scholarship and policy proposals emphasize the importance of revenue-sharing mechanisms, open licensing, and community-benefit metrics to ensure that value created by distributed and data-driven processes is fairly allocated (Gervais, 2022; Soltanibahrehmand, 2024). Recent legal studies suggest that revenue derived from machine-generated works should flow back to both original data contributors and human curators through transparent, collective management organizations (Sun, 2021; Wyczik & Wieczerzak, 2024). At the same time, expanded attribution and anti-distortion clauses protect the moral and cultural rights of marginalized creators whose identity or style may be appropriated by technological systems (Valchuk, 2024). The focus on community benefit also supports open-access regimes, public domain placement, and the safeguarding of knowledge commons, balancing innovation incentives with the need for access, stewardship, and cultural preservation. Such balancing provisions reflect the pragmatic and ethical imperatives of the twenty-first century, anchoring legal protections in measurable contribution, shared utility, and public interest.

International harmonization is essential for effective and predictable copyright governance in a global, digital environment. Research shows that cross-border recognition of provenance credentials, data lineage, and transformation audits reduces forum-shopping and legal uncertainty (Wyczik & Wieczerzak, 2024; Soltanibahrehmand, 2024). Policymakers are advised to develop model treaties or protocols under the auspices of WIPO or similar bodies to enshrine the principles of transformation, transparency, and flexible tiered protection, while allowing for local adaptation (Sun, 2021). Pilot projects in the EU, South Africa, and China demonstrate the feasibility of practice-based and outcome-oriented standards, even in civil law systems that traditionally emphasize moral rights (Khan & Gotora, 2023). By institutionalizing best practices, embedding interdisciplinary panels for dispute resolution, and leveraging automated provenance tools, lawmakers can ensure both legal certainty and creative freedom in hybrid, collaborative, and automated creative processes (Fritz, 2025). Designing copyright for a world without human exceptionalism demands a principled and pragmatic departure from doctrines that privilege intention and private mental states. By rewarding demonstrable transformation, requiring transparency, supporting revenue-sharing, and embedding community benefit, the emerging architecture of copyright law honors both the diversity of creative agency and the complexity of contemporary cultural production. Scholars and policymakers now broadly agree that legal incentives must evolve to reflect the hybrid, networked, and participatory reality of modern authorship. This approach not only resolves doctrinal tensions identified in high-profile cases but also ensures that copyright remains fit for purpose as creative practices continue to diversify.

And as long as these efforts at full transparency and disclosure are understood as preliminary attempts to ease the transition into a world in which the human-AI boundary can no longer be literally spelled out, this system will work well enough.

As copyright doctrine evolves to meet these challenges, stewardship and accountability take on heightened significance, not just for individual creators but for institutions, platforms, and communities that curate, facilitate, or amplify creative work. Research points to the need for robust institutional mechanisms such as collective licensing, data lineage tracking, and third-party verification. These have the potential to ensure the integrity of provenance claims and the fair allocation of both revenue and recognition (Fritz, 2025; Chirag, 2025). By embedding these protocols within copyright infrastructure, legal systems can better guard against fraud, misattribution, and the manipulation of attribution in large-scale, distributed creative environments. Additionally, legal reforms that reward demonstrable stewardship such as active curation, quality control, and ethical management of datasets encourage the emergence of "creative custodians" whose value lies in orchestrating and sustaining the conditions for meaningful and equitable cultural production (Fominova & Bugys, 2024). These reforms further align copyright law with broader social movements for ethical AI, responsible data management, and public-interest technology, strengthening trust in creative ecosystems.

Looking forward, the capacity of copyright law to support a flourishing and just creative landscape will depend on its ability to continually adapt to new technological, economic, and cultural realities. Scholarship in law and innovation studies urges a dynamic, iterative approach: regular review of statutory language, stakeholder consultations, and flexible licensing regimes that can accommodate unforeseen advances in generative technologies and collaborative creativity (Wyczik & Wieczerzak, 2024; Hoshiar & Kiran, 2024). In this spirit, policymakers are encouraged to institutionalize sunset clauses, pilot programs, and experimental governance models that allow for real-time learning and correction as new forms of creative agency emerge (Soltanibahrehmand, 2024; Khan & Gotora, 2023). Such strategies not only foster resilience and relevance but also preserve the core promise of copyright: to incentivize the creation, sharing, and stewardship of knowledge and culture for the benefit of all. By viewing copyright as a living, adaptive social contract rather than a fixed set of privileges rooted in human exceptionalism, lawmakers and creators alike can ensure that creative rights remain responsive to the hybrid, collaborative, and participatory forms of authorship that define the twenty-first century.

This chapter has traced the intellectual and legal evolution of copyright from its roots in Cartesian mentalism to an emerging practice-based, value-oriented regime fit for the complexities of the digital and automated age. The central argument is that the fixation on human intention and originality as private, psychological facts has become increasingly untenable in a world characterized by collaborative creation, distributed agency, and the rise of machine-generated content. Leading research and case law now converge on a model where demonstrable transformation, value creation, and social benefit, not metaphysical authorship, serve as the benchmarks for protection. By foregrounding transparency, provenance, and collective stewardship, this practice-based orientation encourages both innovation and equity, offering more robust incentives for creators while ensuring that new knowledge and cultural forms remain accessible to society at large (Sun, 2022; Wyczik & Wieczerzak, 2024).

Looking forward, the challenge for policymakers, courts, and creators is to construct a copyright architecture that is flexible, transparent, and internationally harmonized. Adaptive tiered protection, open registries of provenance, and multidisciplinary review panels will be essential for navigating the complex realities of hybrid authorship and distributed value generation. And eventually what we call "hybrid authorship" will collapse back into mere authorship, with the transparent act of authorship being the claim of responsibility for output rather than a mechanical disclosure of every "non-human" element. Community benefit, fairness in revenue allocation, and the protection of marginalized voices must remain guiding priorities in the face of rapid technological change (Fominova & Bugys, 2024; Valchuk, 2024). The chapter concludes that letting go of human exceptionalism in copyright is not a concession to technology, but a principled step toward a more inclusive, participatory, and pragmatic regime in which meaning, agency, and ownership are defined not by hidden mental states but by open participation in the ever-evolving practice of creation.

References

Blodgett-Ford, S. J. (2025). Copyright, fair use, and AI technology development: time to sunset the "transformative purpose" test. In *Research Handbook on the Law of Artificial Intelligence* (pp. 673-714). Edward Elgar Publishing.

Brittain, B. (2025). Anthropic wins key US ruling on AI training in authors' copyright lawsuit. *Reuters.* June 24, 2025: https://www.reuters.com/legal/litigation/anthropic-wins-key-ruling-ai-authors-copyright-lawsuit-2025-06-24/.

Bui, L. V. (2025). Advancing patent law with generative AI: Human-in-the-loop systems for AI-assisted drafting, prior art search, and multimodal IP protection. *World Patent Information*, *80*, 102341.

Bulat, N. (2024). Protection of non-original objects generated by artificial intelligence: the Ukrainian copyright law approach. *International Journal of Law and Information Technology*, *32*, eaae010.

Çebi, E., Reisoğlu, P., & Goktas, E. (2023). The influence of artificial intelligence on copyright law. *Interdisciplinary Studies in Society, Law, and Politics*, *2*(2), 33-41.

Cheng, L., & Liu, X. (2023). From principles to practices: The intertextual interaction between AI ethical and legal discourses. *International Journal of Legal Discourse, 8*(1), 31-52.

Cheong, I., Caliskan, A., & Kohno, T. (2024). Safeguarding human values: rethinking US law for generative AI's societal impacts. *AI and Ethics*, 1-27.

Chirag, R. D. (2025). Reinforcing Responsible AI: Provenance and Lineage Verification.

Dimitrova, R. V. (2023, September). Are AI-Assisted Works Copyrightable?. In *2023 International Scientific Conference on Computer Science (COMSCI)* (pp. 1-4). IEEE.

Enarsson, T., Enqvist, L., & Naarttijärvi, M. (2022). Approaching the human in the loop–legal perspectives on hybrid human/algorithmic decision-making in three contexts. *Information & Communications Technology Law*, *31*(1), 123-153.

Fominova, K. E., & Bugys, R. (2024). A work of artificial generative intelligence as an object of copyright protection. *Vilnius University Open Series*, 79-97.

Fritz, J. (2025). Understanding authorship in Artificial Intelligence-assisted works. *Journal of Intellectual Property Law and Practice*, jpae119.

Gervais, D. J. (2021). AI derivatives: the application to the derivative work right to literary and artistic productions of AI machines. *Seton Hall L. Rev.*, *52*, 1111.

Gils, T., Heymans, F., Ooms, W., & De Bruyne, J. (2024). From Policy to Practice: Prototyping The EU AI Act's Transparency Requirements. *Available at SSRN 4714345*.

Han, T. (2023). On the Copyright of Content Generated by Artificial Intelligence. In *SHS Web of Conferences* (Vol. 178, p. 01019). EDP Sciences.

Hoshiar, S., & Kiran, S. (2024, October). Copyright in the Age of Artificial Intelligence: Unravelling the Complexities For the Protection of AI-Generated Work. In *2024 ITU Kaleidoscope: Innovation and Digital Transformation for a Sustainable World (ITU K)* (pp. 1-7). IEEE.

Kasap, A. (2018). Copyright and creative artificial intelligence (AI) systems: A twenty-first century approach to authorship of AI-generated works in the United States. *Wake Forest J. Bus. & Intell. Prop. L.*, *19*, 335.

Khan, R., & Gotora, N. (2023). One (innovation) flew over the law's head: the intersection of artificial intelligence and copyright. *South Afr. Intell. Property Law J*, *11*, 72-87.

Li, W., Song, R., Zhang, B., & Yu, K. (2025). AI Creativity and Legal Protection for AI-Generated Works in Posthuman Societal Scenarios. *Sustainable Futures*, 100749.

Massadeh, F., Alnusair, F., Mahdi Massadeh, A. A., & Ismail, M. (2024). The legal protection of artificial intelligence-generated work: The argument for sui generis over copyright. *Corporate Law & Governance Review*, *6*(1).

Mazzi, F. (2024). Authorship in artificial intelligence-generated works: Exploring originality in text prompts and artificial intelligence outputs through philosophical foundations of copyright and collage protection. *The Journal of World Intellectual Property*, *27*(3), 410-427.

Novaes, R. V., & Ferraz, F. F. (2024, September). Protection of Copyrights in the Era of Generative Artificial Intelligence. In *EPIA Conference on Artificial Intelligence* (pp. 332-343). Cham: Springer Nature Switzerland.

Pokrovskaya, A. (2025, February). The Legal Status of Artificial Intelligence: The Need to Form a Legal Personality and Regulate Copyright. In *Artificial Intelligence and Applications* (Vol. 3, No. 2, pp. 179-191).

Ruhtiani, M., Naili, Y. T., Hidayah, A. N., & Park, H. K. (2025). Generative AI and Copyright Law: A Rule of Law Comparison between Indonesia and South Korea. *Kosmik Hukum*, *25*(3), 428-449.

Sindane, N. (2024). Abezimu/Badimo (ancestors) and copyright law: from the Decolonial Turn to the pluriversal author.

Soltanibahrehmand, R. (2024). Copyright regulations for AI-generated works in the EU.

Sun, H. (2021). Redesigning copyright protection in the era of artificial intelligence. *Iowa L. Rev.*, *107*, 1213.

Torres, A. J., Alberto, J. M. C., Guieb, A. P. J., Paray, A. D., & Villarama, J. A. (2025). Language, identity, and ethics in AI-Driven art: Perspectives from Human Artists in Digital Environments. *Language, Technology, and Social Media*, *3*(1), 17-29.

Valchuk, D. (2024). Artificial intelligence copyright: Problems and solutions. *Modern scientific journal*. https://doi.org/10.36994/2786-9008-2024-3-1.

Wyczik, J., & Wieczerzak, R. (2024). Rethinking Copyright: The Art of Ownership in AI Outputs. *Eastern European Journal of Transnational Relations*, *8*(1), 39-52.

Zakir, M. H., Bashir, S., Nisar, K., Ibrahim, S., Khan, N., & Khan, S. H. (2024). Navigating the legal labyrinth: Establishing copyright frameworks for ai-generated content. *Remittances Review*, *9*(1), 2515-2532.

Zerov, K. (2023). Do generative artificial intelligence systems dream of electric sheep? The concept and conditions of protection of objects generated by generative artificial intelligence systems in Ukraine'. *Theory and Practice of Intellectual Property*. https://doi.org/10.33731/4-52023.289803.

Chapter 8

Criminal Justice After Free Will

Abstract

This chapter examines the profound impact of determinist findings in neuroscience on the foundations and future of criminal justice. By engaging with the arguments and policy proposals of Robert Sapolsky and related scholarship, the analysis traces how evidence undermining metaphysical free will has prompted the decline of retributive frameworks and encouraged the development of models focused on rehabilitation, competence, and social protection. Drawing explicit parallels with shifts in copyright doctrine, the discussion shows that both criminal law and intellectual property have begun to confront the conceptual limitations of blame and the inadequacy of desert-based justice. Practice-based theories of responsibility are developed as ethically coherent and practically effective alternatives to traditional punitive models, emphasizing participation, correction, and public safety over moral condemnation. The chapter explores ways in which neuroscientific research can inform non-retributive policies and support institutional reform, advocating for systems of justice that are empirically grounded, adaptable, and oriented toward human flourishing.

8.1. Sapolsky's Vision: Justice Without Desert

As neuroscientific evidence continues to undermine the foundations of metaphysical free will, the vision of Robert Sapolsky for a justice system without desert (Figure 8.1) offers an actionable framework for reimagining criminal law and punishment in light of scientific realities. The vision here of justice without desert arises from a determinist reading of neuroscience, in which behavior is understood as the product of complex, layered causes rather than uncaused will or inherent moral character. According to this view, a retributive punishment grounded in the notion that people "deserve" to suffer for wrongdoing cannot be justified if agency and culpability are themselves outcomes of biological, genetic, and social factors beyond conscious control (Callender, 2021; Sinha, 2024). Neuroscientific research, including studies on behavioral genetics and brain injuries, has demonstrated that criminality is often shaped by neurological deficits, trauma, and environmental disadvantage, challenging the legal tradition that links punishment to metaphysical free will (Petoft, Abbasi, & Zali, 2023). As Callender (2021) argues, the criminal justice system faces a "Copernican revolution" as scientific evidence makes traditional concepts of desert increasingly untenable. Instead of focusing on blame, Sapolsky and like-minded reformers advocate for systems that prioritize prevention, support, and rehabilitation, drawing on mental health models as guides for criminal intervention (Birks & Douglas, 2018; de Bie & Buchman, 2023). This approach reorients justice toward societal protection and the promotion of well-being, rather than inflicting suffering for its own sake. Recent legal scholarship and policy recommendations call for greater use of neuroscientific data in risk assessment, diversion, and treatment programs (Mamikunian, 2024). The paradigm shift advocated by Sapolsky is rooted in both scientific findings and the ethical imperative to reduce unnecessary harm.

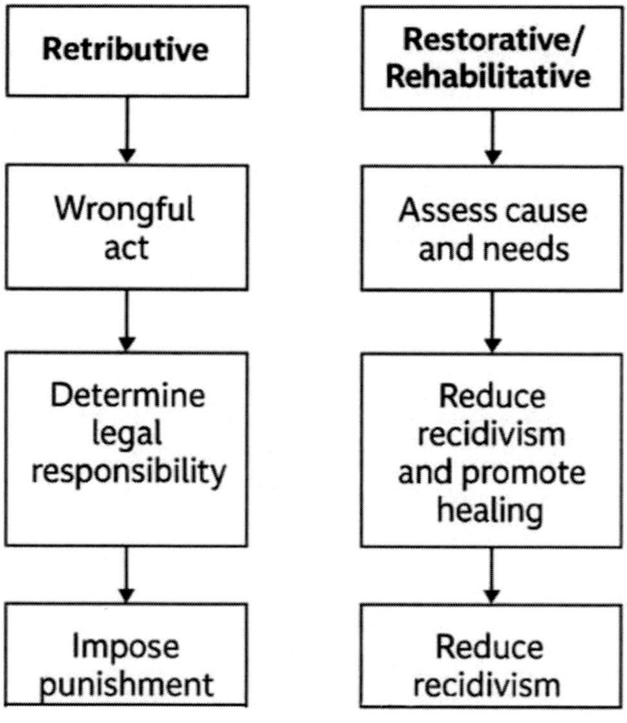

Figure 8.1. Sapolsky Flowchart.

Central to the rejection of desert is the argument that criminal responsibility and punishment must be grounded in empirically validated risk and rehabilitative potential rather than moral condemnation. Empirical studies reveal that most criminal impulses can be traced to identifiable neurological or environmental causes, including mental disorders, substance abuse, or adverse childhood experiences (Petoft, Abbasi, & Zali, 2023; Mamikunian, 2024). The growing use of brain-mapping and neuroimaging techniques in forensic evaluation further supports the claim that behavioral control is often impaired in ways invisible to traditional legal doctrine (Rajbhandari et al., 2024). This evidence aligns with Sapolsky's thesis that, given the causal origins of criminal behavior, justice must focus on treating, preventing, and managing risk rather than demanding suffering due to past actions. International legal developments, including the increasing use of neuro-correctives, community-based rehabilitation, and alternative sentencing, reflect this reorientation from retribution to restoration (de Bie & Buchman, 2023). At the same time, critics caution that deterministic models must avoid eroding personal dignity, autonomy, and legal safeguards (Ligthart, 2022). The more justice systems incorporate neuroscientific knowledge, the more they move away from the logic of desert and toward forward-looking, harm-reduction strategies.

Sapolsky also challenges common intuitions about blame, desert, and "the natural lottery." Recent behavioral studies have shown that public support for harsh punishment often relies on beliefs about free will and just deserts, even in cases where disadvantage, trauma, or genetic "bad luck" are salient (Berryessa, 2022). Experiments demonstrate that people continue to attribute responsibility and endorse severe penalties for those deemed "unlucky" in the genetic or social lottery, suggesting a stubborn resistance to integrating neuroscientific findings into popular moral judgment (Card, 2010; Verplaetse et al., 2009). This tension between empirical evidence and retributive intuitions complicates efforts to move toward a system that is truly blame-free or desert-free. However, Sapolsky's model, supported by critical psychology and neuroethics, proposes that even if some beliefs about free will persist as "necessary illusions" for moral life, policy and law should be grounded in the best available scientific evidence rather than folk intuitions (Sinha, 2024; Zawadzki, 2023). This pragmatic strategy emphasizes the role of public education, transparent communication, and incremental reform in shifting societal norms.

Ethical analysis and international legal scholarship increasingly favor preventive, rehabilitative, and restorative practices over punitive retribution.

New models of "neurointerventions" and brain-based rehabilitation in criminal justice are evaluated primarily on their capacity to reduce recidivism and promote social integration, not on the satisfaction of backward-looking moral claims (Birks & Douglas, 2018; de Bie & Buchman, 2023). Proposals for medical and behavioral interventions are guided by respect for autonomy, proportionality, and the rights of offenders, balancing the imperative to protect society with the need to avoid unjust coercion (Ligthart, 2022; Forsberg, 2021). Critics argue for strong human rights safeguards, emphasizing the importance of consent, bodily integrity, and ongoing oversight (Ligthart, 2022; Kirchmair, 2019). Likewise, the ethical foundation for justice without desert rests on the premise that legal and institutional responses should be measured by their forward-looking benefits, not by the desire to impose suffering for its own sake. This vision of justice without desert offers a scientifically informed and ethically compelling alternative to traditional criminal justice. By grounding policy in neuroscience and social science, and focusing on prevention, rehabilitation, and community protection, this model seeks to reduce harm and promote flourishing for both offenders and society (Callender, 2021; Mamikunian, 2024). While challenges remain in reconciling public intuitions and safeguarding rights, the determinist paradigm provides a roadmap for institutional reform that is responsive to scientific knowledge and committed to social resilience. In an era where scientific insights into agency and behavior are reshaping law and ethics, justice without desert stands as both a challenge and an invitation to reimagine the aims of criminal law for the twenty-first century.

The adoption of a justice system without desert also encourages a more interdisciplinary and holistic approach to public safety and well-being. As neuroscientific models illuminate the links between socioeconomic disadvantage, trauma, and neurodevelopmental outcomes, legal and policy interventions increasingly target upstream causes such as poverty, education gaps, and community violence rather than focusing solely on individual blameworthiness (Birks & Douglas, 2018; de Bie & Buchman, 2023). This shift fosters collaboration among neuroscientists, social workers, educators, and criminal justice professionals, who work together to design evidence-based interventions that mitigate risk and build social capital. Research in restorative justice and public health demonstrates that strategies emphasizing social support, skill-building, and the repair of relationships are more effective at reducing recidivism and promoting reintegration than punitive models grounded in desert (Petoft, Abbasi, & Zali, 2023; Mamikunian, 2024). These reforms not only reduce harm but also enhance social trust, public legitimacy, and the prospects for collective flourishing. By reframing justice as a matter of social investment and preventive care, Sapolsky works to align legal practice with contemporary science and ethical theory, promoting justice that is compassionate, effective, and sustainable.

Moreover, the broader societal adoption of justice without desert signals a fundamental transformation in how agency, responsibility, and personhood are conceived within the law. This new paradigm recognizes that agency is not an isolated or mysterious force, but the emergent product of biology, environment, and social context, a view that supports policies designed to expand opportunities, support autonomy, and reduce inequality (Callender, 2021; Sinha, 2024). The focus on support and prevention over retribution encourages legal and social institutions to prioritize the conditions that enable responsible agency, such as equitable access to mental health care, education, and meaningful work (Birks & Douglas, 2018; Ligthart, 2022). While resistance to abandoning desert may persist due to deep-seated cultural narratives, the determinist approach offers a compelling alternative: one in which law is measured by its capacity to heal, restore, and protect, rather than to punish. The challenge for reformers will be to balance respect for dignity and autonomy with the imperative to address the true causes of harm, ultimately creating a justice system that reflects both scientific understanding and humane values.

This paradigm shift toward justice without desert also prompts a reconsideration of the aims and legitimacy of punishment in a democratic society. Rather than measuring justice by the degree of suffering imposed, the new model prioritizes evidence-based interventions that protect society, restore victims, and empower offenders to reintegrate as responsible participants in communal life. Such a framework aligns with contemporary ethical standards that demand proportionality, dignity, and the minimization of harm as core legal values (Forsberg, 2021; Ligthart, 2022). As neuroscience, psychology, and social science converge on the need for systemic, preventive responses to crime, the legitimacy of retributive punishment weakens in favor of policies that foster public safety through rehabilitation, restorative practices, and social investment. Sapolsky theories call for a continuous, collaborative re-evaluation of criminal law's purposes, ensuring that legal responses remain responsive to scientific knowledge, social needs, and the evolving moral consensus of a pluralistic society.

8.2. Neuroscientific Evidence and the Erosion of Blame

As advances in neuroscience challenge traditional notions of free will, criminal responsibility, and moral agency, an accumulating body of evidence is prompting both scholars and legal practitioners to reconsider the ethical and practical role of blame in the justice system. Neuroscientific research over the past decade has provided increasingly detailed accounts of the biological, psychological, and environmental determinants of behavior, calling into question the presumption that individuals are autonomous agents fully deserving of blame (Petoft et al., 2023). Studies utilizing fMRI and EEG techniques have demonstrated that mental disorders, coercion, substance use, and even somnambulism can erode or override conscious control, thereby undermining traditional foundations for blame in criminal responsibility (Reddy, 2025). This growing recognition of "loss of free will" in both forensic and psychiatric contexts has led many legal systems to expand the scope of exoneration or mitigation for offenders with demonstrable neurological impairments (Dianti et al., 2024). As Johnson (2024) notes, the compatibility between neuroscientific determinism and philosophical theories of free will continues to spark debate, but the legal implications are already being felt: the more courts and clinicians rely on neuroscientific evidence, the less tenable retributive and blame-based frameworks appear. While some theorists defend the need for "basic desert" and the conditional appropriateness of blame (Menges, 2023), a practice-based approach increasingly urges that responsibility be anchored in prevention, proportionality, and rehabilitation.

Critical psychology and neuroethics scholars argue that free will, as traditionally conceived, may be best understood as a "necessary illusion" that supports moral and social order but fails to correspond to the actual causal complexity of human behavior (Sinha, 2024). The rise of neurolaw, a movement advocating for the reorientation of legal doctrine around neuroscientific facts rather than metaphysical beliefs, reflects a paradigm shift from moral retribution to humane treatment and empirical risk management (Opderbeck, 2021). Some caution that this transition risks losing a rich account of human meaning and relationality if it devolves into reductive materialism (Goldberg, 2011; Pardy & Patterson, 2013). Yet, from a policy perspective, the momentum is toward systems that focus on treatment, harm reduction, and forward-looking interventions. As Callender (2021) and Deeley (2022) argue, behavioral genetics and neuroimaging are increasingly used in forensic contexts to guide diversion, mental health referrals, and alternative sentencing, measures aimed at reducing recidivism and improving social integration. These developments signal a move away from blame as moral condemnation and toward responsibility as a pragmatic, socially grounded process. This process does not depend on making the "black box" of the brain transparent, but on making the procedures for intervention, rehabilitation, and reintegration transparent and accountable to the community.

Legal and ethical commentary further emphasize the importance of interdisciplinary collaboration in navigating the shifting terrain between neuroscience and the law (Johnson, 2024). The application of neuroscientific evidence in courts raises methodological, philosophical, and procedural questions about the reliability, interpretation, and ethical use of such data. Nevertheless, the integration of neuroscience into criminal justice is widely viewed as an opportunity to move beyond retribution and to develop evidence-based policies that reflect the causal realities of human behavior (Khilyuta, 2022). Proposals for public engagement, education, and ongoing research are seen as essential for ensuring that reforms are informed, transparent, and equitable. Comparative research across jurisdictions such as Indonesia, Norway, and Iran shows that expanded consideration of neurological factors in criminal responsibility can lead to more nuanced, humane, and just outcomes, especially for offenders with intellectual or mental disabilities (Dianti et al., 2024; Petoft et al., 2023).

Ethicists and philosophers continue to debate the implications of these developments for the concept of blame itself. Some, such as Coren (2024), distinguish between suffering as a consequence of wrongdoing and the appropriateness of blame as a social response, arguing that it may be possible to reject the former while retaining the latter in specific cases. Others suggest that technologies such as neurointerventions and predictive diagnostics complicate the very foundations of autonomy and moral agency, raising new questions about the scope and limits of responsibility (Adomaitis & Grinbaum, 2024). What remains clear is that as neuroscience reshapes our understanding of action, agency, and control, the legitimacy of blame must be reassessed in light of empirical findings and ethical reflection. The erosion of blame in the era of neuroscience reflects a broader transition toward justice systems that are preventive, rehabilitative, and proportionate. The growing reliance on neuroscientific data in legal and policy contexts marks a decisive shift away from moralistic, desert-based responses and toward models that prioritize social well-being, individualized intervention, and respect for human dignity (Johnson, 2024; Callender, 2021). The challenge for the coming decade will be to ensure that justice systems remain both scientifically informed and ethically sensitive, navigating the complex interplay between causal explanation, personal agency, and collective accountability.

The evolving landscape of neurolaw also necessitates new approaches to legal education and professional training, as practitioners must now integrate neuroscientific literacy into their ethical and evidentiary decision-making. Law schools, judicial institutes, and continuing education programs are increasingly incorporating neuroscience modules and case studies, equipping judges, attorneys, and policymakers with the tools needed to interpret neuroimaging evidence, assess expert testimony, and navigate the evolving standards of culpability and mitigation (Johnson, 2024; Opderbeck, 2021). This interdisciplinary fluency is vital for protecting against both the over- and under-valuation of neuroscientific data, a phenomenon sometimes termed "neuroexceptionalism," and for ensuring that legal decisions remain grounded in scientific rigor and due process (Pardy & Patterson, 2013). At the same time, public communication and transparency are essential: as research in psychology demonstrates, community attitudes toward blame, punishment, and reform can shift dramatically with exposure to neuroscientific explanations for behavior (Adomaitis & Grinbaum, 2024; Berryessa, 2022). By fostering open dialogue between scientists, legal professionals, and the broader public, justice systems can balance the demands of accountability, compassion, and legitimacy in a post-blame paradigm.

The erosion of blame demands more than reform; it requires a fundamental reconstruction of the relationship between the individual and the collective. A justice system that abandons metaphysical blame can no longer operate as a reactive mechanism for assigning punishment after harm has occurred. Instead, it must become a proactive, systemic framework focused on cultivating the conditions for responsible agency. This implies a significant expansion of social responsibility, where the focus shifts from the isolated 'criminal act' to the social, economic, and neurobiological determinants that shape behavior. A post-blame world, informed by a Sapolskyan and Wittgensteinian perspective, is one that takes seriously the creation of what might be called an "infrastructure of care," universal access to mental healthcare, trauma-informed education, and equitable economic opportunities. Justice, in this light, is not the act of retribution but the collective, ongoing project of building a society where the capacity for competent, pro-social participation can flourish. This transforms criminal justice from a tool of moral condemnation into an engine of public health and social reconstruction.

The "necessary illusion" of free will for the purposes of maintaining some sense of responsibility and justice can be compared to the "necessary illusion" of authorship as laid out in prior chapters. The requirements of transparency and disclosure have important roles to play, but they rest on the fiction that human action (and authorship) can be parsed and spelled out and assigned merit, praise, blame, payment, punishment, etc. The erosion of blame as a central pillar of justice may enable societies to address the root causes of criminality and social harm more effectively. As neuroscientific understanding of addiction, impulse control, trauma, and cognitive development deepens, policy reforms can target prevention and early intervention, redirecting resources from punitive incarceration toward mental health care, social support, and community-based alternatives (Callender, 2021; Petoft et al., 2023). Such a reorientation has the potential to reduce recidivism, break cycles of disadvantage, and promote collective well-being, in line with the best empirical evidence available. The challenge will be to ensure that these reforms preserve respect for autonomy, legal safeguards, and due process for all involved, especially as new technologies blur traditional boundaries between agency, control, and prediction (Coren, 2024; Goldberg, 2011). Ultimately, the integration of neuroscience into law and policy offers a path toward a justice system that is not only more humane and effective, but also more scientifically grounded and ethically responsible, reflecting the complex, determined nature of human agency in the twenty-first century.

8.3. From Retribution to Reconstruction: The Practice-Based Alternative

The global turn from retribution toward restorative and reconstructive models marks one of the most significant paradigm shifts in contemporary criminal law. Research in Indonesia and elsewhere demonstrates that restorative justice, with its emphasis on rehabilitation, reconciliation, and community engagement, increasingly replaces punitive frameworks that focus on blame and suffering (Djanggih, Syam, & Gunawan, 2023; Putri & Hasbaj, 2024). New guidelines and policies such as Indonesia's Supreme Court Regulation No. 1 of 2024 explicitly prioritize the restoration of victims and the rehabilitation of offenders, reflecting a growing consensus that the aims of justice are best served through social healing and reintegration, not punishment for punishment's sake (Putri & Hasbaj, 2024). International practice has also shown that public prosecutors now play a central role in steering cases toward restorative solutions, seeking peaceful settlements, and supporting recovery over simple retribution (Karyatin & Sinaga, 2024). These trends are supported by both legal analysis and empirical evidence: where restorative approaches are used, rates of recidivism decline and community satisfaction increases (Hastuti, Sriwidodo, & Basuki, 2024). Restorative justice programs often include mediation, victim-offender dialogue, and negotiated agreements that directly address harm, facilitate accountability, and empower all parties involved. This practice-based orientation aligns with neuroethical critiques of retributive punishment, which argue for interventions that respect dignity, autonomy, and human rights (de Bie & Buchman, 2023). The convergence of legal, ethical, and neuroscientific insights underscores the superiority of reconstruction over retribution in building just and resilient societies.

Reconstructive justice is further legitimized by evidence that blame and punishment, when untethered from prevention or restoration, can perpetuate cycles of harm and marginalization. Comparative analyses show that the most successful justice systems now emphasize rehabilitation, community reintegration, and diversion over lengthy incarceration or harsh penalties (Mudrecka, 2024). For example, recent changes to juvenile law in Poland and elsewhere lower the age of criminal responsibility for the most serious crimes but simultaneously introduce new measures for support, education, and resocialization, signaling a synthesis of care and accountability (Mudrecka, 2024). Islamic and civil legal traditions also increasingly accommodate restorative approaches, demonstrating their compatibility with diverse moral and religious frameworks (Permana, Marpaung, & Harahap, 2025). The expansion of restorative justice to address school violence and peer conflict further highlights its potential to foster prosocial skills and reduce harm at all levels of society (Peovska, 2023). In practice, family- and community-based models offer promising alternatives to court-centered processes, accommodating the interests of victims, offenders, and broader communities (Syarifuddin, Purba, & Putra, 2024). These developments challenge the assumption that only retribution can deter crime or promote justice. Instead, justice becomes a collective project of healing, prevention, and inclusive participation.

Practice-based justice also answers concerns about procedural fairness, proportionality, and the prevention of systemic bias. By inviting victims, offenders, and communities to participate in dialogue, negotiation, and reparation, restorative models allow for more flexible, context-sensitive solutions (Djanggih, Syam, & Gunawan, 2023; Hastuti, Sriwidodo, & Basuki, 2024). The use of alternative dispute resolution such as victim-offender mediation enables personalized responses that account for unique harms and social dynamics. Notably, new legal frameworks stress the importance of balancing the interests of all parties while safeguarding public safety, equality, and legal certainty (Putri & Hasbaj, 2024). Prosecutorial discretion is increasingly directed toward identifying cases appropriate for diversion and rehabilitation, moving away from "zero tolerance" or blanket punitive responses (Karyatin & Sinaga, 2024). These reforms are echoed in neuroethical and legal scholarship, which recommends integrating medical, psychological, and social resources into the criminal process to foster autonomy and accountability without coercion (de Bie & Buchman, 2023). By grounding justice in participation, correction, and support, rather than abstract principles of desert, practice-based alternatives offer a more adaptable and responsive system.

One of the enduring challenges for reconstructive justice is public and political resistance, often fueled by fears of leniency, recidivism, or moral hazard. However, recent commentary and research stress that community education, stakeholder involvement, and evidence-based evaluation can address these concerns and increase public trust (Hammond, Thatcher, & Fido, 2024; Peovska, 2023). Transparent procedures, ongoing monitoring, and clear criteria for eligibility ensure that restorative interventions remain accountable, effective, and legitimate. Scholars also highlight the importance of racial justice frameworks, intersectionality, and anti-discrimination policies to ensure that reconstructive approaches serve all communities equitably (Hunt & Shepherd, 2023). The success of reconstruction depends on its capacity to reconcile the needs of victims, offenders, and society, cultivating a culture of empathy, mutual responsibility, and social repair. At the same time, the movement from retribution to reconstruction marks a critical juncture for criminal justice in the neuroscientific age. Practice-based approaches centered on rehabilitation, restoration, and collective participation provide a compelling alternative to punitive, desert-driven models (de Bie & Buchman, 2023). These models are supported by legal innovation, empirical evidence, and ethical analysis, and have proven adaptable across legal cultures and institutional settings. As justice systems continue to evolve, the integration of restorative and reconstructive principles will be vital for building fairer, safer, and more compassionate societies.

The practice-based orientation of reconstructive justice is also transforming how legal systems conceptualize accountability and social order. Instead of presuming that deterrence is best achieved by instilling fear of punishment, research demonstrates that long-term reductions in crime and violence are more closely associated with social investment, restorative dialogue, and the rebuilding of trust within communities (Peovska, 2023; Hammond, Thatcher, & Fido, 2024). Programs that empower communities to participate in setting standards, facilitating reparative processes, and supporting reintegration provide not only more effective justice but also greater social cohesion and resilience (Syarifuddin, Purba, & Putra, 2024). By shifting the emphasis from punitive exclusion to constructive engagement, these models foster a sense of shared responsibility for the conditions that produce harm, as well as for the solutions that repair it. As legal scholars and neuroethicists argue, this systemic approach mirrors insights from neuroscience, which locate the roots of harmful behavior in social determinants and developmental trajectories, rather than in isolated acts of will (de Bie & Buchman, 2023; Hastuti, Sriwidodo, & Basuki, 2024). The result is a justice paradigm that is not only more humane but more sustainable, equipping institutions to address the underlying drivers of conflict and prevent cycles of retaliation.

At the philosophical and ethical level, the move toward reconstructive justice invites a broader rethinking of what it means to do justice in pluralistic, rapidly changing societies. This shift challenges the notion that justice is best served by exacting retribution on behalf of the state or community, proposing instead a model in which law becomes an instrument of social learning, reconciliation, and ongoing improvement (Hunt & Shepherd, 2023; Putri & Hasbaj, 2024). Through participatory practices, communities can articulate and refine their values, identify sources of harm, and collaboratively construct paths to repair. The procedural flexibility of restorative justice accommodates the unique circumstances and histories of participants, ensuring that solutions are tailored, proportionate, and forward-looking (Djanggih, Syam, & Gunawan, 2023). This approach is increasingly echoed in legal reforms, policy documents, and international guidelines, which stress the importance of dignity, agency, and inclusive dialogue. As reconstructive justice gains ground, it not only promises to reduce recidivism and social costs, but also to foster a more reflective, adaptive, and just society equipped to meet the ethical challenges of the neuroscientific and technological age.

8.4. What Courts Can Learn from Copyright's Evolution

As copyright law has evolved from rigid, author-centric doctrines to practice-based and restorative models, courts in criminal justice can draw powerful lessons on adaptability, procedural innovation, and the prioritization of community repair over mere retribution. Recent legal scholarship underscores the value of restorative justice approaches in both copyright and criminal law, where mediation, negotiation, and restitution increasingly supplement or replace traditional punitive processes (Putra, 2023; Nasution, Jubair, & Wahid, 2022). In the realm of copyright infringement, restorative justice efforts now focus on repairing harm to both moral and economic rights, highlighting the potential for analogous reforms in criminal law to center victim and community needs (Putra, 2023). Empirical studies show that mediation and restorative solutions in both domains can resolve disputes more efficiently, reduce recidivism, and improve satisfaction for all stakeholders involved (Dona et al., 2025). These developments align with comparative research from juvenile justice and corporate disputes, where restorative frameworks are credited with reducing repeat offenses and fostering a culture of accountability, dialogue, and social integration (Abubakar et al., 2024; Febrianna, 2024).

Legal reformers increasingly advocate for formalizing restorative justice not only in commercial and copyright cases but also in mainstream criminal adjudication, supporting the design of institutional mechanisms that address the needs of both victims and perpetrators (Wibisana et al., 2024; Halim & Ismoyo, 2023). This shift from punishment toward repair is also mirrored in the treatment of children and marginalized communities, where the best interests of the individual and the community now guide diversion, mediation, and restorative sentencing (Kadir, 2023; Nasution, Jubair, & Wahid, 2022). Courts are encouraged to develop clear guidelines for restitution and restorative outcomes, allowing judges and prosecutors discretion to facilitate fair resolutions while preventing abuse of authority (Mazjah, 2024). These safeguards echo regulatory reforms in the digital marketplace, where transparent rules for mediation and arbitration have improved enforcement and reduced case backlogs (Putra, 2023).

Both copyright and criminal courts are discovering that restorative models can be tailored to a wide range of offenses from traffic accidents and school violence to business crimes and digital piracy (Soekorini, 2022). Successful implementation requires institutional investment in training, procedural guidance, and monitoring to ensure fairness and consistency, as well as sensitivity to the needs and rights of victims (Febrianna, 2024). Experience from Indonesia and other jurisdictions reveals that public education and stakeholder engagement are essential for gaining acceptance of restorative approaches, especially where public skepticism or fear of leniency persists

(Maharian, 2024). When well-regulated, restorative practices reduce legal uncertainty, promote healing, and build trust in legal institutions.

The development of restorative justice in both copyright and criminal domains demonstrates that law can be both principled and adaptable, evolving with changes in technology, society, and ethical expectations. Research shows that restorative justice not only addresses immediate harm but also prevents escalation, repeat offenses, and community disconnection (Nasution, Jubair, & Wahid, 2022). For criminal courts, the lesson is to embed mediation, restitution, and community-based repair into the justice process, treating punitive sentencing as a last resort. Drawing inspiration from the adaptive responses of copyright to digital disruption, criminal justice systems can benefit from flexible, transparent frameworks that prioritize repair, inclusion, and social well-being (Putra, 2023). The evolution of copyright law toward practice-based and restorative models provides a practical and philosophical template for criminal courts seeking to move beyond blame and desert. By adopting mediation, structured restitution, and victim-centered procedures, courts can foster fairer, more resilient, and socially meaningful outcomes (Abubakar et al., 2024). The comparative evidence shows that as law adapts to new realities, restorative justice becomes a transformative approach for building systems that serve the needs of all members of society.

This convergence between copyright and criminal justice also highlights the necessity of ongoing legal education and interdisciplinary training for judges, mediators, and legal professionals. As courts increasingly draw on lessons from restorative models in intellectual property, there is a growing need to cultivate expertise in negotiation, trauma-informed practice, and collaborative problem-solving (Putra, 2023; Wibisana et al., 2024). Training programs that incorporate insights from psychology, social work, and community organizing can empower legal actors to facilitate dialogue, recognize diverse harms, and support the healing of all affected parties. Research underscores that procedural transparency strengthens public trust and ensures that both copyright and criminal remedies are perceived as fair and legitimate (Febrianna, 2024; Mazjah, 2024). These interdisciplinary strategies also enable legal systems to be agile, adapting their procedures to accommodate technological disruption, cross-border disputes, and the evolving needs of diverse communities. The idea of procedural transparency could be a useful analogue for copyright and transparency as well, prompting attention to established processes for claiming and establishing authorship rather than spelling out every detail of the chain of human action and responsibility. Just as criminal justice can move beyond the need to render a defendant's mind perfectly transparent, so too can copyright move beyond the demand for a transparent audit of the author's creative process. In both domains, justice is served by transparent procedures and public acts of accountability.

Additionally, the mutual reinforcement of practice-based and restorative approaches offers a vision of law as a living, participatory institution, rather than a static arbiter of blame or exclusion. Comparative studies demonstrate that jurisdictions which institutionalize restorative options enjoy lower rates of recidivism, greater stakeholder satisfaction, and stronger social cohesion (Abubakar et al., 2024; Dona et al., 2025). By embedding feedback mechanisms, ongoing evaluation, and opportunities for participatory reform, courts can ensure that restorative justice remains flexible, accountable, and responsive to new challenges. This transformative perspective ultimately affirms the core lesson from copyright's evolution: that law's legitimacy and efficacy are maximized when it prioritizes engagement, inclusion, and the restoration of social trust over retributive or exclusionary outcomes. In so doing, both copyright and criminal justice systems can better fulfill their roles as engines of creativity, social repair, and collective flourishing.

This chapter has traced the disruptive impact of neuroscientific determinism and the corresponding erosion of blame-based justice on contemporary criminal law. Through an engagement with Sapolskyan determinist arguments and a critical examination of neuroscientific and legal research, the discussion has illuminated the conceptual and ethical limitations of retributive models built on desert. Across sections, the text has shown that the more scientific evidence displaces the myth of autonomous will, the greater the impetus for justice systems to pivot toward prevention, rehabilitation, and the construction of social well-being. The comparative analysis presented with developments in copyright law demonstrates that a transition from mental-state criteria to practice-based, outcome-oriented frameworks is both feasible and normatively desirable. Legal reform is increasingly guided by interdisciplinary research and evidence-based practice, moving away from punitive responses and toward solutions that reflect the realities of causation, context, and capacity.

The broader consideration emerging from this inquiry is that just systems must be designed to promote flourishing, repair, and accountability within communities, not to satisfy outdated metaphysical intuitions about blame or desert. The embrace of restorative and reconstructive models, informed by neuroscience and comparative legal practice, opens new possibilities for justice that are transparent, flexible, and fundamentally humane. Courts, policymakers, and practitioners are called to build institutions that prioritize engagement, rehabilitation, and public safety over moral condemnation. The chapter concludes that, as scientific understanding of agency evolves, so too must the structures of justice: the future lies in frameworks that are empirically informed, ethically responsive, and oriented toward the inclusive, collective work of social reconstruction.

References

Abubakar, L., Afriana, A., Rajamanickam, R., & Fakhirah, E. L. (2024). Restorative Justice in Corporate Dispute Resolution as Business Actor in Indonesia. *Journal of Indonesian Legal Studies*, *9*(1), 187-216.

Adomaitis, L., & Grinbaum, A. (2024). Neurotechnologies, ethics, and the limits of free will. *Integrative Psychological and Behavioral Science*, *58*(3), 894-907.

Berryessa, C. M. (2022). Losing the lottery of life: Examining intuitions of desert toward the socially and genetically "unlucky" in criminal punishment contexts. *Behavioral Sciences & the Law*, *40*(3), 403-432.

Birks, D., & Douglas, T. (Eds.). (2018). *Treatment for crime: Philosophical essays on neurointerventions in criminal justice*. Oxford University Press.

Callender, J. S. (2021). Neuroscience and Criminal Justice: Time for a" Copernican Revolution?." *Wm. & Mary L. Rev.*, *63*, 1119.

Card, C. (2010). *The unnatural lottery: Character and moral luck*. Temple University Press.

Coren, D. (2024). Blame-Free Desert: Śāntideva's Actual-Sequence View. *Res Philosophica*, *101*(4), 835-841.

de Bie, A. L., & Buchman, D. Z. (2023). Why neuroethical analyses of invasiveness in psychiatry should engage with mental health service user movement knowledges and considerations of social in/justice. *AJOB neuroscience*, *14*(1), 25-28.

Deeley, Q. (2022). 6 Free will and criminal responsibility. *Journal of Neurology, Neurosurgery & Psychiatry*, *93*(12), e3.

Dianti, P. O. V., Andini, M. A. P., Windari, R., & Da Silva, E. B. (2024). Comparison of Indonesian and Norwegian Laws regarding Criminal Responsibility of perpetrators with Intellectual/Mental Disabilities. *Jurnal Suara Hukum*, *6*(1), 68-90.

Djanggih, H., Syam, E. S., & Gunawan, S. (2023). The Prosecutor's Legal Policy In Enacting Restorative Justice On Criminal Case. *Russian Law Journal*, *11*(3), 1349-1357.

Dona, F., Ariyani, E., Junaidi, J., Zahriani, L., & Fattaah, A. (2025). Implementing Restorative Justice in Criminal Case Resolution: A Socio-Legal Research. *Al-Ahkam: Jurnal Ilmu Syari'ah Dan Hukum*, *10*(1), 20–38. https://doi.org/10.22515/alahkam.v10i1.10263.

Febrianna, C. A. D. (2024). Pemenuhan Asas Keadilan Dalam Penyelesaian Kasus Tindak Pidana Kecelakaan Lalu Lintas Melalui Keadilan Restoratif di Kejaksaan Negeri Sragen (Studi Kasus Perkara Nomor: PDM-12/SRGN/EKU. 2/03.2023).

Forsberg, L. (2021). Anti-libidinal interventions and human rights. *Human Rights Law Review*, *21*(2), 384-408.

Goldberg, D. S. (2011). Against reductionism in law & neuroscience. *Hous. J. Health L. & Pol'y*, *11*, 321.

Halim, A., & Ismoyo, S. (2023). Analysis of restorative justice in the criminal justice system. *Enigma in Law*, *1*(1), 12-16.

Hammond, C., Thatcher, A. S., & Fido, D. (2024). The "depraved killers" penalty: a commentary on the 2023 UK sentencing changes to individuals charged with sexually motivated or sadistic murders. *Safer Communities*, *23*(4), 430-443.

Hastuti, A., Sriwidodo, J., & Basuki, B. (2024). Penerapan Peraturan Kejaksaan Nomor 18 Tahun 2021 Terkait Rehabilitasi Narkotika Berdasarkan Keadilan Restoratif. *SINERGI: Jurnal Riset Ilmiah*, *1*(3), 124-132.

Hunt, J. S., & Shepherd, S. M. (2023). Racial justice in psycholegal research and forensic psychology practice: Current advances and a framework for future progress. *Law and Human Behavior*, *47*(1), 1.

Johnson, E., (2024). The Philosophical Implications of Neuroscience Research on Free Will and Moral Responsibility. *International Journal of Philosophy*, *3*(2), 14–26. https://doi.org/10.47941/ijp.1871.

Kadir, A. (2023). Konsepsi Perlindungan Hukum Terhadap Anak Yang Menjadi Pelaku Dan Korban Kekerasan Seksual Dalam Sistem Peradilan Pidana Anak. *Jatijajar Law Review, 2*(1).

Karyatin, A., & Sinaga, O. (2024). Analysis of the Implementation of Restorative Justice by the Prosecutor's Office of the Republic of Indonesia in the Framework of the Direction of Criminal Law Political Reform in Indonesia. *Journal of Law, Social Science and Humanities*, *2*(1), 153-171.

Khilyuta, V. V. (2022). Neurobiology and Free Will in Criminal Law. *Actual Problems of Russian Law*, *17*(5), 134-148.

Kirchmair, L. (2019). How (not) to argue for the Relation between Natural Sciences and Law. *ARSP: Archiv für Rechts-und Sozialphilosophie/Archives for Philosophy of Law and Social Philosophy*, *105*(4), 523-535.

Ligthart, S. (2022). *Coercive brain-reading in criminal justice: An analysis of European human rights law*. Cambridge University Press.

Maharian, S. G. (2024). Restorative Justice in the Reform of the Indonesian Criminal System (Case Study of Violence Against Children in the Selebar Police Sector Area, Bengkulu City). *Journal of Law, Politic and Humanities*, *4*(5), 1865-1871.

Mamikunian, I. (2024). Neuroanatomy in the Justice System. *Journal of Student Research*, *13*(2). https://doi.org/10.47611/jsr.v13i2.2519.

Mazjah, R. M. I. (2024). Mitigating the Risk of Prosecutiontermination Based on Restorative Justice from Transactional Aspects. *Journal of World Science*, *3*(6), 675-683.

Menges, L. (2023). Responsibility, free will, and the concept of basic desert. *Philosophical Studies*, *180*(2), 615-636.

Mudrecka, I. (2024). Ustawa o wspieraniu i resocjalizacji nieletnich z perspektywy współczesnych trendów w postępowaniu z nieletnimi. *Lubelski Rocznik Pedagogiczny*, *43*(1), 177-191.

Nasution, N. P. A., Jubair, J., & Wahid, A. (2022). The Restorative Justice: Ideality, Reality, and Problems in The Indonesia Criminal Justice System. *Rechtsidee*, *10*(2), 10-21070.

Opderbeck, D. W. (2021). *The End of the Law?: Law, Theology, and Neuroscience*. Wipf and Stock Publishers.

Pardo, M. S., & Patterson, D. (2013). *Minds, brains, and law: The conceptual foundations of law and neuroscience*. Oxford University Press.

Peovska, N. (2023). The role of restorative practices in reducing school violence.

Permana, Y., Marpaung, W., & Harahap, A. M. (2025). The Role of Restorative Justice in Juvenile Criminal Law Islamic Law Analysis. *JURNAL AKTA*, *12*(1), 85-94.

Petoft, A., Abbasi, M., & Zali, A. (2023). Loss of free will in the Iranian criminal justice system: Interdisciplinary analysis of law and neuroscience. *Social Neuroscience*, *18*(5), 292-296.

Putra, M. R. A. (2023). Criminal Law Enforcement of Book Copyright Infringement in Digital Market Places in The Ecosystem E-Commerce Through Restorative Justice. *Ius Poenale*, *4*(2), 139-154.

Putri, N. N., & Hasbaj, M. E. (2024). Legal Policy On The Implementation Of Restorative Justice Principle In The Criminal Justice System Pursuant To Supreme Court Regulation Number 1 Of 2024. *Jurnal Rechten: Riset Hukum dan Hak Asasi Manusia*, *6*(1), 1-17.

Rajbhandari, B., Regmi, S., Dahal, K., & Shrestha, S. (2024). The Intersection of Neuroscience and Criminology: Role of Brain Mapping in Addressing Criminal Behavior by Nepal Police. *JNMA: Journal of the Nepal Medical Association*, *62*(278), 709.

Reddy, K. J. (2025). *Foundations of Criminal Forensic Neuropsychology: Bridging Mind, Law, and Criminal Justice*. Springer Nature.

Soekorini, N. (2022). Restorative Justice in the Application of Criminal Law. *KnE Social Sciences*, 607-615.

Sinha, C. (2024). Critical psychology and the brain: Rethinking Free will in the legal context. *Integrative Psychological and Behavioral Science*, *58*(4), 1751-1768.

Syarifuddin, S., Purba, I. G., & Putra, P. S. (2024). Implementation of Restorative Justice in Settlement of Criminal Actions in the Criminal System in Indonesia. *Jurnal Akta*, *11*(1), 106-118.

Verplaetse, J., DeSchrijver, J., Vanneste, S., & Braeckman, J. (2009). *The moral brain*. Heidelberg: Springer Verlag.

Wibisana, A. A. N. A., Wisnumurti, A. A. G. O., Budiartha, I. N. P., & Dewi, A. A. S. L. (2024). Legal reform on the concept of restorative justice in the criminal justice system. *Jurnal Pembaharuan Hukum*, *11*(2), 264-281.

Zawadzki, P. (2023). Is punishment backward? On neurointerventions and forward-looking moral responsibility. *Bioethics*, *37*(2), 183-191.

Chapter 9

AI Liability and Systemic Responsibility

Abstract

This chapter addresses the challenges of accountability and liability in environments shaped by autonomous and semi-autonomous systems. It contends that traditional legal and ethical frameworks are insufficient to address the diffusion of responsibility inherent in complex, technologically mediated networks. The analysis argues for the necessity of systemic models of accountability that prioritize institutional design, human oversight, and procedural transparency, rather than ascribing moral agency to technological systems themselves. By distinguishing between transformative and extractive uses of automated technologies, the chapter develops nuanced criteria for assessing liability, ethical risk, and organizational governance. Through a close examination of contemporary case studies, recent court rulings, and evolving regulatory proposals, the discussion highlights the limitations of attributing outcomes exclusively to machines or individuals. The chapter advocates for forward-looking frameworks that are adaptive to uncertainty, distributed causation, and collective agency, equipping policymakers, engineers, and legal scholars with actionable strategies for managing moral and legal responsibility in a determined technological landscape.

9.1. The Impossibility of Machine Moral Agency

Despite significant advances in machine learning and autonomous systems, recent scholarship overwhelmingly concludes that genuine moral agency remains unattainable for machines, demanding a fundamental rethinking of accountability and liability in an era of distributed, technological action. A growing consensus among philosophers and legal scholars holds that machines, however advanced, lack the necessary conditions for moral agency: intentionality, consciousness, and the capacity for ethical reasoning (Saraiva, 2024). Artificial systems can simulate choice, adapt to context, and even "learn" from feedback, but these processes are preconscious, algorithmic, and ultimately a-rational, missing the self-reflective and motivational dimensions central to moral subjecthood (Mukta, 2025). As a result, it is impossible to ascribe blame, guilt, or praiseworthiness to machines in any robust sense, even when their actions produce profound societal consequences (Walker-Munro & Assaad, 2023). This view is reinforced by case studies in autonomous vehicles, healthcare algorithms, and lethal autonomous weapon systems, which show that public intuitions, courts, and regulators consistently resist attributing moral fault to non-human agents (Sung, 2023). Instead, responsibility is distributed among designers, operators, manufacturers, and institutional actors, making collective and procedural accountability rather than individual machine agency the foundation of ethical oversight (Mukta, 2025; Kellmeyer, Mueller, & Burgard, 2022).

Legal reforms and policy proposals increasingly reflect this reality. The recently adopted EU AI Liability Directive, for example, imposes strict liability on developers and users of highly autonomous systems, not because the system itself can be at fault, but to ensure redress for harms that are difficult to trace to a single human actor (McDonald, 2023). This shift toward systemic and fault-based liability is designed to bridge what scholars call the "responsibility gap," where causal efficacy is distributed across humans, machines, and organizational processes, yet no single agent possesses the epistemic or volitional conditions required for traditional liability. Critics warn that this approach risks both over- and under-attribution of blame, unjustly punishing developers for unforeseeable outcomes or leaving victims uncompensated when harm falls outside conventional categories (McDonald, 2023; Kellmeyer, Mueller, & Burgard, 2022). Some propose a limited form of legal personhood for certain systems akin to that granted to corporations and focused on procedural and compensatory, rather than moral, accountability (Lai, 2021). Yet the dominant view remains that legal and ethical frameworks must remain human-centric, with oversight, transparency, and explainability as prerequisites for any system deployed in morally significant domains (Sung, 2023).

Ethical analysis echoes these legal and philosophical trends. Hwang (2024) reviews the limitations of deontological, utilitarian, and virtue-ethical frameworks when applied to machines, arguing that these theories presuppose forms of subjectivity and reflective endorsement that artificial systems cannot attain. Alternative approaches such as relational ethics and distributed responsibility emphasize the shared obligations of all stakeholders involved in the design, deployment, and use of autonomous systems (Floridi, 2016; Strasser, 2022). The World Health Organization's (WHO) 2021 guidance on ethics and governance of autonomous systems in healthcare further recommends clear rules for human decision-making, ownership of responsibility, and robust regulatory oversight (Wei et al., 2022). Transparency, explainability, and the maintenance of human dignity are repeatedly highlighted as necessary for trust and legitimacy, with the ultimate goal of keeping moral and legal subjecthood squarely in the human domain (Saraiva, 2024).

Debates persist around edge cases and the future trajectory of autonomous systems. Some researchers speculate that as machine autonomy and complexity increase, new frameworks for "dependent legal personhood" may become necessary that will enable AI systems to be sued, held liable, or subject to regulatory action even as ultimate moral agency remains with human overseers (McDonald, 2023; Mukta, 2025). However, the philosophical case for this remains contentious, as most argue that personhood implies forms of agency, intention, and social recognition that artificial systems fundamentally lack (Kellmeyer, Mueller, & Burgard, 2022). Recent interdisciplinary research advocates for a patient-oriented morality and a "distributed responsibility" model, in which responsibility is assigned according to the real distribution of risk, benefit, and control across sociotechnical networks (Floridi, 2016). As system complexity grows, the risk of "responsibility gaps" likewise increases, reinforcing the need for robust, transparent procedures and ongoing interdisciplinary review.

The impossibility of machine moral agency then is not simply a technical limitation but a normative boundary that shapes the design of legal, regulatory, and ethical systems. Consensus research across law, ethics, and technology emphasizes that explainability, human-centric oversight, procedural accountability, and collective governance are the keys to managing risk and ensuring justice in environments shaped by autonomous systems. Rather than attributing agency to machines, the challenge is to develop institutional architectures such as strict liability, regulatory audits, and interdisciplinary review boards that allocate responsibility according to real-world influence and capacity for control. Only by centering human judgment, participation, and oversight can societies ensure that the rise of autonomous systems remains compatible with foundational values of justice and accountability.

The growing sophistication of AI systems and their pervasive integration into daily life underscore the urgency of rethinking how responsibility and accountability are distributed. Scholars point out that as machine actions become more complex and impactful, ranging from life-and-death decisions in healthcare to allocation of financial credit or legal entitlements, the challenge is not to anthropomorphize machines but to craft layered systems of oversight that are responsive to real patterns of risk and influence (Kellmeyer, Mueller, & Burgard, 2022; McDonald, 2023). This often entails establishing traceability protocols, mandatory documentation of design choices, and continuous monitoring for harm, so that responsibility remains anchored in human and institutional domains (Saraiva, 2024; Floridi, 2016). Emerging regulatory frameworks such as the EU AI Act and sector-specific guidelines from the WHO and national authorities are converging on best practices that include stakeholder engagement, redress mechanisms, and public transparency as central pillars for safe and just AI deployment (Wei et al., 2022). These policy innovations further reinforce the understanding that no amount of computational complexity can substitute for the uniquely human capacities for ethical reasoning, empathy, and reflective judgment, capacities that are essential for moral agency and social legitimacy.

The impossibility of machine moral agency reinforces the primacy of practice-based and participatory approaches to ethics and law. Instead of searching for agency within the "mind" of the machine, reformers are encouraged to design institutions that support responsible human participation, foster ethical cultures within organizations, and incentivize collective learning and vigilance (Mukta, 2025; Strasser, 2022). By foregrounding context, human oversight, and shared accountability, this model offers a robust and adaptable strategy for managing the ethical risks posed by autonomous systems while sustaining trust and legitimacy. The broader lesson is that technology must remain embedded within human-centered systems of care, justice, and governance in which agency and responsibility are distributed according to practical capacity, access to knowledge, and power to intervene. As societies adapt to increasingly complex sociotechnical networks, it will be this commitment to procedural rigor, transparency, and shared stewardship that ensures the responsible integration of intelligent systems, rather than the pursuit of unattainable machine morality.

9.2. Human Accountability in a Determined World

While the impossibility of machine moral agency directs responsibility back to human and institutional actors, the challenge remains to clarify how accountability can be meaningfully assigned in a determined, technologically complex world. Recent research highlights that in environments shaped by algorithmic decision-making and automation, the foundations of accountability must rest on human oversight, transparency, and collective governance, rather than the illusion of absolute individual control (Mukta, 2025; Walker-Munro & Assaad, 2022). The "responsibility gap" created by distributed causation and emergent system behavior makes it impossible to locate blame in a single actor, especially as human involvement is often indirect, mediated through teams, code, and institutional processes (Santoni de Sio & Mecacci, 2021). In response, legal scholars advocate for the design of procedural mechanisms such as audit trails, mandatory reporting, and regulatory oversight to ensure that those with meaningful influence over design, deployment, and monitoring are accountable for downstream outcomes (Saraiva, 2024). This systemic approach also requires organizations to embed ethical review and ongoing risk assessment into the lifecycle of technological projects, assigning explicit roles for intervention, correction, and mitigation (Tariq, Ashraf, & Rashid, 2025). By distributing responsibility across developers, operators, and overseers, these frameworks align accountability with real-world influence and capacity to prevent harm. The result is a "networked" model of liability, where institutions are held responsible for establishing, maintaining, and updating robust systems of oversight, rather than merely identifying a single culpable individual (Mukta, 2025). This model is not without challenges, including bureaucratic inertia and the risk of diluted accountability, but it offers a more just and realistic alternative to outdated metaphysical frameworks.

One could imagine a version of this approach eventually becoming the approach to publication and copyright. As it becomes impossible to found authorship on internal mental states and increasingly impossible to distinguish the AI contribution to authorship from the human one, a book or any creative work will be understood as a system with contributors asserting responsibility for different layers or parts of the process. The responsibility for a song "going wrong" or causing damage is different from a company's product causing harm, but the authorship system and the product development system may have productive conceptual overlap.

The shift to collective and institutional accountability is reinforced by recent policy developments in sectors such as healthcare, finance, and transportation. For example, the WHO's guidelines on AI governance in medicine recommend that responsibility be allocated to clinical teams and institutional leaders who approve, implement, and monitor digital systems not to the algorithms themselves (Wei et al., 2022). In financial services, regulators have introduced mandatory transparency requirements, independent audits, and the documentation of decision pathways to ensure that human actors remain answerable for automated outcomes (Saraiva, 2024). Legal scholars argue that these models should be adapted across domains, ensuring that engineers, managers, and policy-makers are incentivized to maintain vigilance, update safety protocols, and intervene when automated systems fail or cause harm (Mormann, 2021). The emphasis on procedural traceability and documentation makes it possible to reconstruct decision chains after adverse events. Crucially, the goal of this reconstruction is not the metaphysical task of identifying a single, blameworthy origin point but the practical task of locating which part of a public, institutional process needs correction. This form of transparency serves accountability and systemic learning, not retribution. The proceduralist model grounds accountability in verifiable action and oversight, aligning with empirical findings that effective risk management and ethical conduct require ongoing institutional commitment rather than episodic intervention. This is the essence of procedural transparency. It rightly abandons the impossible task of achieving transparency into the "mind" of a system or the complete causal history of a failure, focusing instead on making the governance and redress mechanisms themselves transparent and accessible.

Critical analyses warn, however, that accountability systems risk becoming mere formalities unless they are paired with meaningful stakeholder engagement and cultural change. Public trust in algorithmic systems depends not only on technical safeguards, but also on the willingness of organizations to engage in transparent, inclusive, and participatory governance (Purves & Davis, 2022). Research in organizational ethics and technology governance suggests that whistleblower protections, stakeholder forums, and independent ethics committees are crucial for surfacing risks, ensuring responsiveness, and preventing regulatory capture (Hwang, 2024). In this regard, the call for "human-in-the-loop" systems is not simply a technical requirement, but a normative imperative for sustaining accountability in an age of distributed agency (Saraiva, 2024). By democratizing oversight and embedding ethical dialogue into project lifecycles, institutions can ensure that accountability is not just procedural, but substantively responsive to the interests and values of those affected by technological change (Kellmeyer, Mueller, & Burgard, 2022).

The philosophical dimension of accountability in a determined world also invites a rethinking of agency and desert. As determinist insights from neuroscience, philosophy, and social science weaken the case for metaphysical blame, ethical discourse is increasingly oriented toward outcome responsibility, role responsibility, and capacity responsibility. These categories reflect the practical realities of collective action and complex causation, assigning accountability based on the real ability to influence, intervene, and correct rather than abstract notions of free will (Saraiva, 2024). Scholars argue that this approach, while perhaps less emotionally satisfying than blame, is better suited for addressing harms, incentivizing ethical conduct, and promoting organizational learning in sociotechnical systems (Mukta, 2025; Hwang, 2024). Human accountability in a determined world is best secured through systems and cultures that incentivize vigilance, transparency, and collective responsibility rather than through futile searches for individual fault. As technologies grow more autonomous and outcomes more complex, the effective assignment of responsibility will depend on procedural safeguards, institutional commitment, and ethical reflection at every stage of system development and deployment (Wei et al., 2022). In this new landscape, accountability is a distributed and dynamic process that recognizes the social, legal, and organizational conditions that enable or impede responsible action. The challenge for the future is to ensure that these frameworks remain adaptive, participatory, and robust as the boundaries of agency and causation continue to evolve.

The success of these new accountability regimes hinges on their capacity for continual adaptation and reflexive learning. Effective oversight is not a one-time checklist but an ongoing commitment to monitoring, audit, and iterative reform in response to emerging risks and changing technologies (Tariq, Ashraf, & Rashid, 2025; Saraiva, 2024). Organizations that foster a culture of openness where mistakes are reported, analyzed, and addressed collaboratively are more likely to maintain public trust and adapt to future challenges. Comparative research suggests that the most resilient and ethical institutions are those that actively seek input from a diverse array of stakeholders, including affected communities, external experts, and independent regulators (Purves & Davis, 2022; Hwang, 2024). These inclusive processes help surface blind spots, mitigate power imbalances, and ensure that accountability mechanisms remain substantively rather than merely procedurally robust. As algorithmic systems become further embedded in everyday life, the challenge for policymakers will be to balance efficiency and innovation with safeguards that empower users, support whistleblowers, and provide accessible avenues for redress.

This evolving conception of accountability also reconfigures the ethical relationships between humans, institutions, and technology. Rather than treating responsibility as a static, legalistic assignment of blame, practice-based frameworks understand it as an ongoing negotiation shaped by the realities of distributed agency, networked causation, and social complexity (Santoni de Sio & Mecacci, 2021; Kellmeyer, Mueller, & Burgard, 2022). The democratization of oversight and the embrace of collective stewardship foster systems in which individuals and organizations are incentivized to act ethically, to learn from failure, and to prioritize the well-being of those affected by technological change. Such models are more consistent with empirical insights from neuroscience and social science, which stress the importance of environmental, cultural, and institutional factors in shaping behavior and outcomes. In the end, human accountability in a determined world becomes less about finding fault and more about fostering the conditions for responsible, responsive, and resilient action. This approach is essential for sustaining justice, trust, and legitimacy in the age of autonomous systems and distributed intelligence.

9.3. The Bartz Distinction: Transformative Use vs. Extractive Accumulation

The emergence of the Bartz standard, drawing a sharp line between transformative use and extractive accumulation (Table 9.1), will become a defining lens for courts and policymakers as they navigate the complex terrain of liability, authorship, and value in automated and hybrid creative environments. The *Bartz v. Anthropic* litigation and related cases have crystallized a foundational tension in copyright: the distinction between transformative use, which adds social or expressive value, and extractive accumulation, which merely amasses or repurposes existing works for private gain. Legal and philosophical analysis now foregrounds this distinction as the linchpin for determining legitimate versus illegitimate appropriation in the digital and automated era (Centivany, 2024; Wyczik & Wieczerzak, 2024). Transformative use is defined not just by technical alteration but by a demonstrable change in purpose, function, or context that yields new meaning, insight, or utility for audiences or markets (Murray, 2023; Park, 2023). This aligns with the Supreme Court's 2023 ruling in *Andy Warhol Foundation v. Goldsmith*, where the Court clarified that merely derivative or sequential use—even if novel in appearance—does not suffice for fair use unless a genuinely new expression or utility is realized (Park, 2023). In contrast, extractive accumulation encompasses practices such as wholesale scraping, mass ingestion of copyrighted data for algorithmic training, and the untransformed reproduction of content, activities often justified by scale or technical complexity yet lacking any added cultural or social value (Wagh, Peerzada, & Rote, 2023; Syrbo & Krapivina, 2025). Researchers warn that extractive practices not only undermine the rights and incentives of original creators but also risk flooding the marketplace with commoditized, low-value works that stifle innovation and diversity (Centivany, 2024; Rosati, 2024). Courts will now increasingly be required to scrutinize the intent, outcome, and societal benefit of uses, distinguishing those that foster creativity and public enrichment from those that simply mine existing value without giving back. The Bartz distinction offers a practice-based paradigm, emphasizing community-recognized transformation over mere algorithmic novelty.

Table 9.1. Transformative use vs. extractive accumulation

Criteria	Transformative Use	Extractive Accumulation
Input Sources	Selective, purposeful use of existing materials	Mass scraping of publicly available or proprietary datasets
Intent	To add new expression, meaning, or insight	To replicate, replace, or monetize original works without alteration
Public Benefit	High: enhances knowledge, creativity, or commentary	Low or indirect: benefits central platform owners
Control Mechanism	Cites, credits, or builds upon source with human oversight	Often opaque, no clear attribution or opt-out
Legal Framing	Often defended as Fair Use or Fair Dealing	Legally contested under copyright or data protection laws
User Involvement	Human in the loop (curation, prompt design, editing)	Minimal or no human intervention after data ingestion
Risk to Rights Holders	Low to moderate: risk managed through transformation and credit	High: source work often substituted or devalued
Judicial Trend	Increasingly recognized as legitimate in case-by-case analysis	Under growing scrutiny, with courts leaning toward regulation

The doctrine of transformative use, as it has developed since the landmark decisions in *Google v. Oracle* and *Andy Warhol Foundation v. Goldsmith*, sets a high bar: protected works must not only look or sound different but must serve different functions, express new messages, or provide meaningful commentary or critique (Murray, 2023). In the context of generative systems, this means that outputs curated by human designers, prompt engineers, or collaborative teams are often evaluated for the degree to which they demonstrate interpretive intervention, context adaptation, or audience engagement (Mazzi, 2024). Extractive accumulation, by contrast, is typically characterized by large-scale, automated processes such as the scraping of millions of works for training datasets or the generation of outputs that mirror existing works without substantial alteration or contextual shift (Syrbo &

Krapivina, 2025). Legal scholarship shows that extractive accumulation tends to produce "market harm" by substituting for the original work, saturating markets, and reducing opportunities for original authors to benefit from their creative labor (Wagh, Peerzada, & Rote, 2023). Judges and policymakers are urged to draw lines not simply around the presence or absence of human involvement but around the presence or absence of value creation, public benefit, and meaningful transformation (Rosati, 2024). These standards increasingly drive both infringement litigation and regulatory policy, as demonstrated by recent EU, UK, and US initiatives (Centivany, 2024). As new cases arise, legal scholars stress the importance of nuanced, case-by-case analysis, weighing the social, cultural, and economic impacts of each use. The core message: transformation and contribution, not extraction and accumulation, must guide future copyright doctrine.

Empirical and comparative research further illuminates the practical consequences of extractive versus transformative uses in creative economies. For example, studies on licensing and royalty distribution reveal that extractive practices often result in inequitable outcomes, concentrating wealth and control among platform owners and technology firms while excluding original creators from the value chain (Khan & Gotora, 2023). In contrast, transformative uses such as those that remix, collage, parody, and engage in adaptive reinterpretation have been shown to drive innovation, enable cultural dialogue, and enrich public discourse (Wyczik & Wieczerzak, 2024). Researchers argue that fair use and compulsory licensing mechanisms should be retooled to recognize the special status of transformative projects, while subjecting extractive accumulation to stricter scrutiny and regulatory oversight (Centivany, 2024). At the same time, the border between these categories remains porous, especially as generative systems evolve and hybrid forms of authorship proliferate (Mazzi, 2024; Park, 2023). Legal frameworks must remain adaptive, allowing for iterative refinement as technology and artistic practice continue to change. This includes developing clear documentation and provenance standards to help courts and regulators trace the lineage and context of both human and machine outputs (Syrbo & Krapivina, 2025). Only by building systems that balance innovation incentives with protection against exploitation can copyright maintain its relevance and legitimacy in the digital era.

International legal harmonization is emerging as a key priority in addressing the challenges posed by extractive accumulation and global-scale transformative use. Scholars note that divergent approaches to data mining, fair use, and derivative rights risk creating legal uncertainty, regulatory arbitrage, and inconsistent incentives for creators and platforms (Khan & Gotora, 2023; Mazzi, 2024). Recent proposals advocate for the expansion of open licensing regimes, reciprocal recognition of transformative standards, and the development of international registries to track data provenance and transformation (Wyczik & Wieczerzak, 2024). In addition, transparency obligations, robust disclosure requirements, and independent oversight bodies are recommended to ensure accountability and public trust in the management of creative assets. Case law from Europe and Asia demonstrates that the adoption of transparent, practice-based criteria for evaluating transformation and extraction is both feasible and effective at balancing the interests of creators, users, and society (Rosati, 2024). Researchers further emphasize that stakeholder engagement and public consultation are essential for ensuring that legal reforms reflect the lived realities of diverse creative communities (Syrbo & Krapivina, 2025). As legal systems adapt, the Bartz distinction will become increasingly central. The legitimacy of new creative forms depends not on formal authorship but on the public's ability to recognize and value substantive contribution.

This distinction between transformative use and extractive accumulation provides an empirically and ethically grounded standard for copyright and liability in a world of hybrid, automated, and distributed creativity. Scholars, courts, and policymakers are converging on the view that future systems of intellectual property must reward demonstrable transformation, cultural dialogue, and social benefit, while regulating or penalizing practices that merely accumulate and commoditize preexisting value (Wyczik & Wieczerzak, 2024; Centivany, 2024). By focusing on outcomes and social utility, the Bartz standard enables more adaptive, equitable, and innovation-friendly creative economies. At the same time, it challenges technologists, legal practitioners, and cultural institutions to develop mechanisms for transparent provenance, accountable stewardship, and community engagement. In the years ahead, the continuing evolution of this distinction will determine not only the scope of copyright protection, but also the legitimacy and vitality of global creative industries.

As courts and legislatures refine the Bartz distinction, there will be a growing recognition that a purely technical or quantitative approach cannot capture the full social and cultural significance of transformation versus extraction. Practice-based analysis urges evaluators to consider the lived realities of creative communities: Does a use enable new forms of participation? Does it empower marginalized voices or foster inclusive dialogue? Does it stimulate meaningful exchange and innovation within cultural, scientific, or educational domains (Rosati, 2024; Wyczik & Wieczerzak, 2024)? For example, a remix or parody that enables critical commentary or democratizes access to art may be more valuable to society than a high-volume, algorithmic scraping operation that merely replicates existing works for profit. Legal scholars and cultural theorists advocate for the continued development of qualitative guidelines incorporating public interest, diversity of expression, and the enrichment of communal knowledge as explicit criteria for transformative use (Centivany, 2024; Park, 2023). Such frameworks move beyond simplistic metrics of novelty or difference, instead rewarding creative acts that serve broader societal purposes. In doing so, the Bartz standard also acts as a bulwark against the growing commodification of information and culture in automated and data-driven economies.

Moreover, the Bartz distinction serves as a call to action for the design and stewardship of digital infrastructure. Platform owners, developers, and curators are increasingly tasked with implementing provenance tracking, transparency dashboards, and participatory governance tools that empower users and creators to shape how their works are used, credited, and compensated (Mazzi, 2024; Khan & Gotora, 2023). Collaborative curation and open peer review can help ensure that transformative practices are nurtured while extractive tendencies are monitored and, where necessary, curbed through policy or technological interventions. These proactive strategies contribute to a creative ecosystem in which value is continually added and shared, not simply harvested and enclosed. Ultimately, the Bartz distinction stands not only as a legal doctrine but as a living, adaptive principle that links copyright to the evolving practices, values, and aspirations of digital society. As hybrid authorship and generative creativity become the norm, the ongoing refinement and robust application of this standard will be crucial for ensuring justice, equity, and vitality in global creative production.

9.4. Forward-Looking Frameworks for Uncertain Agency

As legal systems grapple with the unpredictable outcomes of distributed agency in automated environments, consensus is emerging that adaptive and resilient frameworks, not static rules, are needed to manage liability and responsibility (Chesterman, 2024). The rapid evolution of machine learning and autonomous decision-making introduces a persistent "responsibility gap," in which no single party (developer, operator, or user) can fully predict, control, or be held individually liable for system behavior (Gallese, 2022)

(Figure 9.1). Rather than focusing on traditional knowledge or intent, scholars now urge the adoption of strict or tiered liability regimes, where responsibility is allocated according to influence, capacity, and risk across the lifecycle of system development and deployment (Wang, 2023). The European Union's ongoing reform efforts, such as the AI Act and revised product liability directives, reflect this movement toward proactive governance, mandating ex ante risk assessment, ongoing surveillance, and mandatory insurance or compensation schemes (Chesterman, 2024). These proposals recognize that uncertainty is an inherent feature of digital agency and demand flexible, auditable, and transparent mechanisms for remediation and redress. Legal frameworks must also accommodate international complexity, harmonizing rules for cross-border data use, supply chains, and networked liability (Fikri & Amelia, 2024). As systemic risk and distributed harm become the norm, governance models must be robust to unexpected failures and designed to learn from emergent hazards, not just respond after the fact (Thatikonda, 2025). The focus is shifting from fault to resilience and collective stewardship.

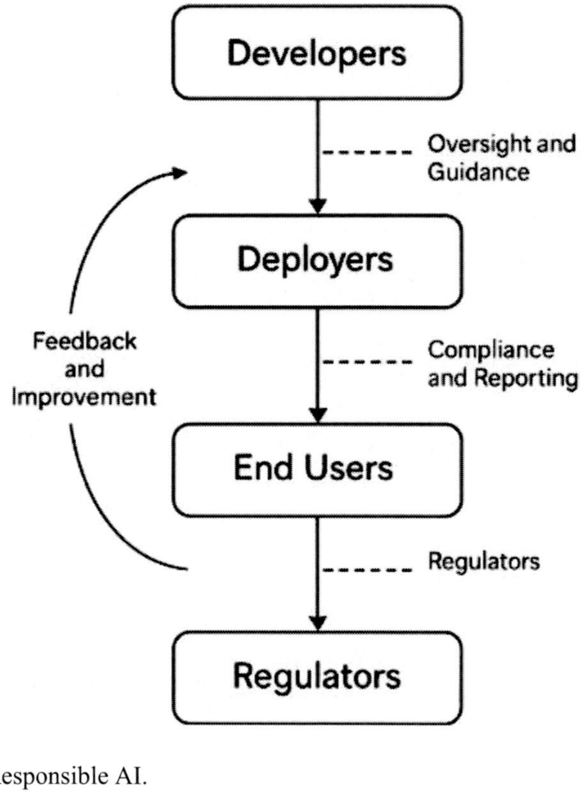

Figure 9.1. Responsible AI.

Scholars emphasize that forward-looking frameworks must prioritize explainability, auditability, and the creation of "traceable" pathways for the purpose of assigning procedural responsibility (Kellmeyer, Mueller, & Burgard, 2022). The goal of such reconstruction is not the metaphysical task of identifying a single origin point for a failure but the practical task of locating which part of a public, institutional process needs correction. Traceability, in this framework, serves accountability, not blame. Instead of seeking individual fault in black-box models, legal standards should require developers and operators to maintain detailed documentation, conduct independent audits, and embed real-time feedback loops for system correction (Sharkey, 2024). A promising approach is the integration of strict product liability, which holds producers and deployers responsible for harms regardless of intent, provided a causal link to system operation can be established. Some commentators propose hybrid liability models, combining elements of vicarious, strict, and joint-and-several liability to reflect the distributed realities of contemporary technological systems (van Eck & Agbeko, 2023). These models can be reinforced through compulsory insurance, collective risk pools, or statutory compensation funds for victims of autonomous or unpredictable harm (Chesterman, 2022). The aim is not only to ensure that victims receive timely redress, but also to incentivize all actors in the value chain to adopt best practices, invest in safety, and collaborate on risk mitigation. Such frameworks must be continually updated as technologies evolve, reinforcing a culture of adaptive governance and proactive responsibility.

In the case of copyright, the equivalent of "seeking individual fault" is "assigning individual authorship," and "proactive responsibility" would be something like the author claiming responsibility for the authored work, even if the provenance of the language, imagery, ideas, and emotional experience created by the work is not spelled out in any exhaustive way. The notion of transparency may involve documentation of tools used in production, labeling some aspect of a work as coming from the author's thoughts or dreams and another aspect as coming directly from an AI model. However, as argued throughout this book, this form of disclosure is a transitional phase. The ultimate goal of a practice-based framework is not this granular, metaphysical accounting but a simpler and more robust transparency: the public act of an author or institution standing behind their work and accepting responsibility for it within a community of practice. Transparency will need to move away from the metaphysical assumptions which have informed much of copyright law if creativity is to be saved from being a laborious audit of every phrase or brushstroke.

The complexity of systemic agency and distributed harm also calls for an expanded understanding of legal and moral responsibility. Recent research distinguishes between causal, outcome, role, capacity, and liability responsibilities, highlighting the need to assign obligations not just to individuals, but to groups, organizations, and networked systems (Custers, Lahmann, & Scott, 2025). This nuanced taxonomy supports the design of interdisciplinary oversight boards, ethics committees, and sector-specific regulators, charged with monitoring emerging risks, setting sectoral standards, and ensuring continuous learning from failures (Chesterman, 2024). Experts also stress the need for dynamic impact assessments, scenario planning, and stakeholder engagement to capture diverse interests, anticipate unintended consequences, and build public trust (Abbott, 2023). Education and legal consciousness play a critical role: promoting a culture of responsibility among developers, operators, and users increases the chances that responsible behavior will be internalized and sustained (Malko et al., 2022). The ultimate objective is to foster legal cultures where positive responsibility, not just fear of punishment, motivates proactive compliance and ethical design.

Forward-looking frameworks must also address issues of privacy, data protection, and algorithmic bias, especially as smart systems mediate sensitive decisions in healthcare, finance, and law enforcement (Fikri & Amelia, 2024; Thatikonda, 2025). Research highlights the necessity for specialized agencies and international protocols that can monitor, investigate, and penalize misuse or negligence in real time (Fikri & Amelia, 2024). Multilayered safeguards (privacy-by-design, bias audits, and external review) should be mandated to mitigate the risks of large-scale harm, data breaches, and systemic discrimination (Thatikonda, 2025; Wang, 2023). As machine rationality and "electronic persons" blur the boundaries of legal subjectivity, forward-looking legal regimes must resist premature grants of personhood or rights, focusing instead on ensuring that all automated agency is subject to human-anchored oversight and public accountability (van Eck & Agbeko, 2023). The lessons from the B2B sector, digital markets, and healthcare all point to the value of continuous adaptation and sector-specific standards.

Finally, the future of legal and ethical governance in the era of uncertain agency is inherently pluralistic and collaborative. No single doctrine, jurisdiction, or regulatory tool is sufficient to manage the evolving landscape of distributed intelligence and automated systems (Chesterman, 2024; Abbott, 2023). Instead, effective governance demands a mosaic of adaptive laws, interdisciplinary expertise, stakeholder engagement, and global cooperation. The persistent challenge of the "responsibility gap" requires legal systems to be not only reactive but also anticipatory, investing in foresight, learning from near-misses, and empowering regulators to act decisively amid uncertainty. By embracing uncertainty and building mechanisms for continuous review, legal systems can foster resilient, ethical, and inclusive societies that are equipped to flourish amid technological change.

A key to the success of these adaptive frameworks is the recognition that legal and ethical governance is not a static end state, but a continuous, iterative process. Regulatory sandboxes, pilot projects, and rolling reviews allow policymakers and industry to test, refine, and improve standards in real-world contexts before scaling them up (Abbott, 2023; Chesterman, 2024). This experimentalist approach enables legal systems to stay abreast of technological advances while avoiding regulatory paralysis or overreaction. At the same time, flexible redress and compensation mechanisms can help absorb and distribute unforeseen risks, minimizing harm while maintaining public confidence in emerging technologies (van Eck & Agbeko, 2023; Wang, 2023). Transparency and open reporting are essential in this process, both to ensure accountability and to allow all stakeholders to learn from system failures and unexpected outcomes. Such institutionalized learning fosters a culture of humility, responsibility, and collective vigilance that is better suited to the evolving challenges of distributed agency than punitive, retrospective blame.

In addition, forward-looking governance frameworks must embed values of justice, equity, and human dignity at every stage of system design and deployment. As scholars note, it is not enough to ensure technical reliability or regulatory compliance; legal systems must also prioritize the rights and interests of those most vulnerable to technological risk, such as marginalized communities, workers, and consumers (Fikri & Amelia, 2024; Thatikonda, 2025). This requires participatory mechanisms for affected groups to influence policy, proactive monitoring for disparate impacts, and robust remedies for those who suffer harm. Only through this combination of anticipatory regulation, ongoing oversight, and inclusive participation can societies ensure that the benefits of distributed agency are shared broadly, while its risks are responsibly managed and equitably addressed. In sum, the challenge of uncertain agency is an opportunity to build legal systems that are not only resilient and adaptive, but also deeply responsive to the plural and evolving needs of global society.

This chapter has illuminated the urgent need for adaptive, forward-looking frameworks to manage accountability and liability in the age of systemic, uncertain agency. As artificial systems become more autonomous, interconnected, and complex, the traditional focus on individual blame or intent is no longer sufficient for assigning responsibility or ensuring justice. The scholarship reviewed here consistently advocates for robust, procedural safeguards such as traceable audit trails, interdisciplinary oversight, and mandatory risk assessment that distribute accountability across the network of developers, operators, users, and regulators. Rather than seeking scapegoats or artificially personifying machines, these frameworks encourage collective vigilance, transparency, and the cultivation of a legal culture oriented toward prevention, resilience, and social learning. The evolving distinction between transformative and extractive uses of automation further demonstrates that genuine value and legitimacy depend on demonstrable contribution, openness, and continual adaptation to new risks and realities.

Reflecting on these considerations, the chapter concludes that a just and effective approach to liability in a determined, technological landscape must be pluralistic, dynamic, and collaborative. Courts, legislators, and designers are called not only to anticipate the unpredictable effects of distributed agency but also to build institutions capable of continuous learning, inclusive participation, and ethical governance. Embracing the uncertainty inherent in automated and networked environments is not a weakness but a strength, provided legal systems remain nimble, participatory, and globally harmonized. By focusing on system-level accountability and the proactive management of risk, societies can foster both innovation and justice, ensuring that the benefits of technology are shared widely while the burdens and harms are equitably addressed. In the end, systemic responsibility for uncertain agency is less about control than about stewardship: designing, monitoring, and evolving the structures within which meaningful, fair, and accountable action remains possible for all.

References

Abbott, R. (2023). We, the Robots? Regulating Artificial Intelligence and the Limits of the Law by Simon Chesterman. *International & Comparative Law Quarterly, 72(*1), 272-273.

Centivany, A. (2024). Mining, Scraping, Training, Generating: Copyright Implications of Generative AI. *Proceedings of the Association for Information Science and Technology*, *61*(1), 68-79.

Chesterman, S. (2024). From ethics to law: why, when, and how to regulate AI. In *Handbook on the Ethics of Artificial Intelligence* (pp. 113-127). Edward Elgar Publishing.

Custers, B., Lahmann, H., & Scott, B. I. (2025). From liability gaps to liability overlaps: shared responsibilities and fiduciary duties in AI and other complex technologies. *AI & society*, 1-16.

Fikri, A., & Amelia, T. (2024). Indonesia's Legal Policy on Protecting Personal Data from Artificial Intelligence Abuse. In *SHS Web of Conferences* (Vol. 204, p. 07002). EDP Sciences.

Floridi, L. (2016). Faultless responsibility: On the nature and allocation of moral responsibility for distributed moral actions. *Philosophical Transactions of the Royal Society A: Mathematical, Physical and Engineering Sciences*, *374*(2083), 20160112.

Gallese, C. (2022, November). Suggestions for a revision of the European smart robot liability regime. In *4th European Conference on the Impact of Artificial Intelligence and Robotics, ECIAIR 2022* (pp. 29-35). Academic Conferences and Publishing International.

Hwang, J. (2024). Ethics of artificial intelligence: Examining moral accountability in autonomous decision-making systems. *World Journal of Advanced Research and Reviews*. https://doi.org/10.30574/wjarr.2024.23.3.2884.

Kellmeyer, P., Mueller, O., & Burgard, W. (2022). The Cambridge Handbook of Responsible Artificial Intelligence: Interdisciplinary Perspectives. *The Cambridge Handbook of Responsible Artificial Intelligence: Interdisciplinary Perspectives (CUP 2022, open access)*, 505.

Khan, R., & Gotora, N. (2023). One (innovation) flew over the law's head: the intersection of artificial intelligence and copyright. *South Afr. Intell. Property Law J*, *11*, 72-87.

Lai, A. (2021). Artificial intelligence, LLC: Corporate personhood as tort reform. *Mich. St. L. Rev.*, 597.

Mazzi, F. (2024). Authorship in artificial intelligence-generated works: Exploring originality in text prompts and artificial intelligence outputs through philosophical foundations of copyright and collage protection. *The Journal of World Intellectual Property*, *27*(3), 410-427.

McDonald, L. (2023). AI systems and liability: An assessment of the applicability of strict liability & A case for limited legal personhood for AI. *St Andrews Law Journal*, *3*(1), 5-21.

Mormann, F. (2021). Beyond algorithms: toward a normative theory of automated regulation. *BCL Rev.*, *62*, 1.

Mukta, S. (2025). Moral Agency and Responsibility in Artificial Intelligence: Can Autonomous Systems Be Held Ethically Accountable. *Journal of Artificial Intelligence General science (JAIGS) ISSN: 3006-4023*, *8*(1), 198-207.

Murray, M. D. (2023). Generative ai art: Copyright infringement and fair use. *SMU Sci. & Tech. L. Rev.*, *26*, 259.

Park, K. (2023). A Study on Appropriation Art and Application of Transformativeness under Fair Use Clause of the Korean Copyright Act - Focusing on the Implication of Andy Warhol Foundation v. Goldsmith. *Korea Copyright Commission*. https://doi.org/10.30582/kdps.2023.36.4.297.

Purves, D., & Davis, J. (2022). Public trust, institutional legitimacy, and the use of algorithms in criminal justice. *Public Affairs Quarterly*, *36*(2), 136-162.

Rosati, E. (2024). Infringing AI: Liability for AI-generated outputs under international, EU, and UK copyright law. *European Journal of Risk Regulation*, 1-25.

Santoni de Sio, F., & Mecacci, G. (2021). Four responsibility gaps with artificial intelligence: Why they matter and how to address them. *Philosophy & technology*, *34*(4), 1057-1084.

Saraiva, L. (2024). Moral agency and responsibility in ai systems. *International Journal of Philosophy*, *3*(1), 25-36.

Sharkey, C. M. (2024). A Products Liability Framework for AI. *Columbia Science and Technology Law Review*, *25*(2).

Strasser, A. (2022). Distributed responsibility in human–machine interactions. *AI and Ethics*, *2*(3), 523-532.

Sung, J. (2023). Artificial intelligence in medicine: Ethical, social and legal perspectives. *Annals of the Academy of Medicine, Singapore*, *52*(12), 695-699.

Syrbo V. A., Krapivina D. A. (2025). Transformations of Copyright and Neighboring Rights in the Digital Era. *Bulletin of Kemerovo State University. Series: Humanities and Social Sciences.* no. 1. pp. 161-172. DOI: https://doi.org/10.21603/2542-1840-2025-9-1-161-172.

Tariq, B., Ashraf, M. R., & Rashid, U. (2025). Ethical Imperatives in AI Design: A Comprehensive Framework for Risk Mitigation and Responsible Innovation. *Ubiquitous Technology Journal*, *1*(2), 61-73.

Thatikonda, K. (2025). Distributed Intelligence for Distributed Systems Resilience: A Meta-Analysis of Artificial Intelligence Driven Self-Healing Systems. *International Journal of Scientific Research in Computer Science, Engineering and Information Technology*. https://doi.org/10.32628/cseit25112448.

van Eck, M., & Agbeko, F. (2023). Electronic persons in contracts. *Obiter*, *44*(4), 808-827.

Walker-Munro, B., & Assaad, Z. (2023). The Guilty (Silicon) Mind: Blameworthiness and Liability in Human-Machine Teaming. *Cambridge L. Rev.*, *8*, 1.

Wagh, S., Peerzada, S., & Rote, P. (2023). AI And Copyright. *Tuijin Jishu/Journal of Propulsion Technology*. https://doi.org/10.52783/tjjpt.v44.i3.2053.

Wang, R. Of Machine Rationality: Artificial Intelligence's Legal Identity and Liability. *Available at SSRN 4330550*.

Wei, B. R., Xue, P., Jiang, Y., Zhai, X. M., & Qiao, Y. L. (2022). World Health Organization guidance Ethical and Governance of Artificial Intelligence for health and implications for China. *Zhonghua yi xue za zhi*, *102*(12), 833-837.

Wyczik, J., & Wieczerzak, R. (2024). Rethinking Copyright: The Art of Ownership in AI Outputs. *Eastern European Journal of Transnational Relations*, *8*(1), 39-52.

Part IV: The Post-Inner-State World

Chapter 10

Designing Ethical AI Systems

Abstract

Chapter ten interrogates the inadequacy of prevailing paradigms of ethical AI design, particularly the widespread reliance on "meaningful human control," and introduces a more philosophically and practically substantive alternative centered on "meaningful human practice." Against the backdrop of rapid technological acceleration and proliferating demands for trustworthy AI, the chapter contends that the dominant focus on aligning system outputs with modeled psychological states or subjective preferences risks reducing value alignment to an impoverished, technical exercise divorced from the actual practices that confer meaning and legitimacy. The chapter conducts a critical examination of major guidelines and standards for AI ethics—including the EU AI Act, OECD Principles, and IEEE Ethically Aligned Design—illuminating both their contributions and their limitations in operationalizing ethical aims. Building on this analysis, the chapter articulates a blueprint for ethical system design grounded in context-sensitivity, community engagement, and norm negotiation, advocating for design principles that prioritize transparency, responsiveness, and the capacity for iterative stakeholder participation. It is argued that only by relocating value alignment from the domain of private mental states to the sphere of public practice can smart systems become robust, just, and democratically accountable. In concluding, the chapter positions practice-based design not as an ancillary desideratum, but as the central criterion for responsible and sustainable algorithmic governance in an era defined by uncertainty, plurality, and unprecedented technological agency.

10.1. Meaningful Human Control vs. Meaningful Human Practice

The debate over "meaningful human control" in the context of automated and algorithmic systems has evolved rapidly in recent years as scholars have increasingly interrogated not only the technical criteria for human oversight, but also the deeper normative commitments that underpin what it means for control to be meaningful in ethical, legal, and practical terms. While much contemporary policy and engineering work has prioritized human-in-the-loop mechanisms or procedural safeguards to ensure traceability and accountability, the latest research demonstrates that such approaches often fall short of addressing the profound gaps between mere supervisory authority and genuine participation in practice. Recent literature calls for a pivot from static models of "control" to dynamic, practice-centered frameworks that emphasize the situated, iterative, and socially embedded character of responsible human engagement.

First, the conceptual foundation of meaningful human control has been subject to intensive philosophical scrutiny, revealing that the term is often invoked without careful attention to its diverse and sometimes conflicting purposes. Davidović (2023) contends that clarifying the intended function (whether safety assurance, moral responsibility, dignity, or legal liability) is essential for institutionalizing appropriate forms of human control in system design and governance. Without specifying purpose, efforts at control risk devolving into ritualistic or symbolic measures, masking "responsibility gaps" and undermining public trust in algorithmic decision-making infrastructures. This critique has profound implications for regulatory regimes in high-stakes domains such as automated vehicles, health care, and public administration, where the inclusion of humans is sometimes reduced to "quasi-automation" or rubber-stamping, generating gray zones of liability and limited moral agency.

Second, empirical and theoretical studies converge on the importance of aligning human oversight not simply with the formal opportunity to intervene, but with the actual capacity to track and influence the morally salient reasons underpinning system behavior. This is operationalized in recent frameworks that distinguish between the "tracking" of human reasons, ensuring that the system's actions respond to relevant human values, goals, and situational judgments, and the "tracing" of outcomes to specific individuals or groups who can be held accountable (de Sio et al., 2023). Experimental research by Van den Bosch et al. (2025) operationalizes these insights in collaborative settings, demonstrating that subjective, normative, and moral control can be reliably measured and are sensitive to variations in team design and task allocation. Their findings indicate that meaningful human control is maximized when human agents are engaged in contextually rich, morally loaded decision points, rather than relegated to passive oversight or after-the-fact review.

Third, the latest scholarship reveals that meaningful control is not a static attribute, but an emergent property of ongoing practice shaped by expertise, training, institutional culture, and the evolving nature of human-technology relations. Hybrid intelligence research, for instance, emphasizes the co-evolution of human and automated systems, where "control" is achieved not through pre-scripted interventions but through reciprocal adaptation, mutual learning, and the cultivation of trust, transparency, and responsiveness (Järvelä et al., 2025). Studies of real-world applications such as semi-autonomous vehicles and health care triage systems demonstrate that user perceptions of safety, trust, and efficacy depend less on the mere availability of override options and more on the extent to which system actions are intelligible, open to negotiation, and aligned with user and community values (Suryana et al., 2024).

Fourth, research into the limitations and unintended consequences of current "control" frameworks underscores the need for a practice-based orientation. Parmer (2024) argues that the deepest forms of meaningfulness arise from participation in open-ended practices rather than the mere achievement of isolated, credit-assignable outcomes. In automated workplaces, the relegation of humans to monitoring roles often leads to skill erosion, diminished sense of agency, and "moral crumple zones," where humans bear responsibility without real influence over outcomes. Practice theory calls for the reintegration of human actors into processes of learning, improvisation, and situated judgment, an orientation that is echoed in Wittgensteinian philosophy where the meaning and normativity of action are rooted in shared forms of life and rule-governed participation.

Fifth, the imperative to move from "meaningful human control" to "meaningful human practice" finds its most compelling justification in the demand for democratic legitimacy and social sustainability. Nikiforova et al. (2023) highlight the risks associated with highly automated, data-driven public services that bypass opportunities for collective deliberation and stakeholder engagement. Only by embedding system design in iterative, context-sensitive, and participatory practices can we ensure that technology remains aligned with evolving community norms, protects against the ossification of power, and supports ongoing negotiation of meaning, risk, and value. The future of ethical automated systems lies not in perfecting supervisory interfaces, but in fostering the socio-technical conditions for a meaningful practice that requires ongoing interdisciplinary inquiry and the critical reinvention of institutional routines.

A growing body of empirical research demonstrates that systems designed around meaningful human practice rather than mere supervisory control are more likely to foster trust, compliance, and adaptive safety across a range of automated domains. Studies in aviation, finance, and health care have shown that meaningful engagement is best sustained through participatory design, continuous user training, and institutional cultures that reward feedback, transparency, and joint problem-solving (Järvelä et al., 2025; Suryana et al., 2024). These environments empower users to recognize and respond to evolving risks, rather than simply overseeing automated outputs as passive monitors. This participatory orientation also supports the development of shared vocabularies, ethical guidelines, and operational routines that make both human and machine agency more intelligible and corrigible. Research on human-machine collaboration highlights that robust agency emerges from practices where all actors, both human and nonhuman, are accountable within shared, negotiated contexts, allowing for ongoing adjustment and distributed learning (de Sio et al., 2023; Parmer, 2024). As such, the pivot from "control" to "practice" is not simply a theoretical refinement, but an essential step for building more resilient, adaptive, and ethically legitimate socio-technical systems. This pivot also clarifies the meaning of transparency in ethical design. Instead of aiming for a transparent "human in the loop" who can audit every algorithmic step, we should aim for transparent practices of engagement where stakeholders can contest, shape, and hold the entire socio-technical system accountable.

As in other chapters, the comparison with authorship is productive here. As it becomes increasingly possible to be the author of a text merely by "pushing a button" and supervising the text as it spools out from the machine, any kind of robust agency on the part of the human author is corroded. The temptation is to see a binary choice between "writing every word by hand" or handing everything over to the AI, but exploring all the possible approaches for "ongoing adjustment" and participating in the act of authorship is sure to lead to a better future. The human in the authorship process will sometimes be supervisory and at other times corrective in a hands-on way. The assertion of agency will have to allow for engagement at many different layers or levels of the produced text if anything like responsibility for the text will be possible in an age of automated authorship to varying degrees.

The shift to practice-based frameworks further redefines how responsibility and legitimacy are constructed in increasingly automated societies. Instead of centering liability and agency in isolated individuals, this approach frames accountability as a relational and institutional achievement distributed across designers, operators, stakeholders, and the wider community (Nikiforova et al., 2023). Legal and policy reforms increasingly mandate the creation of participatory channels, iterative testing, and stakeholder forums to ensure that the design, deployment, and monitoring of automated systems reflect evolving values and contextual realities. As a result, meaningful human practice becomes the ground for new forms of ethical governance, democratic oversight, and social innovation. The ongoing challenge for scholars, practitioners, and policymakers is to develop metrics, standards, and infrastructures that capture the richness and fluidity of these practices, ensuring that the future of automation is not only technically proficient, but also just, responsive, and genuinely human-centered.

10.2. Value Alignment as Social Construction

The imperative of value alignment in the governance of autonomous systems has increasingly moved from an engineering challenge, often conceived as a matter of technically encoding or inferring individual psychological preferences, toward a richer, socially constructed process rooted in community negotiation and public deliberation. Contemporary research underscores that values are neither static nor reducible to private states; rather, they emerge, evolve, and are sustained within the ongoing interactions of communities, shaped by institutional norms, cultural scripts, and the situated experiences of diverse actors (Järvelä et al., 2025). In practical terms, this means that the process of aligning automated system outputs with "human values" is not a matter of finding some pre-existing set of preferences to model, but rather a recursive process of facilitating participation, debate, and adaptation within the affected communities (Nikiforova et al., 2023). The social constructionist perspective holds that any notion of "value" is only meaningful in light of the practices, discourses, and institutional arrangements through which it is enacted and contested.

Recent empirical studies on the deployment of automated systems in public service delivery, education, and health care reinforce the argument that successful value alignment depends on proactive, iterative engagement with stakeholders, and not on the one-off elicitation of stated preferences (Martínez-Maldonado, 2023). These findings indicate that community norms around fairness, transparency, and legitimacy are continuously co-constructed through collective practice and that automated decision systems must be capable of adapting to the evolving moral landscape of their context of use.

This dynamic, participatory process is especially crucial in pluralistic societies where values are often contested and subject to negotiation. As such, the research consensus now advocates for system designs that enable contestability, feedback, and revision, rather than merely optimizing for initial survey-derived utility functions.

Current theoretical work argues that value alignment cannot succeed if it is conceived as a technical problem of maximizing coherence with a fixed set of psychological or behavioral markers. Robbins (2024) demonstrates that attempts to define meaningful human control or value alignment in narrow, individualistic terms invariably overlook the distributed nature of norm formation and the context-dependence of moral evaluation. The consequence is a profound risk of what sociologists term "moral crumple zones," in which responsibility is assigned to individuals without the institutional scaffolding necessary for genuine ethical agency. In this light, value alignment must be reframed as a feature of social practices subject to negotiation, contestation, and evolution rather than as a static mapping from inner states to algorithmic outputs.

Research on hybrid intelligence and human-centered learning analytics further corroborates that values are enacted and transformed through joint human–machine interaction and participatory sense-making. Järvelä et al. (2025) argue that the most promising advances in responsible automation occur when systems are designed not to mimic or anticipate fixed preferences but to support reflective processes that help communities articulate, test, and revise their values in response to new possibilities and challenges. This approach recognizes that "alignment" is less about the convergence on a single, unchanging set of goals and more about cultivating the institutional and procedural capacities for collective adaptation and ethical learning over time.

The social constructionist approach to value alignment demands a new orientation in both research and policy, one that privileges ongoing community engagement, transparency, and institutional reflexivity over mere technical precision. Nikiforova et al. (2023) point to the dangers of automating public services without adequate participatory mechanisms, noting that the legitimacy and sustainability of such systems depend on their ability to remain responsive to the lived experiences and moral expectations of their users. Only by embedding value alignment within a dynamic framework of social negotiation and practice can automated systems remain attuned to the diversity and evolution of human values in contemporary societies.

This reconceptualization of value alignment as a social and iterative process has important ramifications for the design and governance of automated systems. It calls for the institutionalization of practices such as citizen assemblies, participatory design workshops, and community oversight panels that allow affected groups to articulate their priorities, contest decisions, and negotiate trade-offs in real time (Martínez-Maldonado, 2023; Nikiforova et al., 2023). Such mechanisms enable ongoing recalibration of system objectives and metrics, ensuring that automated systems remain sensitive to evolving expectations and social learning. The role of designers, engineers, and policymakers is therefore transformed: rather than acting as neutral technicians, they become facilitators of dialogue, translators of community insight, and stewards of value pluralism. In turn, systems that incorporate these practices are better equipped to navigate value conflicts, address disparities in power, and adapt to new ethical challenges as they arise.

A practice-based approach to value alignment allows the creation of more resilient and trustworthy technology ecosystems. By grounding value definition and implementation in actual community engagement and public reasoning, these frameworks help to build legitimacy and shared ownership over the direction of technological change (Robbins, 2024; Järvelä et al., 2025). Trust is sustained not by opaque claims of "alignment" but by transparency about how values are defined, how competing interests are balanced, and how dissent is addressed within institutional processes. Empirical studies show that users are more likely to accept and benefit from automated systems when they perceive a genuine capacity for feedback, correction, and ethical negotiation, features that cannot be engineered from above but must be cultivated through lived practice and institutional reflexivity. Sustainable value alignment is less a technical achievement than a socio-political accomplishment.

Finally, the social constructionist paradigm underscores the urgent need for interdisciplinary collaboration in both research and policymaking. Ethicists, social scientists, legal scholars, technologists, and community advocates must work together to devise flexible frameworks and methodological tools for surfacing, debating, and revising value priorities (Martínez-Maldonado, 2023; Nikiforova et al., 2023). This includes developing new standards for participatory assessment, conflict resolution, and collective learning, as well as investing in capacity-building to empower marginalized communities in shaping technological futures. As algorithmic and automated systems continue to shape the fabric of social life, only a socially constructed, practice-based approach to value alignment can ensure that these technologies serve the public good by remaining open, corrigible, and responsive to the needs and aspirations of the communities they are meant to serve.

10.3. Building Systems Around Practices, Not Psychology

The inadequacy of psychological modeling as the cornerstone for the ethical design of automated systems has become increasingly clear in the last several years as research exposes the limitations of attempts to "align" complex sociotechnical infrastructures with isolated preferences or inner mental states. Engineers and ethicists have long sought to elicit, encode, or infer "user preferences," but the failure of these methods in diverse application domains ranging from autonomous vehicles to algorithmic governance suggests a foundational misapprehension of the contexts in which meaning, responsibility, and legitimacy arise (Robbins, 2023). Recent scholarship increasingly insists that ethical system design must be oriented not to the presumed contents of individual psychology but to the public, iterative, and practice-based patterns through which values, competence, and agency are realized and revised (de Sio et al., 2023).

Hybrid intelligence research exemplifies this paradigm shift by demonstrating that adaptive, trustworthy, and accountable systems emerge most robustly through iterative co-design with stakeholders, practitioners, and communities (Merchán-Cruz et al., 2025). Such co-design processes move beyond the capture of abstract psychological preferences and instead engage directly with the lived realities, tacit expertise, and institutional routines that characterize complex practices. Martínez-Maldonado (2023) notes that effective learning analytics in educational technology depend less on behavioral prediction and more on sustained collaboration between system designers and users to refine and revise the affordances of the system in light of emerging challenges and evolving community goals. Evidence from empirical studies of human-automation interaction in high-consequence domains such as aviation and clinical medicine also reveals a recurring danger. When psychological modeling dominates, humans are often relegated to marginal or supervisory roles that foster both skill atrophy and a sense of "responsibility without power" (Holford, 2022). The phenomenon of the "moral crumple zone" arises precisely where humans are expected to intervene effectively without the continuous engagement or practice required to maintain situational awareness and skill (Santoni de Sio & Van den Hoven,

2018). In contrast, systems oriented around practices foster the ongoing cultivation of expertise, flexibility, and improvisational judgment.

A growing body of work on "meaningful human control" also demonstrates the limitations of control conceived solely as psychological awareness or the technical ability to override system decisions. Robbins (2023) and Veluwenkamp (2022) argue that control only becomes meaningful when humans are embedded in the flow of practice, when their situated reasons, collective routines, and institutional responsibilities shape the trajectories of system action. Engineering efforts must be guided by ethnographic, organizational, and practice-theoretic research to discern where, how, and with whom agency and accountability are actually enacted. The importance of building around practices is further illustrated by current research on human-centered AI and collaborative automation. The Dagstuhl Perspectives Workshop (2022) reports that effective "human-in-the-loop" design is possible only when technical teams develop a granular understanding of user workflows, communication protocols, and the dynamic division of labor in real-world contexts (Mackay, Shawe-Taylor, & van Harmelen, 2023). Merely appending psychological checkboxes or override buttons fails to create genuine opportunity for influence, especially when organizational culture, legal standards, and collective practices are neglected.

Innovative research in public sector automation highlights the dangers of automating services based on abstracted "user journeys" or supposed preference models without regard to the complex, historically contingent practices of public administration. Nikiforova et al. (2023) show that proactive and personalized public services can generate new forms of exclusion, opacity, and contestation if they are not subject to iterative engagement with the communities they affect and the frontline workers who implement them. Their research suggests that the legitimacy and sustainability of automated systems depend on the institutionalization of participatory processes for debate, adaptation, and collective problem-solving. Crucially, practice-based design does not entail abandoning empirical rigor or technical sophistication; it calls for multidisciplinary engagement integrating insights from social science, law, organizational studies, and cognitive ergonomics to build systems that are intelligible and actionable in context. Calvert et al. (2020) operationalize meaningful human control in the domain of automated driving systems through a framework that emphasizes traceability, accountability chains, and the mapping of design decisions to real-world practices of driver training, licensing, and oversight.

This orientation is equally vital in new domains such as learning analytics and educational technology. Martínez-Maldonado (2023) emphasizes that representative participation, the balancing of stakeholder input with technological innovation, and attention to power dynamics are essential if learning analytics are to promote agency, safety, and trust. These are outcomes that cannot be derived from models of individual cognition alone. The literature in hybrid intelligence further supports the view that co-evolution and mutual learning between humans and intelligent systems are only possible when technology is embedded in the collaborative, regulated, and adaptive processes that define authentic practice (Krinkin & Shichkina, 2022; Krinkin, Shichkina, & Ignatyev, 2023).

Studies of the lived experience of system users such as Tesla's "Full Self-Driving" Beta drivers reveal that user perceptions of trust, safety, and moral legitimacy are closely tied to the alignment between system behavior and the practices, expectations, and reasons that are meaningful in context. Suryana et al. (2024) report that breakdowns in this alignment, especially in morally or physically hazardous situations, erode trust, highlighting the limits of psychological control in the absence of embedded practice. The shift to practice-based design carries implications for legal theory and public accountability as well. Wagner (2019) and Parmer (2024) argue that binary patterns of liability and achievementist models of meaningful work are increasingly inadequate in automated environments. The "practice view" instead foregrounds open-ended, collective, and creative processes through which responsibility and meaning are negotiated and maintained. Law and policy must adapt by institutionalizing structures for contestation, transparency, and the ongoing re-evaluation of system purpose. Lastly, the most promising directions in the research literature call for ethical, legal, and technical systems that remain corrigible and open to critical interrogation and modification by practitioners and stakeholders in light of new information, shifting community norms, and unforeseen consequences (Van den Bosch et al., 2025). Practice-based design is, in this sense, both a pragmatic and a normative imperative. It is the only viable route to systems that are not just operationally effective but also ethically, institutionally, and democratically legitimate in the pluralistic societies of today.

As this research trajectory matures, it becomes evident that embedding practice-based design principles throughout the system lifecycle creates the conditions for sustained adaptability, fairness, and public legitimacy. When design processes systematically include feedback from diverse practitioners and affected communities, automated systems can evolve alongside changing values, regulatory environments, and social expectations (Nikiforova et al., 2023; Martínez-Maldonado, 2023). This iterative, dialogic orientation helps identify blind spots, unanticipated consequences, and new forms of risk or exclusion early in development, fostering a culture of anticipatory governance rather than reactive crisis management. Practice-based approaches enhance resilience in the face of system failures, enabling more effective and context-sensitive responses when breakdowns or ethical dilemmas arise. They support the cultivation of organizational learning, distributed expertise, and continuous improvement, attributes that are indispensable as technologies become more complex and their impacts more far-reaching (Krinkin & Shichkina, 2022). By privileging lived experience and institutional participation over the static abstraction of preferences, these frameworks make possible an ongoing alignment between automated systems and the plural, evolving needs of society. In this way, building around practices not only fulfills technical requirements but also anchors automation in the open-ended, democratic negotiation of meaning, value, and legitimacy.

This shift from psychology to practice is not merely a different method for achieving value alignment; it inaugurates a new and more ambitious goal for the human-AI relationship. Instead of viewing AI as a tool to be controlled or a mind to be simulated, the practice-based paradigm positions it as a potential collaborator in the expansion of collective intelligence. When systems are designed to participate in our shared routines of inquiry, deliberation, and creation, they do more than automate tasks. They become part of the dynamic feedback loops through which our practices themselves evolve. An AI integrated into a scientific research practice does not just analyze data; it can surface novel hypotheses and reveal hidden biases in human interpretation. An AI in a legal practice does not just draft documents; it can highlight inconsistencies and foster more equitable application of rules. This creates the possibility of a truly symbiotic relationship where human judgment and machine processing co-evolve, augmenting our collective capacity for complex problem-solving. In this vision, ethical AI is not about constraining machines to fit a static model of human values, but about designing them to participate in the open-ended, creative, and self-correcting practices through which human flourishing is achieved.

10.4. The Wittgensteinian Approach to AI Ethics

A Wittgensteinian approach to AI ethics fundamentally reorients the discourse on value, agency, and responsibility by locating meaning not in internal psychological states but in the public practices through which rules, norms, and forms of life are negotiated and sustained. This orientation resists the reduction of ethics to the introspective intentions of designers, users, or regulators, and instead frames legitimacy as a function of how systems are embedded in collective routines and institutional practices (Robbins, 2023). Recent research has operationalized these insights by foregrounding the critical role of "meaningful human control," understood as both the ability to track the practical reasons relevant to system use and to trace the outcomes of automated actions back to specific agents or institutions (de Sio et al., 2023). In practical terms, this entails a shift from psychological modeling or predictive analytics to the construction of socio-technical infrastructures that enable communities to interpret, contest, and revise the standards by which automation is governed. Suryana et al. (2024) demonstrate that perceptions of trust and safety in semi-autonomous driving systems are tied not to user beliefs or affective states but to the responsiveness of the system to shared norms and expectations in contextually specific situations. These findings indicate that the legitimacy of automated action is achieved not through internal states but through public engagement with (and accountability to) the norms of the community.

A growing body of empirical and conceptual research further illustrates how Wittgensteinian principles are now shaping digital governance frameworks. Van den Bosch et al. (2025) provide a nuanced measurement of "meaningful human control" by distinguishing among subjective, normative, and moral control in human–machine teaming, demonstrating that transparency—understood as the public contestability of the practice itself—and participatory engagement are vital for ethical legitimacy. Legitimacy is conferred not by a transparent view into the system's inner workings but by the transparency of the social and institutional processes governing its use and correction. The framework developed in their pandemic triage study reveals that engagement and control are maximized when the design foregrounds negotiation and collective reasoning, rather than prescriptive rules or unreflective automation. In public sector applications, Nikiforova et al. (2023) caution that proactive, data-driven services risk alienating communities unless opportunities for ongoing contestation and adaptation are institutionalized. Their findings reinforce the Wittgensteinian imperative that ethical standards are only meaningful when they remain corrigible and open to reinterpretation in light of lived experience.

This rejection of fixed, absolute meanings in favor of dialogic, evolving rule application is increasingly seen as essential to addressing both the "responsibility gap" and the risks of moral ossification in automated systems. Santoni de Sio and Mecacci (2021) argue that value alignment cannot be accomplished through the static encoding of universal values; instead, it must arise from continuous engagement with plural and sometimes conflicting forms of life. This practice-theoretic view is echoed by Cavalcante Siebert et al. (2023), who advocate for "actionable properties" in system development that enable explicit, context-specific negotiation of norms and responsibilities. As systems become increasingly entangled with legal, medical, and educational institutions, only those architectures that sustain participation, correction, and contestation will be ethically resilient.

Recent advances in the social construction of responsibility in AI and automated systems further extend Wittgenstein's legacy by insisting that agency and normativity are produced and maintained through the interplay of technical affordances and institutional practices. Parmer (2024) shows that achievementist models, focused on individual psychological success, fail to explain why meaningful work and agency persist in environments of extensive automation. Instead, meaningfulness is found in open-ended practices where roles, rules, and standards are collectively renegotiated in response to changing circumstances. This has direct implications for system design: Automated decisions should be justified not merely by reference to abstract policy or algorithmic outputs but through public reason-giving, institutional dialogue, and mechanisms for appeal or redress. Robbins (2024) likewise argues that only by enabling users to contest, question, and reframe the purposes of systems do we achieve genuine ethical legitimacy.

Finally, the most forward-looking research underscores that the Wittgensteinian paradigm is not simply an academic critique but a practical blueprint for ethical governance in the age of automation. The call for corrigibility, participatory design, and the iterative revision of norms is now evident in regulatory proposals such as the EU AI Act, as well as in emerging standards for explainability and transparency in system development. Cavalcante Siebert et al. (2023) contend that "actionable properties" for meaningful human control are features that enable procedural transparency. This requires systems to be designed not just for compliance or for providing a transparent audit of their internal states, but for facilitating ongoing negotiation, reflection, and adaptation within the social practices that govern their use. The legitimacy and justice of automated systems must be measured by their capacity to remain open to revision, situated in the lived practices of diverse communities, and accountable to the standards those communities negotiate together, a fundamentally Wittgensteinian vision for the future of AI ethics.

In practice, this Wittgensteinian vision compels both technologists and regulators to shift from static compliance regimes to dialogical, participatory processes that treat norms as evolving, collectively maintained achievements. This approach requires the continuous creation of forums where stakeholders can collaboratively interpret, critique, and revise the principles guiding system development and deployment (Van den Bosch et al., 2025; Nikiforova et al., 2023). Such mechanisms make possible not only the correction of specific failures but also the recalibration of institutional values and objectives in response to social change, technological innovation, or new forms of risk. The Wittgensteinian paradigm empowers communities to "own" the rules governing their technological environments, fostering democratic legitimacy, trust, and a sense of shared stewardship over the purposes and constraints of automated systems. The result is an ethics of practice that is dynamic, context-sensitive, and responsive to the plural and shifting needs of the societies in which AI operates.

The integration of Wittgensteinian principles into AI ethics offers a roadmap for the construction of resilient, accountable, and socially embedded systems. Rather than aiming for perfect alignment with any predetermined value set, the most successful systems are those that can accommodate dissent, foster debate, and adapt to the lived complexity of real-world environments (Santoni de Sio & Mecacci, 2021; Cavalcante Siebert et al., 2023). By embedding contestability and corrigibility into the design of algorithmic systems, engineers and institutions create opportunities for ongoing reflection, community learning, and substantive public engagement. This ethos of continuous negotiation transforms the challenge of AI ethics from one of static rule enforcement to a vibrant, participatory endeavor in which meaning, agency, and legitimacy are enacted through ongoing collective practice. The Wittgensteinian approach not only clarifies how systems can be ethically governed but also models how democratic societies can flourish in an age of technological transformation.

The analysis undertaken in this chapter reveals that the ethical legitimacy and social sustainability of automated systems cannot be reduced to narrow conceptions of "meaningful human control" predicated on technical interventions or psychological modeling. Rather, the latest research compels a reorientation toward frameworks grounded in "meaningful human practice," whereby value alignment and responsible agency are understood as ongoing achievements of context-sensitive, participatory engagement. Empirical studies demonstrate that community norms, institutional routines, and dialogic negotiation form the foundation for genuine ethical oversight, enabling systems to remain corrigible, adaptive, and responsive to the lived realities of diverse stakeholders. Efforts that privilege fixed preference elicitation or surface-level override mechanisms risk entrenching responsibility gaps, eroding trust, and undermining both human agency and public legitimacy. In contrast, design principles inspired by Wittgensteinian philosophy emphasizing rule-following, context, and the open-ended evolution of practices provide the scaffolding for systems that support transparent, accountable, and democratic participation.

In reflecting on these considerations, this chapter affirms that the future of ethical system design depends on embracing the complexities of social construction, institutional reflexivity, and the pluralism of community values. Automated systems must not be conceived as closed solutions, but as sites of ongoing contestation and co-creation subject to revision as norms, risks, and collective aspirations evolve. The challenge is not merely technical, but deeply philosophical and practical, to build infrastructures that foster the capacity for collective learning, contestability, and mutual recognition. By embedding ethical deliberation within the fabric of practice, and by foregrounding transparency, stakeholder engagement, and public accountability, society can move beyond the illusion of isolated control toward the realization of responsible, sustainable, and just technological agency in the age of automation.

References

Calvert, S. C., Heikoop, D. D., Mecacci, G., & Van Arem, B. (2020). A human centric framework for the analysis of automated driving systems based on meaningful human control. *Theoretical issues in ergonomics science*, *21*(4), 478-506.

Cavalcante Siebert, L., Lupetti, M. L., Aizenberg, E., Beckers, N., Zgonnikov, A., Veluwenkamp, H., & Lagendijk, R. L. (2023). Meaningful human control: actionable properties for AI system development. *AI and Ethics*, *3*(1), 241-255.

Davidovic, J. (2023). On the purpose of meaningful human control of AI. *Frontiers in big data*, *5*, 1017677.

de Sio, F. S., Mecacci, G., Calvert, S., Heikoop, D., Hagenzieker, M., & van Arem, B. (2023). Realising meaningful human control over automated driving systems: a multidisciplinary approach. *Minds and machines*, *33*(4), 587-611.

Holford, W. D. (2022). An ethical inquiry of the effect of cockpit automation on the responsibilities of airline pilots: Dissonance or meaningful control?. *Journal of Business Ethics*, *176*(1), 141-157.

Järvelä, S., Zhao, G., Nguyen, A., & Chen, H. (2025). Hybrid intelligence: Human–AI coevolution and learning. *British Journal of Educational Technology*, *56*(2), 455-468.

Krinkin, K., & Shichkina, Y. (2022, August). Cognitive architecture for co-evolutionary hybrid intelligence. In *International Conference on Artificial General Intelligence* (pp. 293-303). Cham: Springer International Publishing.

Krinkin, K., Shichkina, Y., & Ignatyev, A. (2023). Co-evolutionary hybrid intelligence is a key concept for the world intellectualization. *Kybernetes*, *52*(9), 2907-2923.

Martinez-Maldonado, R. (2023). Human-centred learning analytics: Four challenges in realising the potential. *Learning Letters*, *1*, 6-6.

Mackay, W. E., Shawe-Taylor, J., & van Harmelen, F. (2023). *Human-Centered Artificial Intelligence* (Doctoral dissertation, Dagstuhl Reports, Vol. 12, Issue 6).

Merchán-Cruz, E. A., Gabelaia, I., Savrasovs, M., Hansen, M. F., Soe, S., Rodriguez-Cañizo, R. G., & Aragón-Camarasa, G. (2025). Trust by Design: An Ethical Framework for Collaborative Intelligence Systems in Industry 5.0. *Electronics*, *14*(10), 1952.

Nikiforova, A., Bharosa, N., Draheim, D., & Taveter, K. (2023). PPPS'2023-Proactive and Personalised Public Services: Searching for Meaningful Human Control in Algorithmic Government. In *CEUR workshop proceedings*.

Parmer, W. J. (2024). Meaningful work and achievement in increasingly automated workplaces. *The Journal of Ethics*, *28*(3), 527-551.

Robbins, S. (2024). The many meanings of meaningful human control. *AI and Ethics*, *4*(4), 1377-1388.

Santoni de Sio, F., & Mecacci, G. (2021). Four responsibility gaps with artificial intelligence: Why they matter and how to address them. *Philosophy & technology*, *34*(4), 1057-1084.

Santoni de Sio, F., & Van den Hoven, J. (2018). Meaningful human control over autonomous systems: A philosophical account. *Frontiers in Robotics and AI*, *5*, 323836.

Suryana, L. E., Nordhoff, S., Calvert, S. C., Zgonnikov, A., & Van Arem, B. (2024, June). A meaningful human control perspective on user perception of partially automated driving systems: a case study of Tesla users. In *2024 IEEE intelligent vehicles symposium (IV)* (pp. 409-416). IEEE.

Van den Bosch, K., Van Diggelen, J., Verdult, S., Haije, T., & Van der Waa, J. (2025). Measuring meaningful human control in human–AI teaming: effects of team design in AI-assisted pandemic triage. *AI and Ethics*, *5*(3), 3329-3353.

Veluwenkamp, H. (2022). Reasons for meaningful human control. *Ethics and Information Technology*, *24*(4), 51.

Wagner, B. (2019). Liable, but not in control? Ensuring meaningful human agency in automated decision-making systems. *Policy & Internet*, *11*(1), 104-122.

Chapter 11

The Broader Legal Transformation

Abstract

This chapter offers a critical examination of the transformative pressures reshaping legal principles and doctrines in light of the waning authority of mental-state-centric frameworks for agency and responsibility. Rather than anchoring liability, rights, and justice in inaccessible inner states, the analysis advances a practice-based, post-Cartesian jurisprudence that grounds legal standing, protection, and process in public, corrigible practices and institutional participation. The chapter explores the evolution of foundational constitutional guarantees, including due process and equal protection, illustrating how these can be reconceived to prioritize procedural transparency, collective validation, and pluralistic fairness. Drawing on instructive precedents from the "accidental wisdom" of copyright law, as well as contemporary developments in liability and administrative adjudication, the discussion demonstrates how law can evolve organically toward more adaptive and socially responsive models of legitimacy. Case studies and policy recommendations are interwoven to highlight mechanisms for embedding contestability, deliberative engagement, and forward-looking equity within pluralistic societies. Potential challenges ranging from fears of moral relativism to institutional inertia are addressed through reference to contemporary philosophy of law, theories of social practice, and empirical research on institutional reform. The chapter ultimately envisions a legal order attuned to the realities of distributed, determined agency and communal flourishing, offering a framework for the legitimate allocation of rights and responsibilities in an age of algorithmic governance and social complexity.

11.1. Constitutional Principles Without Mental States

The gradual displacement of mental-state-centric frameworks in law has catalyzed a profound reconsideration of constitutional principles, compelling legal theorists and courts to reconstruct guarantees such as due process and equal protection on a foundation that is public, procedural, and practice-based, rather than anchored in the opaque domain of private intention. Historically, constitutional law has relied heavily on the presumption that mental states such as intent, motive, and animus are essential to the legitimate attribution of responsibility, culpability, and legal protection. This reliance is evident in doctrines such as *mens rea* in criminal law, specific intent in equal protection jurisprudence, and the "bad faith" standard in due process adjudication (LaFave, 1986). Yet, this metaphysical orientation has long faced critique from philosophers (such as Wittgenstein) who argue that meaning and agency are constituted not by inaccessible inner states but by participation in shared forms of life and observable practices. More recent legal theorists, drawing from pragmatist and practice-theoretic traditions, have underscored that public criteria, not private mental content, are necessary for legitimate legal reasoning and the avoidance of arbitrary or discriminatory decision-making (Bersoff, 1992; Golding, 1963; Kane et al., 2021). This critique has gained new force in the context of algorithmic governance and distributed agency, where mental-state attributions are not only epistemically dubious but practically infeasible.

Contemporary research illustrates that constitutional protections grounded in mental states (such as the requirement to prove discriminatory intent in equal protection cases) have frequently failed to secure justice for marginalized groups, precisely because such standards place an insurmountable burden on claimants to demonstrate what cannot be publicly accessed (Bagenstos, 2009). This problem is acute in areas such as policing, housing, and employment discrimination, where formal neutrality in policy masks patterns of exclusion and harm that emerge in practice (Alexander, 2015). Legal scholars now advocate for a transition to impact-based and proceduralist standards, where the focus is on patterns, practices, and outcomes rather than the unverifiable mental states of decision-makers (Siegel, 2013). The evolution of disparate impact doctrine in antidiscrimination law and the emergence of process-based protections in administrative law reflect this practice-oriented turn.

The practice-based reimagining of constitutional guarantees is also evident in contemporary debates over due process, where scholars contend that procedural fairness and transparent participation offer a more justifiable foundation for legitimacy than subjective assessments of intent or animus (Farina, 1990; Hill, 2021). Legal philosophers drawing on Wittgensteinian and pragmatist traditions emphasize that the intelligibility and legitimacy of legal procedures depend on public regularities, visible processes for notice, hearing, and the opportunity to contest or appeal decisions, rather than assumptions about what decision-makers "really" intended (Tsai, 2021). This orientation is increasingly salient as courts confront the rise of automated and algorithmic decision-making systems, where human intention is dispersed, collective, or inscrutable, yet the need for fairness, contestability, and transparency remains acute. Here, transparency must be understood procedurally. The goal is not to make the algorithm's 'reasoning' transparent in a psychological sense, but to make the procedures for its oversight, auditing, and appeal transparent to the public it affects.

Legal innovation inspired by practice-based theory is not merely theoretical; it is reflected in emerging case law and statutory reforms that prioritize transparency, auditable procedures, and robust avenues for stakeholder participation over inquiries into personal motivation. For instance, the evolution of administrative due process in the United States, as seen in decisions addressing "black box" algorithms, demonstrates a growing judicial recognition that legitimacy requires visible, challengeable processes rather than the assurance of benign intent (Crawford, 2021). The same trend is visible internationally, with the European Union's General Data Protection Regulation (GDPR) embedding rights to explanation and contestation, echoing a shift from subjective justification to procedural regularity and participatory rights (Veale, Matus, & Gorwa, 2023). This global movement underscores the viability and necessity of reconfiguring constitutional principles for a world where agency and accountability are increasingly collective, distributed, and mediated by technological systems.

At the conceptual core of this transformation is the insight implied by Wittgenstein and contemporary practice theory that public criteria for legal reasoning, fairness, and responsibility must be accessible, contestable, and responsive to evolving social practice. This means that legal systems must build legitimacy by cultivating forms of life where procedures, outcomes, and interpretations are subject to collective scrutiny, correction, and ongoing negotiation. In moving beyond the metaphysics of mental states, constitutional law is positioned to better safeguard pluralism, inclusion, and democratic accountability. The promise of this transition is a legal order that secures rights, allocates responsibilities, and promotes justice by reference to the evolving, corrigible practices of the communities it serves rather than by speculation about what lies hidden in the minds of officials or litigants.

This practice-based reorientation also aligns constitutional law with broader shifts in administrative, regulatory, and technological governance. As public institutions increasingly rely on algorithmic and data-driven processes, procedural safeguards, such as clear criteria for decision-making, timely notice, and transparent rationales, offer a bulwark against both arbitrariness and opacity (Crawford, 2021; Veale, Matus, & Gorwa, 2023). The capacity for affected individuals and groups to contest outcomes, demand explanations, and participate in review processes is now widely regarded as essential for both legitimacy and accountability in digital and pluralistic societies. These developments underscore that legitimacy is a function of public trust, which can only be sustained when legal standards and processes are open to challenge, correction, and inclusive participation. The future of constitutionalism, therefore, depends less on discerning private motivations and more on sustaining visible, contestable, and adaptive practices of legal reasoning and review.

The turn toward public, procedural, and practice-based standards reinvigorates the democratic purpose of constitutional law. Rather than enshrining static doctrines or insulating decision-makers behind claims of intent, practice-based approaches create space for law to evolve in tandem with shifting community norms, new technologies, and the ongoing negotiation of societal values. They empower courts and legislatures to focus on the consequences and procedural regularity of state action, facilitating a more dynamic and equitable allocation of rights and remedies (Siegel, 2013; Alexander, 2015). By foregrounding the open-ended, corrigible nature of public reasoning, constitutional law not only advances justice but also nurtures the collective capacity for democratic self-correction and renewal. This transformation signals a move beyond the metaphysical opacity of mental states to a jurisprudence grounded in the open, lived practices that make the rule of law meaningful and legitimate.

11.2. Equal Protection in a Post-Libertarian World

As constitutional law pivots from metaphysical notions of free will and intention to public, practice-based standards, the principle of equal protection must also be reinterpreted for an era in which agency, harm, and justice are determined through collective social practices rather than atomistic or "libertarian" conceptions of self-authorship. Historically, the doctrine of equal protection in both American and comparative constitutional law has relied upon assumptions of individual choice and intentionality, often demanding proof of discriminatory motive or conscious animus to trigger heightened judicial scrutiny (Siegel, 2013). This libertarian framework has been criticized for failing to address the systemic and structural forms of inequality that persist in the absence of explicit, individualized intent. Alexander (2015) documents how formal equality doctrines, when coupled with colorblind ideology, allow for profound racial and socioeconomic stratification by focusing legal inquiry on subjective intent rather than objective social outcomes. In this respect, the practice-based turn challenges courts and lawmakers to interrogate patterns, practices, and institutional routines that generate disparate impacts, even when the conscious motivations of individual actors remain inscrutable.

Recent legal scholarship and empirical research underscore the limitations of requiring plaintiffs to prove intent and instead highlight the efficacy of impact-based and structural approaches to equality. Bagenstos (2009) and Act (1964) advocate for models of antidiscrimination law that foreground the social practices and organizational norms through which inequality is produced and perpetuated. The adoption of disparate impact standards in areas like fair housing, employment, and voting rights reflects this evolution, enabling courts to address inequality as a feature of practices and institutionalized policies rather than as a function of private intent. Siegel (2013) demonstrates that such approaches are not only more attuned to the realities of systemic discrimination but also enhance legitimacy and democratic accountability by shifting the burden of explanation to policymakers and institutions.

The post-libertarian reconfiguration of equal protection is also evident in contemporary debates over algorithmic bias and the design of automated decision-making systems. Scholars have shown that, absent explicit discriminatory intent, algorithmic models can nevertheless encode and perpetuate existing patterns of exclusion through data selection, model construction, and institutional deployment (Crawford, 2021). This reality has propelled the adoption of practice-based standards such as auditing, transparency requirements, and the right to contest or explain outcomes, measures which address the relational and procedural foundations of equality. Veale, Matus, and Gorwa (2023) argue that such process-oriented reforms align equal protection doctrine with the collective, public nature of modern harms, enabling law to grapple with distributed and emergent forms of injustice.

Practice-based equal protection also demands a re-examination of judicial remedies and institutional design. Rather than treating equality as a negative liberty to be protected solely against intentional interference, the new paradigm emphasizes proactive monitoring, iterative policy revision, and stakeholder engagement as means of promoting substantive fairness (De Waal,

2021). This includes the establishment of independent review boards, the deployment of participatory processes for identifying and correcting inequities, and the development of flexible standards that can accommodate changing social practices. As Rangoni (2022) argues, equal protection in a post-libertarian world is realized through the collective maintenance of just practices, not through the metaphysical assignment of blame or the search for hidden motives.

The broader transformation of equal protection doctrine in the post-libertarian context reflects a pragmatic commitment to public reason, mutual recognition, and ongoing accountability. Through grounding constitutional equality in the practices, procedures, and institutional routines of public life, law becomes more responsive to the complex realities of systemic injustice, technological mediation, and social pluralism. This approach fosters an ethos of shared responsibility, where equality is not a passive entitlement but an active, collective achievement continually subject to critique, revision, and communal deliberation (Siegel, 2013). As the practice-based paradigm matures, it promises to make equal protection not only more effective but also more just, transparent, and democratically legitimate in the post-libertarian legal order.

The practice-based approach to equal protection also enhances the responsiveness of law to the lived realities of diverse communities. By centering legal standards on patterns of harm, institutional conduct, and group-level outcomes, courts and policymakers can better identify and address both overt and subtle forms of discrimination (Crawford, 2021; Veale, Matus, & Gorwa, 2023). This orientation enables more nuanced remedies such as structural injunctions, consent decrees, and community oversight boards that move beyond symbolic declarations of equality to achieve measurable improvements in access, participation, and redress. Embedding processes of ongoing evaluation and stakeholder consultation within legal frameworks ensures that evolving forms of bias, whether algorithmic or organizational, are continually surfaced and corrected. In this way, equal protection becomes an iterative and dialogic project, grounded in the continual renegotiation of fairness as social conditions change.

The move toward collective and procedural conceptions of equality also prompts a reimagining of the role of courts and legislatures. Rather than serving merely as arbiters of individual grievances, legal institutions increasingly function as facilitators of systemic reform and agents of democratic learning. Through impact litigation, regulatory innovation, and participatory policy design, courts and legislatures are able to set standards, disseminate best practices, and catalyze institutional transformation across sectors (De Waal, 2021; Rangoni, 2022). This broader institutional mission is especially crucial in the context of automated decision-making, where the sources and effects of inequality are often opaque, dynamic, and widely dispersed. The challenge is to build legal architectures that sustain collective vigilance, empower affected groups, and allocate responsibility for ongoing review and remediation, turning the promise of equal protection into a continuous social achievement.

The post-libertarian framework for equal protection, therefore, recognizes that the meaning and realization of equality must remain open to contestation, revision, and democratic renewal. Law cannot afford to treat equality as a static principle or a one-time accomplishment, but must institutionalize mechanisms for periodic review, critical feedback, and inclusive debate (Siegel, 2013). This ongoing openness to collective inquiry and reform is the best safeguard against both complacency and backlash, enabling societies to respond to new injustices and to evolving aspirations for justice. In this sense, the transformation of equal protection doctrine is not merely a technical or doctrinal shift; it is a deepening of democracy itself, a call to embrace equality as a practice of ongoing, pluralistic, and participatory self-governance.

11.3. Due Process and the Practice-Based Alternative

As the jurisprudence of due process adapts to the erosion of metaphysical notions of intent and psychological fairness, practice-based approaches have become central to the ongoing transformation of procedural justice in constitutional law. Traditionally, due process protections in constitutional frameworks, particularly in the United States, have been tethered to a set of assumptions about the subjective motivations and good faith of decision-makers, especially in adjudicatory and administrative settings (Foran, 2023). However, decades of critique have revealed that such reliance on private mental states often fails to secure justice, particularly for individuals and groups lacking institutional power. As Postema (2022) argues, the true core of due process lies not in the assurance of benevolent intentions but in the public visibility, contestability, and accountability of legal and administrative procedures. The practice-based model reimagines procedural justice as an ongoing public achievement, emphasizing mechanisms such as notice, hearing, reason-giving, and opportunities for correction rather than the metaphysical guarantee of internal fairness.

This transformation is especially salient in the governance of automated and algorithmic decision-making systems, where mental-state-based standards are not merely unworkable but conceptually incoherent. Scholars such as Crawford (2021) and Veale, Matus, and Gorwa (2023) have shown that legitimacy in digital and automated procedures can only be sustained by embedding procedural transparency, auditability, and robust appeal mechanisms into the infrastructure of administrative law. This form of transparency is not a quest to make the machine's "reasoning" fully legible (likely an impossible task) but to make the human-led governance structures around it visible, contestable, and accountable. This marks a decisive shift from models of individualized scrutiny where fairness is presumed from official intentions to models where fairness is the emergent property of open, corrigible practices accessible to all participants and stakeholders. Practice-oriented due process is also characterized by a commitment to continual revision, feedback, and public participation. Rather than securing justice through static procedures or formal compliance alone, the new paradigm insists that process legitimacy must be maintained through iterative stakeholder engagement, community oversight, and the regular updating of standards in response to changing conditions (Bottoms & Tankebe, 2012). This is visible in the growing judicial recognition that legitimacy in both criminal and civil contexts depends on procedures for meaningful challenge, the right to a reasoned decision, and the capacity to appeal or demand further justification when new evidence or arguments emerge.

A key example of this practice-based alternative is the evolution of "explainability" and "right to contest" provisions in modern administrative law, particularly in response to algorithmic governance. The European Union's GDPR and emerging legislative frameworks in the United States and elsewhere now enshrine rights to explanation, procedural review, and challenge, replacing faith in official good faith with public, contestable, and revisable standards (Balsamo, 2025). These mechanisms reflect the Wittgensteinian insight that the legitimacy of process arises from the visible regularities of shared practice, not from the unknowable inner workings of decision-makers. Finally, the normative thrust of the practice-based approach to due process lies in its commitment to pluralism, adaptability, and collective agency. Legal philosophers such as Siegel (2013) contend that procedural legitimacy and justice are best secured not through the metaphysical interrogation of intent, but by constructing forums for mutual recognition, dialogue, and revision. Practice-based due process, in this sense, is not a static achievement but a continuous, dynamic negotiation that invites participation and correction by all those subject to the power of law.

One of the central strengths of practice-based due process is its capacity to recognize and accommodate diversity in both individual circumstances and collective needs. Instead of relying on rigid procedural templates or abstract notions of fairness, the practice-based approach supports contextualized, case-specific solutions, allowing for procedural flexibility that honors the realities of those most affected by administrative and judicial decisions (Foran, 2023; Postema, 2022). This flexibility does not mean arbitrariness; it is bounded by public norms of transparency, contestability, and ongoing justification, ensuring that all parties have access to meaningful participation and redress. In settings ranging from social welfare administration to digital rights enforcement, such flexibility has proven essential for sustaining trust and legitimacy, especially as technological and social conditions evolve. The resulting model is one where justice is seen as an active process enacted, maintained, and renewed through the engagement of communities and institutions.

Another advantage of the practice-based model is its emphasis on organizational learning and institutional accountability. Mechanisms such as public hearings, stakeholder forums, and periodic reviews transform due process from a legalistic checklist into a living system for monitoring and improving decision-making (Bottoms & Tankebe, 2012). Feedback gathered through appeals, community oversight, and iterative assessment enables institutions to correct course, identify systemic issues, and refine both their rules and their practices. By embedding learning and adaptation into procedural structures, legal systems become better equipped to address unforeseen challenges, manage complexity, and resist ossification. Such processes are especially crucial in an era of algorithmic governance, where the sources of error and bias can be opaque, shifting, and resistant to one-time correction.

Crucially, the practice-based alternative enhances the ethical legitimacy of due process by foregrounding participation, contestation, and the right to be heard. Legitimacy, on this view, is not derived from the intentions of officials, but from the collective processes through which decisions are made, challenged, and re-examined (Siegel, 2013; Balsamo, 2025). This orientation fosters a culture of mutual respect and accountability, where affected individuals and communities are recognized as active partners in the administration of justice, not passive recipients of its outcomes. Moreover, public and stakeholder engagement generate new sources of information, diverse perspectives, and creative problem-solving that enrich both procedural and substantive justice. As a result, practice-based due process is inherently dynamic, capable of evolving alongside changing social expectations and technological innovation.

Practice-based due process reflects a philosophical commitment to pluralism and democratic self-government. By treating legal procedures as corrigible and open to revision, it institutionalizes humility and the willingness to learn from error, qualities that are essential for justice in complex, plural societies (Postema, 2022; Bottoms & Tankebe, 2012). The shift away from metaphysical guarantees of internal fairness and toward public practices of participation, reasoning, and correction aligns due process with the broader democratic project of collective self-rule. In this sense, the transformation of procedural justice is not merely a technical adaptation to the challenges of automation or bureaucracy; it is a moral and political achievement which makes legal systems more humane, equitable, and attuned to the aspirations of those they are meant to serve.

11.4. Learning from Copyright's Accidental Wisdom

The history of copyright doctrine offers an instructive example of how legal systems can, sometimes inadvertently, evolve away from individualist metaphysics and toward practice-based, pragmatic models of legitimacy, highlighting opportunities for other constitutional domains to adapt in the age of determined agency and collective authorship. Copyright law in its modern form originated with the Statute of Anne (1710), which enshrined the rights of authors but did so with only partial reference to personal intention or creative genius; instead, it foregrounded practical concerns about the encouragement of learning, the regulation of printing, and the broader public interest (Huang, 2009). Throughout the nineteenth and twentieth centuries, courts struggled to define originality and authorship, sometimes falling back on metaphors of individual creativity but more often settling disputes by examining observable practices: publication, attribution, commercial use, and the circulation of works within communities (Netanel & Nimmer, 2011). The emergence of collective, collaborative, and corporate authorship in the twentieth century further undermined the notion that copyright rests solely on personal, mental acts of creation (Al Harrasi & Al Subhi, 2024). Instead, legal legitimacy increasingly derived from demonstrable practices establishing who contributed, how decisions were made, and how the public accessed and understood the work.

Contemporary debates in copyright now revolve around the challenge of protecting creativity in a digital environment where agency is diffuse, automated, and often algorithmic. Scholars such as Samuelson (2021) and Ginsburg (2022) have documented how courts and lawmakers have responded to new technological realities not by reverting to metaphysical definitions of authorship, but by focusing on patterns of use, standards of attribution, and the evolving expectations of communities of practice. The accidental of the law wisdom lies in its gradual acceptance of collective and iterative creation, as well as its increasing reliance on procedural mechanisms that reinforce public, accessible standards rather than elusive intentions. On the other hand, and perhaps most strikingly, the rise of generative algorithms and collaborative digital production has brought copyright into closer alignment with the practice-based orientation advocated in this volume. Courts are now compelled to determine ownership and rights based on workflows, metadata, contractual routines, and industry norms rather than any supposed mental act of originality (Th, 2025). This process mirrors the shift in constitutional law away from individual intent and toward observable, contestable, and corrigible practices. All this highlights the capacity of legal regimes to adapt organically (and sometimes by necessity) to the complexity of modern agency and the collective construction of value.

The accidental wisdom of copyright further extends to its mechanisms for public engagement and contestation. Notice-and-takedown procedures, compulsory licensing, and collective management organizations function not as perfect instantiations of authorial rights, but as adaptive, negotiated solutions to practical problems of access, attribution, and fair use (Netanel, 2011; Singh & Tanwar, 2024). These procedures exemplify how law can build legitimacy by embedding transparency, stakeholder participation, and opportunities for ongoing revision, rather than by clinging to the metaphysics of creative intent. The evolution of copyright provides a living illustration of how legal order can move toward more pluralistic, practice-centered, and public-facing models of fairness and legitimacy. As constitutional law faces analogous challenges in the era of collective, automated, and distributed agency, the lessons of the accidental wisdom of copyright serve as a guide for embedding procedural regularity, transparency, and communal contestation at the heart of modern legal institutions. This is the productive form of transparency this book advocates: not the impossible disclosure of private intent or complete causal history, but the establishment of public, contestable, and adaptive procedures for assigning responsibility. By foregrounding the practices by which value, responsibility, and legitimacy are constructed, legal systems can remain both adaptive and just amid technological and social change.

This evolution in approach to legitimacy on the part of copyright highlights the profound benefits of focusing on practical mechanisms for accountability and adaptability. As legal regimes shift from metaphysical abstractions to observable practices, they become better equipped to accommodate new forms of agency and collective creativity that would otherwise be marginalized or misunderstood under more rigid, individualist frameworks (Al Harrasi & Al Subhi, 2024). The copyright experience shows that legitimacy is not achieved by defending doctrinal purity, but by cultivating structures for transparent attribution, participatory dispute resolution, and collective oversight. These structures, in turn, are resilient because they are continuously open to scrutiny and recalibration in response to new technologies, market realities, and social priorities. Such openness to institutional learning and revision has been central to copyright's adaptability and should be a guiding lesson for constitutional theory and legal design as they confront similarly disruptive changes.

The pragmatic success of these adaptive mechanisms also underscores the importance of institutional pluralism and stakeholder engagement for robust legal governance. The proliferation of industry standards, alternative dispute resolution panels, and cross-border licensing schemes demonstrates that diverse, overlapping forms of participation can complement formal legal rules and fill gaps that statutory or judicial solutions alone cannot address (Samuelson, 2021; Singh & Tanwar, 2024). In the constitutional context, this translates into a need for multilayered forums spanning courts, agencies, legislatures, and community organizations where competing values and practical interests are negotiated, harmonized, and periodically revised. These participatory spaces serve not only to resolve immediate disputes but also to foster a broader civic culture of accountability, innovation, and shared responsibility for the ongoing construction of legal meaning.

As such, this chapter has demonstrated that the displacement of mental-state-centric frameworks from constitutional law is not merely a theoretical exercise, but a necessary and pragmatic adaptation to the realities of contemporary agency, governance, and social complexity. The analysis reveals that as legal systems increasingly encounter distributed, collective, and technologically mediated forms of action, the metaphysical search for intention and individualized culpability becomes not only impractical but also unjust. Instead, legitimacy and fairness in constitutional doctrine now require public, procedural, and practice-based standards anchored in transparent, contestable, and corrigible social practices. This shift is most evident in the reorientation of equal protection and due process toward impact-based, structural, and participatory criteria, as well as in the emergence of procedural mechanisms that enable ongoing adaptation, accountability, and mutual recognition. The lessons drawn from the "accidental wisdom" of copyright further underscore the viability and normative power of legal orders that embed communal contestation, transparency, and institutional reflexivity at their core.

The practice-based turn in constitutional theory and doctrine offers a more pluralistic, adaptive, and democratic vision of justice capable of addressing the ethical and institutional challenges posed by automation, algorithmic decision-making, and communal authorship. Rather than clinging to the elusive metaphysics of mental states, law's future legitimacy lies in its capacity to construct and maintain processes that are visible, participatory, and responsive to the lived experiences and evolving aspirations of diverse communities. By foregrounding procedures over private intentions and by fostering collective engagement in the interpretation and application of legal standards, constitutional law can better realize the promise of equal protection, due process, and creative flourishing in an era defined by rapid social and technological transformation.

References

Act, C. R. (1964). Title VII of the Civil Rights Act of 1964. *Retrieved October*, *21*, 2005.

Alexander, M. (2015). Incarceration in the Age of Colorblindness. New York: The New Press, 2012. *Reason Papers*, *37*(2), 233-238.

Al Harrasi, N., & Al Subhi, N. (2024). Determinants of effective university–industry collaboration: an empirical study of Oman's Higher Education Institutions. *Cogent Education*, *11*(1), 2387951.

Bagenstos, S. R. (2009). *Law and the contradictions of the disability rights movement*. Yale University Press.

Balsamo, F. (2025). Leaving or changing religion in the European Union Law: The impact of the European Data Protection Regulation (GDPR). In *Human Dignity, Religion and the Law* (pp. 110-125). Routledge.

Bersoff, D. N. (1992). Judicial deference to nonlegal decisionmakers: Imposing simplistic solutions on problems of cognitive complexity in mental disability law. *SMUL Rev.*, *46*, 329.

Bottoms, A., & Tankebe, J. (2012). Beyond procedural justice: A dialogic approach to legitimacy in criminal justice. *J. Crim. l. & Criminology*, *102*, 119.

Crawford, K. (2021). *The atlas of AI: Power, politics, and the planetary costs of artificial intelligence*. Yale University Press.

De Waal, C. (2021). *Introducing pragmatism: a tool for rethinking philosophy*. Routledge.

Farina, C. R. (1990). Conceiving due process. *Yale JL & Feminism*, *3*, 189.

Foran, M. (2023). Rights, common good, and the separation of powers. *The Modern Law Review*, *86*(3), 599-628.

Ginsburg, J. C. (2022). Fifty Years of US Copyright: Toward a Law of Authors' Rights?. *AIPLA QJ*, *50*, 635.

Golding, M. P. (1963). Principled decision-making and the supreme court. *Columbia Law Review*, *63*(1), 35-58.

Hill, S. A. I. (2021). Bail reform and the (false) racial promise of algorithmic risk assessment. *UCLA L. Rev.*, *68*, 910.

Huang, H. (2009). On public domain in copyright law. *Frontiers of Law in China*, *4*(2), 178-195.

Kane, N. B., Keene, A. R., Owen, G. S., & Kim, S. Y. (2021). Applying decision-making capacity criteria in practice: A content analysis of court judgments. *PLoS One*, *16*(2), e0246521.

LaFave, W. R. (1986). Substantive criminal law.

Netanel, N. W., & Nimmer, D. (2011). Is Copyright Property?--The Debate in Jewish Law. *Theoretical Inquiries in Law*, *12*(1), 241-274.

Postema, G. J. (2022). *Law's rule: The nature, value, and viability of the rule of law*. Oxford University Press.

Rangoni, B. (2022). Experimentalist governance. In *Handbook on theories of governance* (pp. 592-603). Edward Elgar Publishing.

Samuelson, P. (2021). Withholding Injunctions in Copyright Cases: Impacts of eBay. *Wm. & Mary L. Rev.*, *63*, 773.

Siegel, R. B. (2013). Equality divided. *Harv. L. Rev.*, *127*, 1.

Singh, M., & Tanwar, R. S. (2024). *Intellectual Property Rights: Foundations, Laws, and Practices*. Academic Guru Publishing House.

Th, T. (2025). Evolution of Copyright in the Era of Artificial Intelligence: Analysis of Conflicts of Law and Judicial Precedents. *Journal of Digital Technologies and Law*, *3*(1), 35-64.

Tsai, R. L. (2021). Legacies of Pragmatism. *Drake L. Rev.*, *69*, 879.

Veale, M., Matus, K., & Gorwa, R. (2023). AI and global governance: Modalities, rationales, tensions. *Annual Review of Law and Social Science*, *19*(1), 255-275.

Wittgenstein, L. (2009). *Philosophical investigations*. John Wiley & Sons.

Chapter 12

Living after the Cartesian Ghost

Abstract

This concluding chapter interrogates the philosophical, social, and normative consequences of relinquishing inner-state-centric theories of agency, meaning, and responsibility. It contends that the migration from Cartesian metaphysics to community- and practice-based accounts not only dissolves entrenched conceptual dilemmas but also inaugurates new avenues for individual self-realization, collective agency, and social justice. Through critical analysis, the chapter elucidates the policy ramifications of this paradigm shift, addressing implications for the governance of emerging technologies, educational innovation, and the adaptive design of institutions. Special emphasis is placed on navigating the risks of misapplication and the enduring allure of metaphysical intuitions within both popular and expert discourse. Drawing on contemporary philosophy, empirical research, and real-world case studies, the chapter confronts sources of resistance, evaluating both the ethical costs and transformative potential of a post-Cartesian framework; it affirms that situating agency, normativity, and meaning within public, observable, and corrigible practices constitutes not a diminishment but an expansion of human possibility.

12.1. What We Gain by Abandoning Inner States

The shift from inner-state-centered theories to community- and practice-based accounts of agency, meaning, and responsibility yields significant philosophical, ethical, and practical gains, fundamentally altering our approach to selfhood, justice, and social coordination. First, relinquishing the centrality of private mental states in ethical and legal reasoning allows for the construction of frameworks that are publicly accessible, transparent, and open to collective verification. Philosophers inspired by Wittgenstein and pragmatist traditions have long argued that meaning and normativity are anchored in rule-governed practices, not in inaccessible subjective experiences (Dybowski, Dzięgielewska, & Rzepiński, 2024; Glock, 2024).

Recent legal theory corroborates this orientation, emphasizing that public criteria (not unverifiable intentions) are essential for the fair and legitimate administration of law (Hofius, 2021; Yuningsih & Prihatinah, 2025). By making agency and responsibility dependent on observable actions and institutional practices, we achieve greater procedural justice and reduce the epistemic opacity that often breeds mistrust or arbitrariness. This procedural justice is the only form of transparency that matters in a post-Cartesian world. We gain nothing by demanding a transparent view into the inner lives of others, but we gain everything by building transparent institutions where our shared practices are open to all.

Second, the practice-based approach enhances inclusivity and pluralism by making collective deliberation and social participation the foundation for ethical and political life. When meaning and value are generated through shared practices, the perspectives and experiences of marginalized groups gain epistemic and normative standing that would otherwise be suppressed in individualist, intention-focused models (Siegel, 2013). Empirical studies in legal reform and algorithmic governance demonstrate that impact-based and participatory standards enable more equitable outcomes than those that require proof of subjective intent (Bagenstos, 2009; Heisler & Grossman, 2023). This paradigm fosters practices of mutual recognition, deliberative correction, and collective responsibility, aligning law and ethics more closely with the plural realities of modern society.

Third, abandoning the metaphysics of inner states paves the way for institutional innovation, particularly in the context of rapidly advancing technologies and distributed agency. Automated and algorithmic decision systems, which operate without psychological intention, nevertheless produce real social effects that must be governed by practices of transparency, explainability, and contestability (Crawford, 2021). Practice-based frameworks have proven adaptable to these challenges, permitting the development of regulatory and adjudicatory mechanisms that address harms and distribute benefits without recourse to the fictive certainty of individual mental causation. This is particularly salient for issues such as algorithmic bias, platform accountability, and collaborative authorship, where collective and institutional factors determine outcomes.

Fourth, the relocation of normativity and responsibility from private mental realms to public practices fosters greater social learning and democratic adaptation. Legal philosophers Sabel and Simon contend that institutional legitimacy is best preserved by cultivating procedures for continuous feedback, participatory revision, and stakeholder engagement, rather than by relying on the presumed good faith of decision-makers (Rangoni, 2022). Practice-oriented governance makes room for contestation, error correction, and the open evolution of rules, attributes critical to sustaining justice and legitimacy in complex societies. Such adaptability is less achievable in systems that privilege hidden intentions, which often entrench the status quo and hinder necessary change.

Fifth, this shift enables a more grounded and humane conception of personal fulfillment and agency decoupled from the impossible demand for self-transparency or sovereign autonomy. When agency is understood as a function of participation in shared practices, individuals can pursue meaningful lives through collaboration, mutual support, and the joint construction of value (Järvelä et al., 2025). Empirical research in educational reform and workplace innovation confirms that people thrive in environments where goals, standards, and achievements are negotiated collectively and open to reinterpretation. This not only democratizes meaning-making but also distributes responsibility in ways that are psychologically realistic and socially empowering. As such, the abandonment of inner-state metaphysics equips society to more effectively address risks, resistances, and path dependencies associated with emerging technologies and institutional inertia. By insisting on the primacy of observable, corrigible practices, public policy can better anticipate and respond to unintended consequences, systemic failures, and the persistence of outdated dogmas (Crawford, 2021). This orientation supports an ethos of collective vigilance and creative problem-solving, inviting ongoing reassessment of norms as circumstances evolve. The gains of abandoning inner states are not merely philosophical, but practical, social, and existential, opening new vistas for flourishing, justice, and cooperative transformation.

A further advantage of abandoning inner-state metaphysics lies in the increased accountability and legitimacy that result from anchoring agency and responsibility in observable practice. When decisions and attributions of responsibility are subject to public scrutiny and revision, legal and ethical systems become more robust against both arbitrary power and hidden bias (Hofius, 2021; Siegel, 2013). This transparency not only enhances the credibility of institutions but also empowers individuals and communities to contest, adapt, and shape the standards by which they are governed. As empirical research on participatory governance and algorithmic accountability demonstrates, institutions that prioritize openness and procedural fairness foster greater social trust and more responsive policymaking (Järvelä et al., 2025; Yuningsih & Prihatinah, 2025). In this light, abandoning the search for inaccessible mental states does not diminish the complexity of moral or legal life. It democratizes it, offering more actors a stake in both the process and the outcomes of collective decision-making.

Lastly, the move away from mentalist accounts of agency supports a broader cultural transition toward resilience and adaptability. By embracing models of agency and meaning that are open to correction and grounded in evolving communal practice, societies are better positioned to manage uncertainty, embrace diversity, and cultivate innovation. This cultural shift aligns with developments in digital governance, organizational design, and educational practice, all of which benefit from iterative feedback, co-design, and continuous learning (Rangoni, 2022; Crawford, 2021). The ethos of corrigibility and practical engagement helps prevent the stagnation of norms and the ossification of institutions, ensuring that collective life remains vibrant and capable of responding to new challenges. In the final analysis, the abandonment of inner-state metaphysics is less a loss than an invitation: an invitation to co-create the meaning, values, and responsibilities that define human flourishing in the twenty-first century.

12.2. Community, Practice, and the Sources of Meaning

The relocation of meaning from the isolated mind to the collaborative domain of community and shared practice marks a foundational shift in how individuals, institutions, and societies understand normativity, agency, and value. For instance, philosophical traditions from Wittgenstein through contemporary pragmatists have established that the intelligibility and force of meaning arise not from solitary reflection, but from participation in forms of life where language, rules, and customs are continually negotiated and enacted. This communal orientation is echoed in social epistemology and legal theory, where practices such as reason-giving, critique, and mutual recognition structure the processes by which shared meaning and legitimacy are maintained (Ragoni, 2022). The authority of moral and legal rules depends on their embedding in visible, corrigible practices that invite collective participation and review. Such grounding ensures that meaning is never static but always open to reinterpretation in response to changing circumstances, new evidence, and plural perspectives.

Likewise, research in psychology, education, and organizational studies confirms that practices of joint attention, collaboration, and iterative feedback are essential for individual and collective flourishing. Järvelä et al. (2025) show that environments supporting shared regulation and hybrid intelligence enable the dynamic co-creation of knowledge and values, providing a more robust and adaptive model of learning than inward, individualistic approaches. When agency is understood as an emergent property of participatory practices, personal fulfillment becomes inseparable from engagement in meaningful communal activity. This has profound implications for the design of educational, technological, and organizational systems, requiring a shift toward collaborative, transparent, and participatory structures that facilitate collective sense-making and distributed responsibility. In fact, the sources of meaning in modern life are increasingly found in the procedures, traditions, and institutional routines that govern social interaction. Siegel (2013) notes that democratic legitimacy and justice in pluralistic societies rest on practices of public reason, stakeholder engagement, and ongoing negotiation rather than metaphysical assertions of value. This practice-based orientation is evident in contemporary movements for participatory budgeting, community-based restorative justice, and stakeholder-led governance, all of which ground legitimacy in visible, accountable processes. By emphasizing the procedural sources of meaning, these models enable communities to adapt to changing needs, encourage innovation, and reconcile competing interests without recourse to inaccessible mental content.

Technological and legal developments further reinforce the necessity of grounding meaning in public practices. In the context of algorithmic decision-making, scholars such as Edwards and Veale (2017) argue that the intelligibility and legitimacy of automated systems depend on practices of transparency, explainability, and collective contestation. Legal requirements for audit trails, reasons for decisions, and rights to appeal mirror Wittgensteinian insights into the inherently social and contestable character of meaning. These procedural mechanisms allow affected individuals and communities to make sense of, challenge, and shape technological outcomes in ways that respect pluralism and foster democratic agency. Practice-centered sources of meaning are especially salient in the management of social conflict and the pursuit of justice. Siddiq and Salam (2025) demonstrate that robust legal institutions rely not on the good intentions of officials, but on the visibility, adaptability, and responsiveness of the practices by which rights are adjudicated and remedies distributed. Community-based dispute resolution, participatory policy-making, and transparent regulatory oversight all serve to relocate legitimacy from the metaphysical realm of intention to the public world of collective action. These developments are not only more just, but also more effective in managing diversity, reducing arbitrariness, and building social trust.

The transition to a practice-based account of meaning opens space for a richer conception of human flourishing that honors the irreducible plurality of social life and the transformative power of collective creativity. By situating the sources of meaning in the interplay of communal participation, institutional design, and shared narratives, society gains the tools to navigate uncertainty, address conflict, and adapt to change. This perspective affirms that agency and value are not threatened by the decline of inner-state metaphysics; rather, they are enhanced by the democratization of sense-making and the collaborative negotiation of social goods (West, 2025). In this way, community and practice emerge not only as sources of meaning but as engines of social renewal and creative transformation.

The entrenchment of practice-based meaning is especially significant in times of social upheaval, rapid technological change, or political polarization. When established norms and values are contested or destabilized, the flexibility and resilience of communal practices provide a foundation for reconstituting shared understandings and rebuilding trust (Siddiq & Salam, 2025). Rather than clinging to fixed doctrines or searching for universal mental content, communities that invest in iterative dialogue, inclusive participation, and mutual accountability are better able to weather uncertainty and foster adaptive innovation. This dynamic is evident in fields as diverse as climate action, public health, and urban planning, where participatory governance models yield more legitimate and enduring solutions than top-down mandates or abstract theorizing (Siegel, 2013; Järvelä et al., 2025). In these settings, meaning and agency are co-produced, continually revised through negotiation and lived engagement.

The move toward community and practice as sources of meaning supports a more humane and ethical politics. By foregrounding procedural justice, inclusivity, and ongoing critique, practice-based frameworks reduce the risks of domination, marginalization, and dogmatism that so often attend metaphysical or authoritarian accounts of value. Communities that grow through deliberation, transparency, and contestation are not only more just but also more creative, able to harness the diverse perspectives and skills of their members for collective problem-solving (Ragoni, 2022; West, 2025). This orientation aligns with the best traditions of democratic theory and social epistemology, which hold that legitimate authority is earned, not presumed, and must remain accountable to the practices and needs of the people it claims to serve. The sources of meaning are distributed, corrigible, and open to transformation by those who participate in making and remaking them.

The practice-based account of meaning then has profound existential implications for how individuals find purpose, belonging, and dignity in the modern world. The search for authenticity or meaning is no longer a solitary, introspective quest, but an ongoing, dialogical journey enacted with others through the routines, rituals, and projects that constitute communal life. This vision recognizes that flourishing arises not from isolated insight but from sustained engagement in the practices that bind individuals to communities and give shape to collective aspirations (Järvelä et al., 2025; West, 2025). In this sense, the relocation of meaning to community and practice is both liberating and empowering, opening up new avenues for self-discovery, solidarity, and creative transformation across the full spectrum of social life.

This relocation of meaning from the private mind to public practice amounts to a re-enchantment of the social world. The Cartesian ghost, with its promise of a sovereign inner self, left the external world of institutions and conventions disenchanted, a mere stage for the drama of interiority. The practice-based turn reverses this. It reveals that the true locus of meaning, value, and agency is not hidden "within" us, but is manifestly present in the shared rituals, evolving language games, and collaborative projects that constitute our collective life. This perspective does not diminish the individual; it re-situates them within the rich, tangible network of relationships and practices that make a meaningful life possible. The search for authenticity is no longer a lonely introspective journey but a shared, creative endeavor. In a determined age, where the myth of the uncaused self has dissolved, we find our freedom not by transcending our world, but by participating more deeply, critically, and collaboratively in its ongoing creation.

12.3. Policy Frameworks for a Determined Age

As society embraces community- and practice-based understandings of agency, new policy frameworks are required to govern technological, legal, and educational systems in ways that are transparent, participatory, and robust to the realities of distributed and determined agency. The regulation of emerging technologies, particularly automated and algorithmic systems, necessitates procedural safeguards that foreground explainability, stakeholder engagement, and collective contestation over attempts to ascertain individual intention. Scholars have emphasized the limitations of "black box" systems and the dangers of opacity in algorithmic governance, advocating for legal mandates that require traceable, auditable, and reviewable processes

(Crawford, 2021). Within the practice-based framework of this book, a "traceable" process is one that allows for the assignment of public responsibility and facilitates correction, sharply distinct from the metaphysical goal of tracing an outcome back to a single, originating mental state or line of code. Regulatory initiatives such as the EU's AI Act and the GDPR enshrine rights to explanation and challenge, moving beyond metaphysical conceptions of intent to focus on the practical mechanisms by which affected individuals and communities can scrutinize and influence technological outcomes (Huang, 2025). These frameworks underscore the importance of transparency, participatory oversight, and dynamic adaptation to evolving social contexts.

Legal and institutional reform also increasingly prioritizes participatory mechanisms and iterative review over formal adherence to rules that presume fixed or internal mental states. Pomaza-Ponomarenko et al. (2024) demonstrate that successful regulatory institutions are characterized by public feedback loops, stakeholder deliberation, and procedures for ongoing correction and refinement, rather than by faith in the intentions of individual officials. This approach is evident in the spread of independent oversight bodies, public advisory panels, and experimental "sandbox" regulatory regimes that allow for the testing and revising of policy in real time. On the other hand, educational policy is undergoing a parallel transformation as schools and universities respond to the demands of a determined, technologically mediated society. Researchers in hybrid intelligence and educational technology advocate for curricula and assessment models that emphasize collaborative problem-solving, reflective dialogue, and adaptive learning over individual mastery or presumed psychological traits (Järvelä et al., 2025). Educational frameworks are increasingly designed to support socially shared regulation, iterative feedback, and opportunities for collective sense-making, mirroring broader societal shifts toward community-oriented and practice-based understandings of meaning and achievement. These models not only enhance equity and inclusivity but also prepare individuals for the realities of distributed agency in complex technological environments.

Fourth, policy frameworks for a determined age must also attend to the risks of institutional inertia, regulatory capture, and the reification of practices that perpetuate injustice or exclusion. West (2025) and Siegel (2013) warn that the practice-based turn does not guarantee justice by itself; it requires vigilant mechanisms for transparency, contestation, and the continual re-examination of procedural norms. Effective policy must be designed to resist ossification and to empower marginalized voices in the ongoing negotiation of norms and institutional priorities. This entails fostering open forums for dissent, supporting the emergence of new practices, and building in safeguards for periodic review and reform.

Advances in policy science and adaptive governance provide methodological tools for implementing and monitoring practice-based frameworks. Zhou and Cai (2024) highlight the efficacy of experimentalist governance models, which combine local innovation with central oversight and create platforms for sharing best practices and scaling effective solutions. These models treat policy as an ongoing process of learning and correction, emphasizing empirical assessment, peer review, and flexibility in the face of changing circumstances. Such adaptive approaches are particularly well suited to the complexity and unpredictability of technological, legal, and social transformation in the determined age. Moreover, the broader policy shift away from inner-state metaphysics is ultimately a democratic achievement: it entrusts communities, practitioners, and institutions with the task of constructing and continually refining the public goods that shape collective life. By making practices, procedures, and outcomes the focus of regulation, rather than unverifiable mental states, society gains not only greater transparency and justice but also enhanced resilience and creative capacity. This orientation provides a platform for shared flourishing, allowing for the co-evolution of norms, institutions, and technologies in response to the lived realities and aspirations of diverse populations. In this way, policy frameworks for a determined age become engines of democratic renewal, social learning, and inclusive progress.

The emergence of practice-based, participatory policy frameworks also signals a redefinition of expertise and authority in the governance of technology and society. Rather than relying solely on the technical judgments of centralized regulators or the presumed wisdom of isolated experts, these new frameworks seek to harness the distributed intelligence of diverse stakeholders (developers, users, citizens, educators, and marginalized groups) through ongoing consultation, collaborative design, and public deliberation (Pomaza-Ponomarenko et al., 2024; Zhou & Cai, 2024). This democratization of governance fosters a richer, more grounded form of collective problem-solving, making policy not merely responsive to technological change but generative of new forms of social coordination and ethical innovation. By creating opportunities for feedback, iteration, and bottom-up revision, these frameworks strengthen both the legitimacy and the adaptive capacity of the systems they regulate. Such models are especially effective in complex environments such as those shaped by AI, big data, and digital platforms where the speed and unpredictability of change render static, expert-driven solutions obsolete.

At the same time, the commitment to continual adaptation and review makes policy frameworks more resilient in the face of crises, failures, and rapid transformation. By institutionalizing regular assessments, sunset clauses, and mechanisms for rapid course correction, society can avoid both paralysis in the face of novelty and the entrenchment of outdated or unjust practices (Huang, 2025; West, 2025). This iterative, learning-oriented approach is increasingly recognized as the hallmark of effective governance in a determined age: one that acknowledges the limits of foresight, embraces uncertainty as a stimulus for institutional creativity, and orients regulation toward the open-ended flourishing of communities. In so doing, policy moves from the defense of inherited metaphysics to the proactive cultivation of practices, relationships, and institutions that are both robust and humane. The result is a vision of governance that is not merely reactive or risk-averse but fundamentally committed to the ongoing work of building just, responsive, and future-ready societies.

12.4. The Ongoing Revolution in Mind, Law, and Society

The transformation from inner-state metaphysics to practice-based and community-centric paradigms is more than a theoretical correction; it is an active revolution reshaping the contours of mind, law, and collective life in the twenty-first century. To begin, the revolution in theories of mind and meaning is apparent across philosophy, psychology, and the cognitive sciences. Rather than privileging the solitary mental interior, contemporary research in hybrid intelligence and distributed cognition demonstrates that intelligence, agency, and normativity are realized through patterns of social interaction, language, and shared problem-solving (Järvelä et al., 2025). The mind is increasingly conceptualized as a public phenomenon, a product of engagement in rule-governed practices, rather than a closed, Cartesian theater.

Moving into the legal domain, this conceptual reorientation is changing how institutions understand and distribute responsibility. Legal systems, once wedded to metaphysical concepts of intent and mental causation, are now focusing on procedural transparency, accessible standards, and institutional regularity. The regulatory challenges posed by automated and algorithmic decision-making systems have led scholars to call for robust practices of auditability, explanation, and the right to contest outcomes, all concrete mechanisms that replace private intention with public contestability and review (Edwards & Veale, 2017). Simultaneously, new forms of social order and governance are emerging in response to these intellectual and technological developments. The growth of participatory policy-making, citizen assemblies, and experimentalist governance models foregrounds adaptability, stakeholder engagement, and iterative revision as the core of institutional legitimacy (Siegel, 2013). Rather than relying on hierarchical commands or metaphysical doctrine, these systems build resilience and inclusion by making practices visible, corrigible, and open to plural input.

At the same time, the revolution is not without friction. Entrenched interests, institutional inertia, and persistent metaphysical intuitions about agency and merit pose obstacles to the realization of a practice-based order (Crawford, 2021). Ongoing debates about algorithmic fairness and institutional accountability underscore the need for continuous vigilance, reform, and public deliberation to keep the gains of this revolution alive and equitable. As these new frameworks take root, possibilities for social justice, collaborative creativity, and human flourishing expand. Educational reformers, for instance, are increasingly designing curricula that promote shared regulation, reflective dialogue, and the co-creation of meaning, demonstrating the liberatory and empowering effects of grounding achievement in collaborative practice. Likewise, legal reforms that embed contestation, transparency, and stakeholder participation enable new forms of democratic agency, better adapted to the distributed, pluralistic conditions of modern society.

The ongoing revolution also illuminates the deep connections between epistemology, ethics, and political organization. As social meaning and agency are increasingly recognized as collective and corrigible achievements, disciplines once separated by methodological walls (philosophy, law, neuroscience, organizational science) are being drawn together in the pursuit of shared, practice-oriented inquiry (Järvelä et al., 2025). This interdisciplinarity not only enriches theoretical understanding but also enables the development of practical tools such as participatory design protocols, adaptive regulatory mechanisms, and learning-oriented governance that can respond nimbly to new challenges. In this way, society's capacity to address crises depends on our collective willingness to revise, coordinate, and sustain the public practices that undergird both knowledge and justice.

Moreover, the practice-based transformation creates opportunities for renewing trust and legitimacy in public institutions, particularly in an era of widespread skepticism toward expertise and authority. Institutions that anchor legitimacy in visible, inclusive, and participatory processes are better able to withstand shocks, correct errors, and maintain social cohesion even amid uncertainty (Siegel, 2013; Crawford, 2021). By continually inviting critique, supporting plural perspectives, and building systems that are open to learning, these organizations become more than mere rule-enforcers: they evolve into engines of social renewal, capable of nurturing the conditions for both individual flourishing and collective resilience. This vision of governance is neither utopian nor naïve. It is grounded in an empirical and pragmatic recognition of the limits of both centralized power and unexamined tradition.

The ongoing revolution in mind, law, and society is best understood as a call for a new kind of citizenship that is rooted not in deference to authority or fixed doctrine, but in the ongoing work of participation, correction, and creative engagement with the forms of life that shape our world (West, 2025; Järvelä et al., 2025). It is a revolution that prizes humility, adaptability, and collaborative intelligence, inviting individuals and institutions alike to take responsibility for the future as a shared and open-ended project. In embracing the unfinished, evolving nature of practice-based order, society gains not only a more realistic account of agency and legitimacy but also the resources to cultivate justice, innovation, and meaning for generations to come.

Looking ahead, the ongoing revolution in mind, law, and society must be regarded as an unfinished and generative process calling for sustained engagement, critical inquiry, and creative adaptation. Rather than settling for inherited categories, this transformation invites communities to actively shape the norms, institutions, and meanings that structure collective life. As society continues to move beyond the Cartesian ghost, it gains the resources to meet new ethical, social, and technological challenges through practices that are participatory, corrigible, and open to all. This chapter has demonstrated that the abandonment of inner-state metaphysics in favor of community- and practice-based frameworks constitutes not a diminishment of human agency or meaning, but rather their expansion and deepening. By situating normativity, responsibility, and creativity within publicly accessible, corrigible practices, individuals and societies gain new tools for self-understanding, collaborative achievement, and adaptive problem-solving. This transformation is evident across philosophy, law, education, and governance, where legitimacy and justice are increasingly realized through transparent procedures, participatory engagement, and the continual negotiation of plural values. The revolution in mind, law, and society requires vigilance and creativity, ensuring that the gains of participatory practice are not eroded by institutional inertia or the lingering allure of metaphysical individualism. This includes resisting the lingering allure of a flawed transparency, the impulse to audit every cause and disclose every influence. The true, revolutionary transparency is the one grounded in public accountability, procedural fairness, and the collective courage to stand behind our actions in a complex, determined world.

The ongoing shift to practice-based paradigms invites us to see flourishing, justice, and innovation as collective accomplishments achieved through shared regulation, open dialogue, and institutional adaptability. As technological, legal, and social challenges become ever more complex and interconnected, the resources for meaningful agency and equitable governance will be found not in introspective certainty but in the practices that bind and renew communities. The post-Cartesian era holds out the promise of a more inclusive, responsive, and resilient social order in which the sources of meaning, value, and agency are democratized and continually remade through our participation in the evolving practices of public life.

References

Bagenstos, S. R. (2009). *Law and the contradictions of the disability rights movement*. Yale University Press.

Crawford, K. (2021). *The atlas of AI: Power, politics, and the planetary costs of artificial intelligence*. Yale University Press.

Dybowski, M., Dzięgielewska, W., & Rzepiński, W. (2024). Introduction: Why practice theory and law?. In *Practice Theory and Law* (pp. 1-20). Routledge.

Edwards, L., & Veale, M. (2017). Slave to the algorithm? Why a'right to an explanation'is probably not the remedy you are looking for. *Duke L. & Tech. Rev.*, *16*, 18.

Glock, H. J. (2024). *Normativity, meaning and philosophy: essays on Wittgenstein*. Anthem Press.

Heisler, N., & Grossman, M. R. (2023). *Standards for the Control of Algorithmic Bias: The Canadian Administrative Context*. CRC Press.

Hofius, M. (2021). Practice Approaches in International Political Theory. In *Perspectives on International Political Theory in Europe* (pp. 87-106). Cham: Springer International Publishing.

Huang, H. (2025). Hiding in plain sight: Algorithmic Transparency and Explainability under the GDPR: Legal and Technical Challenges in Applying the GDPR's Provisions on Transparency and Explainability to Algorithmic AI Systems.

Järvelä, S., Zhao, G., Nguyen, A., & Chen, H. (2025). Hybrid intelligence: Human–AI coevolution and learning. *British Journal of Educational Technology*, *56*(2), 455-468.

Pomaza-Ponomarenko, A., Leonenko, N., Cherniahivska, V., Lehan, I., & Puzanova, G. (2024). Dynamics of legal transformatins: Assessment of impact on society and analysis of determinations of changes in the legislative sphere. *Multidisciplinary Reviews*, *7*.

Rangoni, B. (2022). Experimentalist governance. In *Handbook on theories of governance* (pp. 592-603). Edward Elgar Publishing.

Siddiq, N., & Salam, R. (2025). Enhancing Legal Certainty through Legal Reform in Indonesia: Problems and Efforts to Strengthen Legal Institutions. *Strata Law Review*, *3*(1), 1-14.

Siegel, R. B. (2013). Equality divided. *Harv. L. Rev.*, *127*, 1.

West, E. G. (2025). Constitutional Private Law.

Yuningsih, Y., & Prihatinah, T. L. (2025). Reassessing the Legal Validity of Non-Notarial Gifts Between Parents and Children Under Indonesian Law: A Doctrinal and Judicial Perspective. *Jurnal Hukum In Concreto*, *4*(1), 139-156.

Zhou, C., & Cai, R. (2024). Experimentalist governance under hierarchy through leading small groups: a solution to power fragmentation?. *Journal of Asian Public Policy*, 1-25.

Conclusion: The Unexpected Unity

Abstract

This conclusion weaves together the central insights from legal doctrine, neuroscience, and artificial intelligence, arguing that the global shift away from mental-state-based theories signals not an isolated disciplinary trend but a watershed transformation in the philosophical conception of agency, responsibility, and creativity. By advancing a unified, practice-centered account, the volume demonstrates how entrenched dichotomies (human versus machine, theory versus application, mind versus society) are transcended, allowing for a more robust, dynamic, and pragmatic understanding of social and ethical life. The discussion affirms the resilience and versatility of practice-based frameworks, highlighting their ability to resolve enduring theoretical dilemmas and to meet the demands of rapidly evolving technological and institutional landscapes. Attention is given to the broad ramifications for future scholarship, cross-disciplinary synergy, and the design of adaptive policy infrastructures. Rather than defending metaphysical abstractions, philosophy is repositioned as the ongoing work of elucidating the social, technological, and normative forms of life that underpin meaningful agency. The volume concludes by urging sustained critical inquiry and inventive participation in the practices that continually reconstitute our collective world.

C.1. How Copyright, Neuroscience, and AI Reveal the Same Truth

In bringing this volume to a close, it becomes clear that what began as an inquiry into the philosophical underpinnings of law, mind, and machine has culminated in the revelation of an unexpected unity. Across domains as disparate as copyright doctrine, neuroscience, and artificial intelligence, the trajectory is unmistakable: a decisive shift from theories rooted in the opacity of inner mental states to frameworks grounded in the public, observable, and corrigible practices of communities. This transformation is not merely a convergence of scholarly interests, but a sign of a deeper, epochal change in how agency, creativity, and responsibility are understood. The great dichotomies that once divided human from machine, mind from society, and theory from practice are increasingly seen as the products of outdated metaphysics, ill-suited to the complexities of a technologically mediated and institutionally pluralistic world. By tracing the evolution of collective authorship in copyright, focus on distributed cognition in neuroscience, and algorithmic reliance on social practices for legitimacy, we see not a fragmentation of knowledge but a surprising synthesis. This concluding chapter explores how these seemingly unrelated fields expose a common philosophical core: meaning, normativity, and value emerge not from private intention but from shared practice. Through this lens, the final lesson of the volume is not a call for theoretical purity or disciplinary boundaries, but for creative, collaborative engagement with the evolving forms of life that constitute our collective future.

The parallel evolution of copyright law, neuroscience, and artificial intelligence demonstrates that agency, authorship, and responsibility are not anchored in solitary mental events, but in the patterns of collaboration, practice, and interaction that define collective life. Copyright doctrine, for instance, has moved from an emphasis on the romantic notion of the solitary creator toward legal recognition of collaborative, corporate, and algorithmic authorship (Ginsburg, 2020). Neuroscience similarly disrupts the myth of the sovereign, isolated mind by demonstrating that cognition is fundamentally distributed across neural networks, bodies, and social environments (Barrett, 2017). In the realm of AI, legitimacy and ethical governance now depend on embedding systems in transparent, contestable practices rather than attempting to reconstruct or simulate hidden intentions (Veale, Matus, & Gorwa, 2023). Together, these developments expose the inadequacy of metaphysical accounts that privilege private mental states over public, shared realities.

What unifies these fields is a recognition that the sources of meaning, value, and responsibility lie in observable patterns of participation and negotiation rather than in introspective certainties. The move of copyright toward collective authorship was prompted by the rise of collaborative and digital production, where legal disputes increasingly turn on demonstrable contribution, workflow, and social practice, not on unverifiable intention or originality (Jon, 2025). In neuroscience, empirical research on brain plasticity and the social construction of perception affirms that cognition is not a matter of static inner states, but a process shaped by social interaction and cultural tools (Barrett, 2017). The legitimacy of algorithmic systems, likewise, increasingly depends on contestability, explanation, and the visible embedding of machine decision-making within institutional routines that can be collectively reviewed and revised (Crawford, 2021). This unity is not merely conceptual but practical and institutional. All three fields have responded to crises of legitimacy and complexity by developing mechanisms that support public contestation, revision, and distributed accountability. In copyright, this is seen in the evolution of notice-and-takedown systems, collective licensing, and dispute resolution procedures that prioritize accessible, observable processes over metaphysical inquiries into "real" intent (Netanel, 2008). Neuroscience, by mapping the dynamic interactions between brain, body, and environment, has informed therapies and educational practices that emphasize collaborative regulation and social learning (Järvelä et al., 2025). AI ethics now demands "right to explanation" and participatory oversight, creating institutional structures for transparency and iterative correction that parallel the procedural reforms in copyright and the adaptive, social approach of contemporary neuroscience (Edwards & Veale, 2017).

This convergence offers a solution to some of the most persistent theoretical and practical puzzles across disciplines. The dichotomy between human and machine so central to debates over creativity, responsibility, and normativity dissolves when agency is viewed through the lens of practice, participation, and corrigible social forms (Järvelä et al., 2025). The embrace of collective, automated, and corporate authorship on the part of copyright law, the neuroscience model of distributed cognition, and the procedural turn in AI all point to the same truth: value and meaning are enacted, not intuited; achieved, not discovered. The implication is that both policy and theory must privilege accessible, adaptable, and participatory systems capable of supporting ongoing negotiation and revision, rather than rely on hidden or essentialized inner states. Another striking lesson is that robust, pluralistic societies can accommodate technological and epistemic complexity not by policing boundaries between mind and machine, but by cultivating flexible, public-facing practices that sustain legitimacy, fairness, and collective learning. The regulatory responses in copyright and AI, such as independent review panels, public consultation mechanisms, and the demand for procedural transparency, mirror the way neuroscience informs new pedagogies, therapies, and institutional designs (Rangoni, 2022). These developments demonstrate that resilience and adaptability are the fruits of practice-based frameworks, not the fragile product of hidden or unexamined mental content.

The parallel journeys of copyright, neuroscience, and AI reveal that the future of agency, creativity, and responsibility lies in the cultivation of public, contestable, and evolving forms of life. Philosophy, law, and technology all stand to benefit from this unexpected unity, as they move from defending metaphysical mysteries to clarifying and renewing the practices by which communities navigate meaning and value. As new challenges emerge, be they technological, ethical, or social, the ongoing work of creative, collaborative practice will remain the crucible in which agency and legitimacy are forged.

C.2. From Mental States to Social Practices: The Complete Framework

The transition from mental-state-centric paradigms to social practice-based frameworks represents not a mere theoretical pivot, but the establishment of a comprehensive, empirically robust, and adaptable account of agency, normativity, and meaning. Historically, the philosophical tradition anchored action and responsibility in intention, will, or inner states, a view reflected in classic legal doctrines and early psychological theories (LaFave, 1986). Yet, decades of interdisciplinary critique have revealed the epistemic, ethical, and institutional limitations of this orientation. Wittgenstein and his intellectual heirs in philosophy and sociology demonstrated that the meaning of words, actions, and rules is constituted through their use in public, norm-governed practices. This realization is echoed in contemporary law, neuroscience, and AI ethics, where the intelligibility and legitimacy of decisions are increasingly linked to observable, repeatable procedures that can be collectively scrutinized and revised.

In the domain of law, the move to practice-based frameworks has resulted in a reconfiguration of doctrines surrounding responsibility, fairness, and justice. Legal scholars such as Siegel (2013) and Rangoni (2022) argue that public criteria, institutional routines, and contestable procedures are far superior to metaphysical inquiries into "real" intention for ensuring equity and legitimacy. The evolution of due process, equal protection, and disparate impact standards in law, especially in the context of discrimination, automated decision-making, and collective authorship, demonstrates a growing reliance on transparent, participatory, and adaptive legal practices. Such mechanisms ensure that claims to justice and legitimacy are tested against public standards and shared experiences, rather than the unknowable contents of individual minds. This framework finally clarifies the role of transparency. It is not a metaphysical demand for the disclosure of inner states or causal minutiae, but a practical and ethical demand for accountable procedures and the public act of taking responsibility. Neuroscience and cognitive science have similarly reoriented the study of mind from individual states to distributed, relational, and embodied practices. As noted, Barrett (2017) and others show that cognition, emotion, and agency are emergent properties of the dynamic interplay between brains, bodies, and social environments. Research on plasticity, collaborative learning, and hybrid intelligence reveals that agency is best understood as a collective achievement, realized and refined through ongoing interaction, reflection, and adaptation (Järvelä et al., 2025). This scientific consensus further dissolves the myth of the sovereign mind and supports the shift to frameworks that ground responsibility, meaning, and value in public, social forms.

Likewise, issues related to algorithmic governance illustrate the practical necessity of moving beyond inner states. As Edwards and Veale (2017) emphasize, ethical and legitimate machine learning cannot rest on opaque inferences about user or designer intention, but must be built around auditable, explainable, and contestable procedures that allow for stakeholder oversight and redress. This procedural turn is seen in legal mandates for "right to explanation," impact assessments, and participatory algorithmic audits, measures designed to institutionalize transparency, accountability, and the continual revision of standards in response to new risks and collective experiences (Crawford, 2021).

A complete framework rooted in social practices must also acknowledge the risks of ossification, capture, and exclusion that can attend even well-intentioned procedural regimes. Nourse (2023) and Siegel (2013) highlight the importance of periodic review, dissent, and the inclusion of marginalized voices to ensure that institutional routines do not calcify into new forms of injustice. Robust practice-based frameworks must embed mechanisms for transparency, challenge, and creative adaptation, ensuring that justice remains a dynamic, collective accomplishment rather than a static result of formal compliance. The complete framework for understanding agency, normativity, and meaning emerges from the convergence of law, neuroscience, and technology. Agency is not the exclusive product of inner states but an emergent phenomenon of collaborative, observable, and correctable social practices. This framework not only addresses philosophical puzzles and legal dilemmas but provides actionable guidance for the governance of education, technology, and democratic institutions. The resilience, adaptability, and pluralism of such a system lie in its commitment to openness, contestation, and continual learning, qualities that position it to navigate the uncertainties and complexities of an increasingly interconnected world.

C.3. Philosophy's Role in the Coming Transformation

As the epochal shift from inner-state metaphysics to practice-centered frameworks unfolds across law, neuroscience, and artificial intelligence, philosophy is uniquely positioned to guide, critique, and animate the transformation of agency, meaning, and responsibility in contemporary society. In fact, the unique contribution of philosophy in an age of accelerating technological and institutional transformation is neither to adjudicate metaphysical mysteries nor to defend inherited dogmas, but to clarify and critique the evolving forms of life through which agency, meaning, and responsibility are constituted. The displacement of mental-state-centric theories by practice-based, public, and corrigible frameworks positions philosophy not as an external judge but as an active participant in the critical reconstruction of law, science, and social practice. The pages of this volume have traced the arc from Cartesian skepticism and romantic authorship through the pragmatic turn in legal theory, the distributed mind of neuroscience, and the procedural revolution in artificial intelligence. At each juncture, the role of philosophy has been to interrogate the criteria by which meaning and legitimacy are produced, emphasizing transparency, public participation, and the situatedness of normativity within collective practices.

Central to this transformation is philosophy's capacity to reveal the hidden assumptions and unexamined metaphors that often structure both policy and ordinary thinking. The notion of the sovereign, introspective self has long functioned as an anchor for theories of rights, liability, and creativity, yet it has proven ill-equipped for a world of distributed cognition, automated agency, and institutional complexity (Barrett, 2017). Philosophy, by deconstructing these metaphysical holdovers, enables a more nuanced and responsive account of agency that privileges the plurality of social forms, the corrigibility of practices, and the mutual recognition at the heart of democratic life (Rangoni, 2022). In this sense, the public task of the discipline is not the defense of abstraction but the illumination and revision of the conceptual scaffolding of shared reality.

As the book has shown, the coming transformation will not be realized through abstract argumentation alone but through the practical reconstruction of institutions, policies, and collective habits. In law, this means prioritizing participatory mechanisms, procedural justice, and transparent, contestable routines over metaphysical quests for intention or moral purity (Siegel, 2013). In neuroscience and education, it requires shifting from fixed models of ability and achievement to dynamic, collaborative, and adaptive practices that cultivate shared regulation and creative dialogue (Pradeep et al., 2024). In the realm of artificial intelligence, it calls for the design of systems that are not only technically robust but socially embedded and anchored in mechanisms of explanation, redress, and stakeholder governance (Camilleri, 2024). A practice-based philosophical approach also equips society to navigate the persistent risks of exclusion, ossification, and regulatory inertia. Procedures, by themselves, are no guarantee of justice: they require continuous reflection, dissent, and reform if they are not to devolve into mere ritual or to reproduce historical inequities. A critical eye remains necessary for exposing the failures of proceduralism when it serves as cover for arbitrariness or entrenched power, and for generating new conceptual resources for contestation and creative institutional change. By fostering dialogue across disciplines and communities, philosophy cultivates the conditions for genuine pluralism and mutual recognition, values essential to flourishing in a rapidly changing world.

The arguments advanced throughout this volume demonstrate that moving beyond inner-state metaphysics does not entail a loss of agency, responsibility, or creativity; rather, it expands the possibilities for democratic self-governance and collaborative achievement. By making agency a function of visible, corrigible, and collectively negotiated practices, societies gain new tools for addressing the complexities of technological innovation, plural identities, and institutional change (Crawford, 2021). The resilience of such frameworks is evident in their capacity for adaptation, their openness to ongoing critique, and their suitability for navigating the emergent challenges of the digital, automated age. This integrative vision enables interdisciplinary synthesis, drawing together law, neuroscience, AI, and the humanities in a common project of clarifying, refining, and transforming the normative structures that undergird social life. The practice-based paradigm is not a static doctrine but a living methodology, inviting experimentation, dialogue, and critical re-examination as new challenges arise. By embracing the uncertainty and contingency of practice, philosophy animates the ongoing work of democratic renewal and institutional creativity, refusing the false comfort of final answers and instead fostering the habits of reflective citizenship and ethical inquiry.

In reflecting on the arguments and interventions of this book, one sees a unifying thread: the continuous interplay between individual aspiration and collective achievement, between innovation and tradition, between critique and constructive participation. The evolution of copyright from romantic authorship to procedural regularity, the neuroscientific turn toward distributed agency, and the embrace of transparency and contestability in AI ethics all point toward a future in which the value and legitimacy of systems are realized in their openness to participation, scrutiny, and revision. The abiding role of philosophy is to sustain and enrich this process, ensuring that social practices remain responsive to new knowledge, unanticipated risks, and the plural voices of an evolving citizenry.

As the volume closes, the reader is invited to embrace a vision of philosophy as an engaged, forward-looking practice committed to the ceaseless work of clarifying meaning, interrogating power, and cultivating the habits of collective self-government. The coming transformation will demand not only technical ingenuity or policy innovation, but also a revitalized public sphere in which all are empowered to participate in the shaping of the forms of life that define our shared world. Philosophy, in this sense, is both a guide and a companion. It teaches vigilance against dogmatism, humility before complexity, and hope in the generative power of collaborative practice.

The final call to action, then, is both scholarly and civic, to move beyond defensive postures and metaphysical nostalgia and take up the ongoing task of building, contesting, and renewing the social, legal, and technological practices through which agency, meaning, and justice are enacted. In so doing, scholars and practitioners alike can realize the promise of a world where the boundaries between mind and society, theory and application, human and machine are not obstacles to be feared, but resources for shared learning, creative adaptation, and collective flourishing.

References

Barrett, L. F. (2017). *How emotions are made: The secret life of the brain*. Pan Macmillan.

Camilleri, M. A. (2024). Artificial intelligence governance: Ethical considerations and implications for social responsibility. *Expert systems*, *41*(7), e13406.

Crawford, K. (2021). *The atlas of AI: Power, politics, and the planetary costs of artificial intelligence*. Yale University Press.

Edwards, L., & Veale, M. (2017). Slave to the algorithm? Why a'right to an explanation'is probably not the remedy you are looking for. *Duke L. & Tech. Rev.*, *16*, 18.

Ginsburg, J. C. (2025). Humanist Copyright. *J. Free Speech L.*, 6, 91.

Järvelä, S., Zhao, G., Nguyen, A., & Chen, H. (2025). Hybrid intelligence: Human–AI coevolution and learning. *British Journal of Educational Technology*, *56*(2), 455-468.

Jon, W. (2025). Prompting Creativity: Tiered Approach to Copyright Protection for AI-Generated Content in the Digital Age. *Media and Communication, 13*.

LaFave, W. R. (1986). Substantive criminal law. *(No Title)*.

Netanel, N. W., & Nimmer, D. (2011). Is Copyright Property?--The Debate in Jewish Law. *Theoretical Inquiries in Law*, *12*(1), 241-274.

Nourse, V. (2023). The Paradoxes of a Unified Judicial Philosophy: An Empirical Study of the New Supreme Court: 2020-2022. *Const. Comment.*, *38*, 1.

Pradeep, K., Sulur Anbalagan, R., Thangavelu, A. P., Aswathy, S., Jisha, V. G., & Vaisakhi, V. S. (2024, December). Neuroeducation: Understanding neural dynamics in learning and teaching. In *Frontiers in Education* (Vol. 9, p. 1437418). Frontiers Media SA.

Rangoni, B. (2022). Experimentalist governance. In *Handbook on theories of governance* (pp. 592-603). Edward Elgar Publishing.

Siegel, R. B. (2013). Equality divided. *Harv. L. Rev.*, *127*, 1.

Veale, M., Matus, K., & Gorwa, R. (2023). AI and global governance: Modalities, rationales, tensions. *Annual Review of Law and Social Science*, *19*(1), 255-275.

Index

U

W